PRAISE FOR

A TRUTH UNIVERSALLY ACKNOWLEDGED

"Whether you adore Jane Austen for her wit, characters, or astute observations about human nature, this swoon-worthy collection penned by
modern masters of literature will offer even more reasons to love her."
—Minneapolis *Star Tribune*

"Jane Austen . . . remains a hot literary property. *A Truth Universally
Acknowledged* . . . explains her eternal appeal."
—*USA Today*

"This book would make a perfect Christmas present for anyone who
loves Austen."   —*The Economist*

"A collection for both newcomers to the charms of Jane Austen and
those long-time 'Janeites' . . . The writers in this volume explain
their own relationship with Austen and together are a kind of invitation
for us, whether we're Janeites or not, to understand why we are so in
her thrall."   —*Chicago Tribune*

"There are lots of reasons for *reading* this book. . . . The essays are such
pleasures in themselves I have only gratitude to offer the editor."
—*San Francisco Chronicle*

"*A Truth Universally Acknowledged* contains almost as many gems as the
novels encompass."   —*The Miami Herald*

"An ideal nightstand book."   —*The Star-Ledger*

"After reading many of the essays, one is tempted to re-read many of
Austen's books."   —*Tucson Citizen*

"This fascinating volume offers a range of perspectives on the great lady's work, supporting the theory that no one is immune to the allure of Austen." —*BookPage*

"Austenites will enjoy dipping into this collection." —*Booklist*

"Informative and thoroughly entertaining." —*Library Journal*

A TRUTH
UNIVERSALLY
ACKNOWLEDGED

RANDOM HOUSE TRADE PAPERBACKS | NEW YORK

A TRUTH UNIVERSALLY ACKNOWLEDGED

33 GREAT WRITERS ON WHY WE READ JANE AUSTEN

EDITED BY

Susannah Carson

FOREWORD BY

Harold Bloom

A 2010 Random House Trade Paperback Edition

Copyright © 2009 by Susannah Carson

All rights reserved.

Published in the United States by Random House Trade Paperbacks,
an imprint of
The Random House Publishing Group, a division
of Random House, Inc., New York.

RANDOM HOUSE TRADE PAPERBACKS and colophon are
trademarks of Random House, Inc.

Originally published in hardcover in the United States by
Random House, an imprint of
The Random House Publishing Group, a division
of Random House, Inc., in 2009.

Previous publication information for the essays contained
in this book can be found starting on page 293.

Library of Congress Cataloging-in-Publication Data
A truth universally acknowledged: 33 great writers on why we read
Jane Austen / edited by Susannah Carson.
p.   cm.
ISBN 978-0-8129-8001-1
1. Austen Jane, 1775–1817—Appreciation.   2. Austen, Jane,
1775–1817—Influence.   I. Carson, Susannah.
PR4037.T78 2009
823'.7—dc22   2009012904

Printed in the United States of America

www.atrandom.com

2 4 6 8 9 7 5 3 1

Book design by Victoria Wong

Foreword

HAROLD BLOOM

Some literary works are mortal; Jane Austen's are immortal. What makes this so? Austen's work possesses an uncanniness, a certain mode of originality. She created personality, character, and cognition; she brought into being new modes of consciousness. Like Shakespeare, Austen invented us. Because we are Austen's children, we behold and confront our own anguish and our own fantasies in her novels. She seems to explain us for the simple reason that she contributed to our invention. Personality is Austen's greatest originality and the cause of her perpetual pervasiveness.

The precision and accuracy of Austen's representation is Shakespearean. The influence of the heroines of Shakespeare's romantic comedies, Rosalind of *As You Like It* in particular, is palpable upon Elizabeth Bennet of *Pride and Prejudice* and Emma Woodhouse of the equally superb novel she entitles. After Shakespeare, no writer in the language does so well as Austen in giving us figures, central and peripheral, utterly consistent each in her (or his) own mode of speech and consciousness, and intensely different from each other.

The strong selves of Austen's heroines are wrought with a fine individuality that attests to her reserves of power. Had she not died so soon, she would have been capable of creating a Shakespearean diversity of persons, despite her narrowly, deliberately limited social range of representation. She had learned Shakespeare's most difficult lesson: to manifest sympathy toward all of her characters, even the least admirable, while detaching herself even from her favorite, Emma.

Austen is a profound ironist who employs her irony to refine aspects of Shakespeare's invention of the human. Irony seems more than a trope in her work: it seems indeed to be the condition of her language. Subtle as Austen's ironies are, they remain visible because they are so controlled, whereas the Chaucerian-Shakespearean ironies of courtship frequently are too huge to be readily discerned. This hardly is a disadvantage to Austen, since her comic genius surpasses that of anyone in the language since Shakespeare himself. Yet irony hardly accounts for the effect of moral and spiritual power that she so constantly conveys, however implicitly or obliquely.

Austen, following in the footsteps of Richardson's extraordinary novel *Clarissa,* brilliantly moved Shakespearean inwardness into the unitary plot of a single action: courtship between the sexes. Elizabeth and Darcy resolve their agon by an ultimate exchange of spiritual estimates that works to confirm their mutual self-esteem. There is a transcendent strength to Elizabeth's will, and her pride has playfulness in it, a touch even of the quixotic. That Jane Austen is a wise writer is indisputable, but we do not read *Pride and Prejudice* as though it were Ecclesiastes. Austen has no more a political or social agenda than she has a religious one. To read the heroines' stories well, you need to acquire a touch of Austen's own wisdom, because she was as wise as Dr. Samuel Johnson. Like Johnson, though far more implicitly, Austen urges us to clear our mind of "cant." "Cant," in the Johnsonian sense, means platitudes, pious expressions, groupthink. Austen has no use for it, and neither should we. Those who now read Austen "politically" are not reading her at all.

The art and passion of reading well and deeply is waning, but Austen still inspires people to become fanatical readers. We read Austen because she seems to know us better than we know ourselves, and she seems to know us so intimately for the simple reason that she helped determine who we are both as readers and as human beings.

Contents

Introduction

SUSANNAH CARSON

> "I am a Jane Austenite, and therefore slightly
> imbecile about Jane Austen."
>
> —E. M. Forster

Why do we read Jane Austen? What explains our fascination with her novels?

So many writers have been forgotten over the ages, but for two centuries Austen has enthralled her readers. Men and women, teens and adults, academic professionals and those who read for fun: all turn to Austen time and again to find some nourishment for their literary souls that they can find nowhere else.

Austen's major works are *Northanger Abbey, Sense and Sensibility, Pride and Prejudice, Emma, Mansfield Park,* and *Persuasion*. Since their publication between the years of 1811 and 1817, they have been perennial favorites and have never gone out of print. In his biography of Austen, David Nokes reports that the first edition of her first novel, *Sense and Sensibility,* soon sold out, and that *Pride and Prejudice* was the most fashionable novel of the season.[1] After the publication of *Mansfield Park* the Prince Regent requested that she dedicate her next novel to him. This was *Emma,* for which Sir Walter Scott praised her "knowledge of the human heart." *Persuasion* was published posthumously to both domestic and international acclaim.

Austen's real influence on readers over the years cannot be measured. Other writers have admirers; Austen has fans, societies, and even a cult of what Rudyard Kipling first termed "Janeites." Other books are read; Austen's are devoured, digested, and reinterpreted in the everyday lives of her readers. Other worlds are admired; Austen's provide the landscape for further literary and artistic endeavors. In addition to film adaptations, there has been an endless series of sequels, spin-offs, self-help books, dating guidebooks, cookbooks, board games, tarot card decks, figurines, websites, discussion forums, book club meetings, Empire-waist fashions, and so on. All, it would seem, are designed to enable devotees to maintain the illusion that they, too, are part of this special literary world.

Austen's novels lend themselves to a certain kind of involvement which goes far beyond the black and white of the printed page. For many of us, the delights of reading are polychrome, and once we have entered this vibrant world we quite simply never want to leave. Other novels can be read through once and soon forgotten, but our favorite Austen novels haunt us our entire lives, inform our understanding of what it is to be human, and in the end fuse so wholly with our thoughts and feelings that it would be difficult to imagine the sorts of people we might have become had we never encountered them. We read her novels to identify and to improve, to laugh and to sympathize, to enjoy the present and to revisit the past, and at times to escape our own muddled lives for a bit and find the clarity that only the best fiction can provide.

Like Shakespeare, Austen enjoys a popular appeal that is astonishing in both the breadth of readership affected and in the depth of personal response. The ability of Austen to inspire reactions of such passion and variety is evidence of a rare genius. Such fierce partisanship has resulted, for instance, in great debates about which is the "best" novel: *Emma* has always been a great favorite and is often held up as an example of Austen's mastery of the novel form; *Mansfield Park* usually inspires either devotion or irritation, but rarely indifference; that *Pride and Prejudice* "sparkles" no one has ever attempted to deny; *Sense and Sensibility* can claim fewer but just as fervent admirers; the "autumnal" cast and rich emotions of *Persuasion* appeal more to readers as they achieve similarly greater degrees of maturity in their own lives; and yet the youthful satires *Love and Freindship* and *Northanger Abbey* have their fans as well. Some readers are certain there is a fixed hierarchy and take no greater pleasure than in defending their choice and converting their opponents. Others find the question as impertinent and irrelevant as if they had been asked to pick a favorite child. It is, moreover, common that readers find their preferences shift from one novel to another over time. This is natural, for the Austen we discover in adolescence is not the same Austen we return to in later life.

Austen's novels provide not only the aesthetic pleasure of a good read, but also the intellectual engagement of a good think. For a long time I refused help reading Jane Austen, preferring the certain simple delights of reading for fun. I sought help reading Chaucer, Shakespeare, Richardson, Charlotte Brontë, Dickens, and Woolf, but I would not "spoil" my reading of Austen with the dry, critical analysis of scholarly exegesis.

It was therefore with skepticism and the guilty belief that I was somehow betraying Jane that I recently walked into a lecture by Stephen Arkin, chair of the San Francisco State University English department. To begin, he read aloud the opening pages of *Pride and Prejudice*. Mrs. Bennet exclaims that Netherfield Hall is let at last, Mr. Bennet projects indifference, and the two enact conjugal misunderstanding and mutual frustration distilled to the point of perfection. Steve read the familiar lines aloud in a way that not merely had us laughing, but that highlighted Austen's ability to delineate character through ironic exchange. Although this technique can be found in many novels, these famous pages constitute perhaps the best example in the English language. The live reading increased our appreciation of the comedy of the scene, but the basic observation about Austen's mastery of irony would not have been new to the careful reader—and no doubt the packed room was filled with nothing but such careful readers and rereaders.

Then Steve made a point that astonished us all: the disdained Mrs. Bennet is right. She seems ridiculous, simplistic, and even stupid, but she nevertheless predicts the entire story line of *Pride and Prejudice*. It *is* a wonderful thing for their girls that the Hall is let, for not only one but two daughters make marriage matches beyond their expectations. Furthermore, we might roll our eyes at Mrs. Bennet's continued scheming, but by depriving Jane of the carriage in inclement weather, thereby causing her to catch cold and be invited to remain at Netherfield for her recovery, the conniving mother does manage to seal the deal. Although the first laugh is on Mrs. Bennet, we are so busy sniggering at her that we fail to see the justice of her remarks and machinations: the last laugh is on us. We, too, are the targets of Austen's fierce, subtle irony.

The point is so obvious that it is almost invisible, so simple that it can only be seen by the most astute of critics. In this one quick point, Stephen Arkin changed our reading of *Pride and Prejudice*. Although my emotional engagement remained as unspoiled as it ever was, my intellectual appreciation had deepened into a fuller understanding of Austen's ability to structure a novel, to capture human nature, and to layer the levels of her characteristic irony. I hope the essays collected in this volume will afford you similar moments of Austenian awakening.

One way of sifting through the wealth of literature on Jane Austen is to make a rough distinction between those who explain why Austen, her characters, and her world seem so familiar to us, and those who insist we appreciate the differences.

For the first group of critics, the appeal lies in the modern reader's ability to step effortlessly over the threshold of history into Regency England. Austen's strangely familiar world constitutes a timeless pocket of human experience, and her observations concerning human nature are just as valid now as they were then. Far from being cold philosophical insights, these observations take on the warm personalities of her creations. "I had a date with Mr. Collins last night," we might confide to a friend with exasperation, or with glee, "What a Darcy!"; we might call a matchmaker "an inveterate Emma," or a babbler "Miss Bates." Without collapsing into caricature, her vivid portraits can be used to sum up all we might want to say of a person. No simple description of any of these characters would suffice, since even Austen's flattest characters are nuanced throughout the course of the novels. For the critics who idolize the portraitist, Austen paints characters who are so fully realized in their fictional worlds that they appear to step off the page.

We see not only our friends, lovers, and acquaintances, but also ourselves in Austen's novels. Her heroes and heroines especially seem to invite identification. Who can resist believing that she, too, possesses the "fine eyes" of Elizabeth? Or the common sense of Elinor? Who is not tempted to strike Darcy's pose of aristocratic disdain? To fancy himself an irresistible rake like Willoughby? Austen knows us better than we know ourselves because, as noted by Harold Bloom, she has helped to invent us.

Austen has a way of putting things that often strikes us as exactly right—as even better than what we could have come up with to describe our own experiences. When we come upon a passage that hits us with more than ordinary force, we feel unnerved but somehow comforted. There seems to be no distance at all between Austen's world and our own when the only balm for a broken heart is found in Wentworth's letter to Anne in which he at last declares: "You pierce my soul"; when Knightley's cutting "Badly done" rings in our ears after some inconsiderate act; when we justify some act of folly with Sophia's caution, "Run mad as often as you chuse, but do not faint"; when the only antidote to a gloomy day is the satiric mirth packed into the famous first line, "It is a truth universally acknowledged." Such passages seize us, draw us into the novels, and in some mysterious way transform us. By reciting time and again the familiar lines, we not only come to know the characters intimately, but we often arrive at a greater understanding of ourselves. Although we bring our own hope, longing, guilt, and elation to the novels, our reading fashions our sentiments after Austen's unique understanding of human relationships. When we pass from the fictional world back into the real, we hear her turns of phrase, see her characters, and overlay her scenes onto the experiences of our everyday lives.

We like to say that we are the readers of these novels, but in a deeper sense it is these strangely resonant novels that have begun to read us. Austen's entire mode of perception, from the arrangement of words to the arching sweep of the stories, is so persuasive that we often find ourselves converted to the unique sect of what Lionel Trilling terms her "secular wisdom."

For some critics the appeal lies in this closeness, but for other critics the attraction lies in distance. To appreciate the novels we must emphasize and reflect on the great differences between Austen's world and our own. Without denying the timelessness of many of Austen's insights into human nature, these critics point out that new readers can only identify with the characters and situations in these two-hundred-year-old novels up to a certain point. Beyond that, the novels become incomprehensible and require decoding. These critics attempt to explain those aspects with which present-day readers might find it difficult to relate.

If the young Wentworth proposed to Anne today, for instance, would Lady Russell be able to persuade her to reject him? Would we reject him? Understanding why Anne did reject Wentworth's first proposal requires us to recognize that social prospects had greater weight in Austen's world than they do in ours. Would a modern Edward Ferrars maintain a loveless relationship with Lucy Steele? Wouldn't we break off such an engagement? Again, comprehending Edward's faithfulness demands that we acknowledge a code of honor that has all but disappeared. If the stories were retold today, these obstacles would not exist and so the novels themselves would not exist: Anne and Wentworth, Elinor and Edward simply would have married immediately and their stories would have ended before they had even begun. To understand the main conflict in

both of these novels and to enjoy the full satisfaction of their happy resolutions, we must reinvest this obsolete moral code with its full consequence.

This moral code was in part determined by the political climate. For
modern readers, Darcy wears his pride like a leather jacket, but for readers who had lived during the French Revolution and who were still waiting to see what social changes would happen in England, such
ostentatious aristocratic pomp was thought to lead to lower-class resentment and revolution. Social mobility was necessary to ensure a smooth
transition from an age of aristocracy to an age of democracy. For this reason Emma's snobbery is inexcusable, and her rude remark to Miss Bates
at Box Hill is not a mere slip: it exposes Emma's ugly flaw to others as
well as to herself, and so functions as the turning point of the entire
novel. When Wentworth returns from fighting in the Napoleonic Wars,
he has not only secured his future, he has become a national hero. In
these novels, the enormous importance—and seductive power—of Mr.
Darcy's good management of Pemberley, of Mr. Knightley's concern for
the tenants of his abbey lands, and of Captain Wentworth's naval record
can only be fully appreciated against the almost invisible background of
the broader historical movement of English nationalism. Those higher
up on the social scale were welcome to remain there if they took care of
the English citizens and the English soil under their protection, and
those lower down on the social scale were welcome to move up if they
cultivated that soil and protected it from foreign threats. In some ways
conservative, and in other ways forward-thinking, Austen calibrates her
moral codes to correspond to the safety and prosperity of her homeland.

Love is hard enough; money makes matters worse. Today, love is less
likely to be influenced by the cold numbers of dowry income and inheritance than it was in the early eighteenth century. In Austen's novels, romantic relationships are forged both because of and in spite of pecuniary
concerns. Many of Austen's heroines don't have enough money: Fanny
is poor, Elinor and Marianne have gone down in the world, and Jane,
Elizabeth, and Catherine come from modest backgrounds: none are
wealthy enough for their heroes. Their meager dowries are further diminished by division, for there are too many children. The Morlands
have ten, the Prices nine, the Bennets five, and all girls, and the Dashwoods, also all girls, are still too many at three. Some of Austen's heroines do have enough money—but their lot isn't much better. Emma, for
instance, believes she should fall in love with someone of her own rank:

luckily, she can easily exchange Frank Churchill for Mr. Knightley. Anne is less fortunate: having once rejected the prospect-poor Wentworth, it takes her years and an entire novel to win him back. The possession of money can make heroines just as lonely as its lack. Money makes love harder to find, and for that reason it makes the endings more than simply happy—it makes them blaringly triumphant.

For critics who emphasize distance, our fullest understanding of Austen depends on this historical context. Placing Austen back in her own time requires more than superficial tailoring: we cannot dress up in the characters' manners and morals the same way we could, should we be so inclined, dress up in their pelisses and breeches. The best way to understand both ourselves and these fictional early-nineteenth-century beings is to consider how much the world has changed, not just in the outward trappings of coaches, costumes, and architecture, but in the strict but invisible claims of duty, honor, status, family, money, and love.

Why, then, do we read Jane Austen? Some appreciate her timeless truths, some her portrayal of a world now lost—and some both, for the approaches are not incompatible. While it is difficult to say why we read Austen without referring either to time-transcending similarities or to historical differences, any real response to the question will be much more than a measurement of the distance between our world and hers. The essayists of this volume tell us why they read Austen. While personal, their reflections also go a long way toward explaining the phenomenon of Austen's permanent popularity.

Some of the essays have been newly composed by contemporary academics and authors, and others have been culled from the works of some of the greatest critics of the last hundred years. Fresh perspectives are juxtaposed with essays that have stood the test of time. Literary critics and social historians offer the informed comments of close readers, whereas authors and essayists, who are the direct descendants of Austen's ironic line, provide the insight of practitioners.

At the most fundamental level, Austen is an artist and craftswoman. We read *Emma* not only for the initial pleasure it affords, writes David Lodge, but also for the deepening understanding of Austen's skill as an author afforded by each rereading. For W. Somerset Maugham, the eternal vibrancy of *Pride and Prejudice* is wrought by Austen's skilled handling of structure and technique. Austen turns the love plot so adroitly, writes Margot Livesey, that we feel "a whole world order is in question until [the heroine and hero] find each other." Diane Johnson explains how

Austen exploits and transforms traditional narrative techniques such as identification, dialogue, and point of view. Just as these modern novelists admire and then pillage Austen's novels for their own artistic ends, so do filmmakers: Amy Heckerling tells us how she transformed *Emma* into the romantic comedy *Clueless.*

Although in many respects timeless, Austen holds a special place in literary history, and it is helpful to think of the composition of her works, and their transmission, as occurring in time. Brian Southam tells us about his own special place in literary history as collator and editor of Austen's complete works, including his grail-like quest for the original manuscript of *Volume the Second.* My essay repositions *Northanger Abbey* in the broader literary heritage and calls attention to its playful rewriting of received narrative tricks. John Wiltshire discusses the differences between Austen's then-cutting-edge novels and their modern transpositions into backward-gazing heritage films.

The subject matter of Austen's novels is historically embedded, and some essayists situate them with respect to contemporary political events, social currents, and moral values. Donald Greene refutes the claim that Austen is "limited" and that she does not write about "death or sex, hunger or war, guilt or God." To reinvest the terms "sense" and "sensibility" with their full original import, Ian Watt sets them in their cultural background. Lionel Trilling re-situates *Emma* in a burgeoning democratic society in which morals and politics are intertwined: Emma's snobbish discrimination and misplaced meddling disrupts the innocent, idyllic, and quintessentially English landscape of Highbury. Harold Bloom sets Austen at the cusp of the Aristocratic and Democratic Ages: in *Persuasion,* she transforms Richardson's tragic depiction of the Protestant will into ironic comedy.

Although Austen's morals can be explained in part by her times, they are also uniquely hers. Alain de Botton shows us how Austen contrasts status hierarchy with her own moral hierarchy in *Mansfield Park.* The enduring persuasiveness of Austen's strict moral notions of "sanity and sense" intrigues Virginia Woolf. Kingsley Amis faults Austen for the "censoriousness" of *Mansfield Park,* whereas James Collins finds the high moral standards of the novel inspiring. In her reading, Fay Weldon goes so far as to suggest that "perhaps we *should* look to fiction for moral instruction" and value writing as "a sacred charge." Not entirely solemn, morals also fulfill a more lighthearted purpose: C. S. Lewis cites Austen's "hard core of morality" as "just what makes good comedy possible."

For many, Austen's morality is less a strict code of conduct and more an account of mature human interaction. The ridiculous, for Benjamin Nugent, can be found in the contrast between those characters who interact as fully formed individuals and those who, like Mary Bennet, interact as nerds because they are unable to connect with others on a deeper level. A. S. Byatt and Ignês Sodré talk about the timeless relationships in *Mansfield Park:* real family members often fail to understand one another, and alternative family relationships are forged in their place. Austen is a humanist who seems to understand certain eternal truths of human nature.

The subtitle of the collection is pilfered from Lionel Trilling's classic article "Why We Read Jane Austen," in which he reflects on the perennial relevance of her "sacred wisdom." Rebecca Mead imagines her imparting that wisdom, and its accompanying wit, at a dinner party of immortals. The timelessness of Austen's art and insights is commended by J. B. Priestley, who describes her oeuvre as a "version of the perpetual human comedy, in which we all have to play our parts."

Austen's perpetual comedies are of a specific genre: romance. Martin Amis calls *Pride and Prejudice* a "divine comedy of love," and Amy Bloom reads *Persuasion* as a cautionary tale: Austen reminds us that we must never lose sight of "the one necessary and essential love." Jay McInerney observes that "a belief in true love, with passion as its signal component, is precisely what distinguishes Austen heroines from most of their contemporaries"; he confesses to serial crushes on Elizabeth, Fanny, Emma, and Anne.

Austen ends her stories with love and marriage, writes Eva Brann, because she "knows what the angels know—that happiness is more worthy of note than unhappiness." This angelically happy mood imbues the novels with sparkle and life. Austen's heroes and heroines are all in pursuit of what Louis Auchincloss terms "the good life": a life worth living. Austen's novels are about life, and for this reason they are, according to Eudora Welty, "dazzlingly alive."

As a result, Austen herself seems to be magically present and dazzlingly alive in her works. Virginia Woolf calls our attention, in the juvenilia, to the sound of a young girl laughing. Janet Todd observes that "Austen permits this intimacy to us all in an inimitable way." If you make friends with Austen, writes J. B. Priestley, "you have made a friend for life."

You have made not just one friend, I'd like to add, but innumerable friends: all those who are, like E. M. Forster, "slightly imbecile about Jane

Austen." With this shared literary fervor, we greet each other in print and in the world as though we are destined to be friends, as Mrs. Jennings warmly welcomes the Dashwoods into Derbyshire, or as Austen's relative Mrs. Mowll welcomed the young scholar Brian Southam into her home to read Austen's original manuscript over coffee and biscuits.

Opening the cover to this volume is like opening the door to all the clamorous merriment of a book club meeting. Each of these essayists has taken a shot at defining and explaining Austen's place both in the literary canon and in the cultural imagination. Through exchanges with the fellow readers whose voices are included in this volume, I hope you will be encouraged to formulate your own unique and personal response to the timeless question: why do *you* read Jane Austen?

I'd like to thank Stephen Arkin, Lea Beresford, Harold Bloom, Jeanne Bloom, Karen Carson, Al Maggini, Bonnie Nadell, and Jill Schwartzman.

—*SC*

A TRUTH
UNIVERSALLY
ACKNOWLEDGED

Susanna Clarke

WHY WE READ JANE AUSTEN: YOUNG PERSONS IN INTERESTING SITUATIONS

"Human nature is so well disposed towards those who are in interesting situations, that a young person, who either marries or dies, is sure of being kindly spoken of."

So said Jane Austen in *Emma* in the early 1800s, and for the rest of the nineteenth century novelists got a lot of mileage out of young persons who either died or married. Dickens excelled at the young persons who died, Austen did the ones who married.

Stories about love and marriage are full of the good stuff: romance, sexual attraction, jealousy, suspense, misunderstanding. But in the early nineteenth century they had another dimension. All of a woman's future—her happily-ever-after or lack of the same—was implicit in her choice of husband. Such, at least, was the conventional wisdom of the age, and whether or not it was entirely true, clearly many things did depend on whom a woman married—her income, her status, her home, perhaps even her occupations.

If the female characters in Austen's novels sometimes give the impression of considering potential husbands rather dispassionately, there is good reason for it. In many ways they are not only choosing a husband, they are also choosing a career. By their marriage Austen's heroines may become a parson's wife (Elinor, Fanny, and Catherine), a landowner's wife (Elizabeth and Emma), or a ship's captain's wife (Anne). With the exception of Emma, marriage holds out to them not simply a more financially secure life, but the opportunity for a more active, socially responsible one.

Today the idea of marriage is a loaded one; at best it's a closing down of options. Austen's women saw things differently. For them life opened up at the point of marriage. The married state, not the single state, meant liberation. Marriage offered freedom from the confined life of a girl at home. In *Mansfield Park* Maria Bertram marries to gain "Sotherton and London, independence and splendour"—two houses, worldly status, and independence from her parents.

Of course this bid for freedom only worked if you married the right person. Maria did not and found in marriage a prison at least as confining as her father's house. For both sexes, marriage to the wrong person could have disastrous consequences—not simply unhappiness and financial precariousness, but worse still, moral degradation. If you were led to marry someone small-minded, mean, or coarse (whether by your own faulty judgment or the faulty judgment of your friends and relations), you risked those qualities rubbing off on you. It was a danger Austen seems to have felt men were particularly prone to. Of Mr. John Dashwood she says: "Had he married a more amiable woman, he might have been made still more respectable than he was:—he might even have been made amiable himself." Similar things are said of Frank Churchill's uncle, who is married to the perennially disagreeable, ill-tempered Mrs. Churchill: ". . . he would be the best man in the world if he were left to himself . . ."

Even if you somehow proved immune to your partner's vices and you didn't actually acquire them yourself, your personality might be warped by trying to accommodate them, as with Elizabeth's father, Mr. Bennet. Twenty-something years of his wife's nonsensical conversation seem to have given him a faintly masochistic turn: he takes a strange pleasure in never giving her a straight answer, thereby making some of her imaginary frustrations real and provoking her to exclaim even more. These two do not act pleasantly on each other.

With stakes as high as these it's hardly surprising that the action of Jane Austen's six novels so often turns on character. The author, her readers, and her heroines all set themselves to decipher the personality of *this* attractive young man, *that* newly arrived young woman, not as an abstract exercise in aesthetics or moral judgment, but because these young people form a significant part of the available marriage pool and the future happiness of someone—usually someone dear to the heroine— depends on it. Marriage is rarely far from the thoughts of an Austen heroine, but much of the time it is not her own marriage that occupies her.

Elizabeth Bennet, Emma Woodhouse, Anne Elliot, and Fanny Price are all, in their different ways, inveterate people-watchers. When Darcy asks Elizabeth Bennet, "May I ask to what these questions tend?" she replies, "Merely to the illustration of *your* character . . . I am trying to make it out." Nor is it simply the pressure of finding a suitable partner that makes them so curious about other people.

In our largely urban culture we choose those to whom we belong: our friends are likely to have interests and opinions similar to our own. Other family members may live some distance away, and we have a degree of control over how often we see them. Austen's women—and most of her men—don't have this freedom. They live in small, clearly defined societies—a village or country town. Even Emma Woodhouse, who is wealthy, hasn't much choice of companions; she cannot avoid Miss Bates who irritates her, Mr. and Mrs. Cole who bore her, or Jane Fairfax whom she dislikes. In fixed societies it becomes a matter of some necessity to understand one's neighbors, to seek out those most likely to contribute to one's comfort and to learn how best to get on with the rest.

Often there is a newcomer whose character becomes a sort of mystery that requires unraveling. In *Sense and Sensibility* it is Willoughby, in *Emma* Frank Churchill, in *Persuasion* Mr. Elliot, while *Pride and Prejudice* has three: Bingley, Darcy, and Wickham. Darcy has somehow been redefined in recent years as a dark, brooding, romantic hero. I've seen him mentioned with Heathcliff and Mr. Rochester as if they were all points on the same spectrum. But that's not how Elizabeth or Jane Austen sees him. When Elizabeth thinks Darcy is arrogant, she isn't attracted to him. She turns him down. It's only when she sees him as a kind friend, a caring brother, and a good master that she begins to fall in love with him. If he makes other people happy, then he is capable of making her happy too. I doubt that Elizabeth is secretly or subconsciously attracted to a "dark" Darcy. Twenty-first-century women (and men) can afford to romanticize dark heroes because their fates and futures are in their own hands—Elizabeth didn't have that option.

As in a detective story where a tiny detail may hold the key to a murder, some small action may turn out to be a clue to a man's personality. Halfway through *Emma* Frank Churchill goes to London to get his hair cut, and it promptly becomes one of the most overanalyzed haircuts in English literature:

There was certainly no harm in his travelling sixteen miles twice over on such an errand; but there was an air of foppery and nonsense in it which she could not approve. It did not accord with the rationality of plan, the moderation in expense, or even the unselfish warmth of heart which she had believed herself to discern in him yesterday. Vanity, extravagance, love of change, restlessness of temper, which must be doing something, good or bad; heedlessness as to the pleasure of his father and Mrs. Weston, indifferent as to how his conduct might appear in general; he became liable to all these charges . . .

And these, it ought to be said, are just Emma's *first* thoughts on the haircut. Of course she is right and the haircut is a clue—but not in the way she thinks.

Austen's liveliest and most articulate heroines (Elizabeth Bennet and Emma Woodhouse), who congratulate themselves on their superior knowledge of people, are the ones who get it spectacularly wrong. Elizabeth misjudges Darcy, Wickham, and Bingley; Emma goes one better and misjudges everybody including herself. ("With insufferable vanity had she believed herself in the secret of every body's feelings; with unpardonable arrogance proposed to arrange every body's destiny.") But the quiet heroines, the women whom circumstances have conspired to humble (Fanny Price and Anne Elliot) see and understand perfectly. I suspect that "humble" is the key word here. There is a logical connection for Austen between clarity of vision and true humility (a virtue so unfashionable nowadays that we scarcely believe it exists and use it as a synonym for "hypocrisy"). If you no longer believe that you can control a situation or have anything to gain from it, then your chances of perceiving it clearly are much improved. Not that this is a particularly pleasant gift: Fanny and Anne are both cruelly hurt by what they see. Each endures the heartbreak of watching the man she loves court someone else.

Film and television adaptations have misled us into thinking Austen wrote about something called "the Jane Austen world"—a world of picturesque houses, romantic landscapes, carriages, placid servants, candlelit ballrooms, bonnets, and costumes. But these things belong to costume drama; they are what give it visual impact. Austen wasn't a visual writer. Her landscapes are emotional and moral—what we would call psychological; they are not physical.

There is always more negative space around Austen than we think. We know that she did not address social problems, criticize political or social institutions, delve into the lives of the working class, or rise to describe the aristocracy. In fact the list of things Austen didn't write about is much longer than that. She has little to say about dress; even less about landscape. The servants, who must play an enormous part in the daily lives of her characters, are rarely named. How many of the most important houses in her fiction are described? Not Longbourn. Not Hartfield. Even Mansfield Park is barely sketched in ("an handsome house") until Mary Crawford contemplates marrying Tom Bertram in Chapter 5. Then we learn it has: "a park, a real park five miles round, a spacious modern-built house, so well placed and well screened as to deserve to be in any collection of engravings of gentlemen's seats in the kingdom, and wanting only to be completely new furnished . . ." The liveliest, most revealing description of property in Austen generally comes at the point at which some young woman is thinking of marrying the owner, because then it ceases to be part of the physical landscape and takes on an emotional significance; it is part of her possible future (perhaps, as in Mary Crawford's case, the most important part).

What looks like physical description in Austen often turns out to be something else entirely: ". . . Mr Darcy soon drew the attention of the room by his fine, tall person, handsome features; noble mein . . ." This is a curiously opaque set of adjectives. If the police tried to find Mr. Darcy based on this they wouldn't get very far. The truth is that it is not really a description of Darcy at all; it is a description of the effect he had on other people. Most important of all, it is the setup for a joke. At the beginning of the paragraph the people in the ballroom are impressed by what they hear of Darcy's large fortune and attribute every physical perfection to him. By the end of the paragraph he has snubbed them and "not all his large estate in Derbyshire could then save him from having a most forbidding, disagreeable countenance . . ." Wealth and novelty have a bewitching effect on the inhabitants of Meryton, but can easily be trumped by their sense of their own importance.

Take another quintessential Austen scene—the Netherfield ball from *Pride and Prejudice*. It takes up all of Chapter 18 and feels as if it should be a set piece. Any television adaptation of *Pride and Prejudice* will certainly make it a set piece; there will be shadowy rooms, candlelight, flowers, beautiful dresses, lovely girls, and officers' uniforms. But Austen barely touches on the physical aspects of the ball. We get an admission that Elizabeth "had dressed with more than usual care" (in what we do not know) and that she "entered the drawing-room at Netherfield"; later there's a mention of the cold ham and chicken they had for supper. That's it. Austen's ball, the ball of the novel, is all emotion (Elizabeth's humiliation and anger, her surprise at Darcy's unexpected attentions, Jane and

Bingley falling quietly in love in the background), comedy (Mrs. Bennet's triumphing over her neighbors, Mary Bennet's cringe-making piano playing), and shaky moral judgments (Darcy's contempt for Elizabeth's family, Elizabeth's increasing anger toward Darcy). No candles, no dresses, scarcely any dancing.

We have such a strong visual image of the Regency period, and such a strong association of Austen with costume drama, that we barely notice that the bonnets and gowns, carriages and servants—all the Regency paraphernalia—are what we bring to Austen, not the other way round. Generally speaking, one of the pleasures of reading a nineteenth-century novel is crossing over into a world quite different from our own—think of *Oliver Twist*'s vividly imagined criminals, undertaker's shop, and workhouse with its arcane set of parish officials. But the pleasure of reading a Jane Austen novel is like that in only a superficial way. She chose a small canvas—"3 or 4 Families in a Country Village" was how she put it. The "3 or 4 Families" are arranged in the foreground and middle ground. The background (the "Country Village") is sketched in with a few light strokes. But because the humanity of her three or four families—their sufferings and pleasures, their good qualities and bad—is so recognizable to us, so familiar, the veil between her age and ours grows very thin.

Eudora Welty

THE RADIANCE OF JANE AUSTEN

Jane Austen will soon be closer in calendar time to Shakespeare than to us. Within the reading life of the next generation, that constellation of six bright stars will have swung that many years deeper into the one sky, vast and crowded, of English literature. Will these future readers be in danger of letting the novels elude them because of distance, so that their pleasure will not be anything like ours? The future of fiction is a mystery; it is like the future of ourselves.

But, we ask, how could it be possible for these novels to seem remote? For one thing, the noise! What a commotion comes out of their pages! Jane Austen loved high spirits, she had them herself, and she always rejoiced in the young. The exuberance of her youthful characters is one of the unaging delights of her work. Through all the mufflings of time we can feel the charge of their vitality, their happiness in doing, dancing, laughing, in being alive. There is always a lot of jumping; that seems to vibrate through time. Motion is constant—indeed, it is necessary for communication in the country. It takes days to go some of the tiny distances, but how the wheels spin! The sheer velocity of the novels, scene to scene, conversation to conversation, tears to laughter, concert to picnic to dance, is something equivalent to a pulsebeat. The clamorous griefs and joys are all giving voice to the tireless relish of life. The novels' vitality is irresistible for us. Surely all this cannot fade away, letting the future wonder, two hundred years from now, what our devotion to Jane Austen was all about.

For nearly this long already the gaiety of the novels has pervaded them, the irony has kept its bite, the reasoning is still sweet, the sparkle undiminished. Their high spirits, their wit, their celerity and harmony of motion, their symmetry of design appear still unrivaled in the English novel. Jane Austen's work at its best seems as nearly flawless as any fiction could be.

Of course, this in itself may create a gentle threat to the reader's mood of understanding today. This is possible even while we are still able to like, and to turn to, that which we know to be better than *we* could do. And besides writing perfectly, she did so not in the least by accident; the oddness is compounded. Her intelligence was formidable, and it was well nourished by an understanding family. She was beautifully educated at home, was always well read, "intimately acquainted with the merits and defects of the best essays and novels in the English language," Henry Austen has told us in the "Biographical Notice," and "her memory [was] tenacious." Best of all, she had been born, or rewarded, with fairy gifts—not one, but two entirely separate ones. She had the genius of originality, and she had the genius of comedy. And they never fought each other at all, but worked together in a harmony that must have delighted her in a way we rejoice to think about, and a way particularly belonging to the eighteenth century, whose spiritual child she was.

She was, of course, from the first, a highly conscious artist. This the writer of comedy indeed must be, and in comedy was she not supreme? We know, too, from her own remarks, that she looked on the novel as a work of art, and that she gave it the concentration, the devotion, of all her powers.

But it is further well known that Jane Austen's life was not only unusual for an author's, it was unique. And for this, will the future treat her as blindly as we have been known to treat her and take her down because she was a spinster who—having never lived anywhere outside her father's rectory and the later family homes in Bath, Southampton, and Chawton, whose notion of travel was an excursion to Lyme Regis—could never have got to know very much about life? Will they wish to call her a snob?—her life touched intimately only that of the other country gentry in the neighborhood. Or a butterfly?—gossip comes down through all these years that she couldn't do at all without dancing. Her detractors have also declared that even the Battle of Waterloo went by without her notice, so remote was her life; although a novel called *Emma*, published of course anonymously like her others, came out dedicated to the Prince Regent soon after his victory "by His Royal Highness's dutiful and obedient servant, the author." It might be that dedication page that will puzzle the far future: readers of *Emma* may wonder what it was that the Prince Regent had done that was so deserving.

But what must be indelibly certain is that never did it escape Jane Austen that the interesting situations of life can take place, and notably do, at home. The dangerous confrontations and the decisive dialogues can very conveniently happen in country parsonages. The novels she wrote were, in themselves, remarkable examples of this very phenomenon.

Each novel is a formidable engine of strategy. It is made to be—a marvel of designing and workmanship, capable of spontaneous motion at the lightest touch and of travel at delicately controlled but rapid speed toward its precise destination. It could kill us all, had she wished it to; it fires at us, all along the way, using understatements in good aim. Let us be thankful it is trained not on our hearts but on our illusions and our vanities. Who among novelists ever more instantly recognized the absurd when she saw it in human behavior, then polished it off to more devastating effect, than this young daughter of a Hampshire rectory, who as she finished the chapters enjoyed reading them to her family, to whom she also devoted her life? She could be our Waterloo; she *is* our Waterloo. We pray that those readers of the future will not lose or throw away their heritage of absurdity; this alone would render them incapable of knowing what her novels "are all about," and would probably make them hopeless as human beings in the process.

Reading those chapters aloud to her own lively, vocative family, on whose shrewd intuition, practiced estimation of conduct, and seasoned judgment of character she relied almost as well as on her own, Jane Austen must have enjoyed absolute confidence in an understanding reception of her work. The novels still have a bloom of shared pleasure. And the felicity they have for us must partly lie in the confidence they take for granted between the author and her readers—at the moment, ourselves. Odd to our own twentieth-century expectations as this trust may be, it is unshakably effective to this day.

This young novelist's position was in every respect clear. As all her work testifies, her time, her place, her location in society are in no more question than the fact that she was a woman. She wrote from a perfectly solid and firm foundation, and her work is wholly affirmative.

There is probably some connection between this confidence, this positivity, and the flow of comedy. A novelist may be strictly satiric in the presence of strangers, encouraged to more acidity still by a ring of sworn enemies. But when the listeners all have bright faces, ready minds, teasing and affectionate dispositions, mimicking ways, and kindred wars, it would have been hard, even had it occurred to her, to keep up hauteur, to give in to sentimentality, to plunge into unconfined melodrama, to pause for too many sermons along the way. Comedy is sociable and positive, and exacting. Its methods, its boundaries, its *point,* all belong to the familiar.

Jane Austen *needed* very little space, very limited material, to work with; asking for little seems immoderate to us. Given: a household in the country, then add its valuable neighbor—and there, under her hands, is the full presence of the world. As if coming in response to a call for good sense, life is at hand and astir and in strong vocal power. At once there is convenient and constant communication between those two houses. The day, the week, the season fill to repletion with news, arrivals, speculation, and fresh strawberries, with tumult and crises, and the succeeding invitations. Everybody doing everything together—what mastery she has over the scene, the family scene! The dinner parties, the walking parties, the dances, picnics, concerts, excursions to Lyme Regis and sojourns at Bath, all give their testimony to Jane Austen's ardent belief—which our century's city dwellers find odd—that the unit of everything worth knowing in life is in the family, that family relationships are the natural basis of all other relationships.

Her world, small in size but drawn exactly to scale, may of course easily be regarded as a larger world seen at a judicious distance—it would be the exact distance at which all haze evaporates, full clarity prevails, and true perspective appears. But it would be more to the point to suppose that her stage was small because such were her circumstances and that, in fact, she was perfectly equipped to recognize in its very dimensions the first virtue and principle of comedy. The focus she used was for the same end: it was central. A clear ray of light strikes full upon the scene, resulting in the prism of comedy.

And of this prerequisite world she sees and defines both sides—sensibility as well as sense, for instance—and presents them in their turns, in a continuing state of balance: moral, aesthetic, and dramatic balance. This ingenuity in the way of narrative (not to put it too strongly) and this generosity of understanding could be seen in their own brilliant way as other manifestations of her comic gift. The action of her novels is in itself a form of wit, a kind of repartee; some of it is the argument of souls.

Her habit of mind of seeing both sides of her own subject—of seeing it indeed in the round—is a little unusual, too, to writers and readers of our day. And it offers one more good reason, perhaps, why there is little comedy being written now; what is shaped from a single point of view and grows heavily weighted to one side is more likely to turn out a tragedy, or a tragedy by courtesy. But it cannot be allowed that there is any less emotional feeling contained in the novels of Jane Austen because they are not tragedies. Great comic masterpieces that they are, their roots are nourished at the primary sources. They are profound in emotion. Jane Austen was by declared intention a moral, even "improving," writer; if she could have improved us at all, at this far reach, it must be doubted that she would have hesitated. Nor did moralizing keep out life. In her novels the strong feelings she knew, respected, and made evident in her characters and their situations were given their full weight. Far from denying the emotions their power, she used her intuitive and narrative restraint and employed it to excellent advantage. Nothing of feeling has been diminished. There is passion, the stronger for being concealed until it can be concealed no longer; there is desperation, intense suffering such as Marianne Dashwood's and Jane Fairfax's. But the effect of the whole is still that of proportions kept, symmetry maintained, and the classical form honored—indeed celebrated. And we are still within the balustrades of comedy.

All the differences between people then and people now are not external, of course—differences never are. In Jane Austen's time they quite literally saw the world differently.

She was "a warm and judicious admirer of landscape," says Henry Austen's "Biographical Notice"; and for Jane Austen the novelist "judicious" can be taken to mean that landscape was appraised for its suitability in the calendar of events, when excursions called for fine prospects as they did for cold collations. In the novels everything keeps its place, and the place of landscape is in the middle background, in size proportionally small, but drawn and furnished to specification, as truly as was Northanger Abbey built for Catherine Morland to read Mrs. Radcliffe in.

Landscape may be simply a setting, convenience laid out. There is Elizabeth's favorite grove in *Pride and Prejudice;* it is the one Mr. Darcy walks in—and walks for some time—in the hope of meeting Elizabeth in order to give her, with his look of haughty composure, the letter he wrote her at eight o'clock—those two pages written in a very close hand

and beginning "Be not alarmed, Madam." As a grove it is not visible, rather it is suitable. Lady Catherine de Bourgh, paying her call upon the Bennets, condescends to say, "Mis' Bennet, there seemed to be a pretty-ish kind of little wilderness on one side of your lawn. I should be glad to take a turn in it." And here, on the other hand, is Lady Catherine de Bourgh's park: "Every park has its beauty and its prospects; and Elizabeth saw much to be pleased with, though she could not be in such raptures as Mr. Collins expected the scene to inspire, and was but slightly affected by his enumeration of the windows in front of the house, and his relation of what the glazing altogether had originally cost Sir Lewis De Bourgh."

Between Jane Austen's time and ours lies the Romantic movement, but it doesn't matter: it does not lie between her page and our minds. She has command over our vision, and any description of the surround is irrelevant to *Pride and Prejudice:* what we are being afforded are views of character. Thus landscape provides an excuse to Mrs. Elton for bringing her brother Mr. Suckling's barouche-landau into the conversation. The seaside is the cause of rapture in Louisa Musgrove's breast, so that she has to be jumped down the steps by Captain Wentworth, to unlooked-for misfortune.

But it may be harder for us to see what she wants us to when she shakes her finger in our faces. She moralized; she could also be cynical, even at the rare moment coarse—she was, once again, of her day. (And the coarseness of an earlier age shocks the later, perhaps because an ugliness that isn't our own seems to have been something unintentional.) But in her writing there deeply lies, as deeply as anything in her powers, a true tenderness of feeling. Though it could be at the odd moment turned into the other thing, even into cruelty, seldom indeed did it suffer the fatal lapse into what is unlifelike. But our occasional blank aversion from her, now, shows us simply how precarious is the passage of time.

The century that produced Jane Austen was even seamier and more brutal in many ways than our own, and although we, too, boast of an opposite extreme, ours is not *their* opposite extreme: we have nothing in our own best that corresponds to the orderliness, the composure, of that life, or that meets its requirements of the small scale, the lovely proportions, the intimacy, the sense of personal security. And not only is our fare different, our palate is different.

Think of today's fiction in the light of hers. Does some of it appear garrulous and insistent and out-of-joint, and nearly all of it slow? Does now and then a novel come along that's so long, arch, and laborious, so ponderous in literary conceits and so terrifying in symbols, that it might have been written (in his bachelor days) by Mr. Elton as a conundrum, or, in some prolonged spell of elevation, by Mr. Collins in a bid for self-advancement? Yes, but this is understandable. For many of our writers who are now as young as Jane Austen was when she wrote her novels, and as young as she still was when she died, at forty-one, ours is the century of unreason, the stamp of our behavior is violence or isolation; non-meaning is looked upon with some solemnity; and for the purpose of writing novels, most human behavior is looked at through the frame, or the knothole, of alienation. The life Jane Austen wrote about was indeed a different one from ours, but the difference was not as great as that between the frames through which it is viewed. Jane Austen's frame was that of *belonging to her world.* She could step through it, in and out of it as easily and unself-consciously as she stepped through the doorway of the rectory and into the garden to pick strawberries. She was perfectly at home in what she knew, as well as knowledgeable of precisely where she was on earth; she even believed she knew why she was here.

Nothing can change his own life for the writer. Reading can roam the centuries and pleasure itself at will, but writing, the writing of novels, is of its own time only. To each of us alive, our own world is with us, as was Jane Austen's world entirely with her. To any novelist, that which is less important than his own world's presence—its ruthless presence, its blotting-out nearness and newness—is simply irrelevant.

Yet there is left the reconcilable element. Pride and Prejudice, Sense and Sensibility, Persuasion: looked at not only as titles but as the themes they are, they might be called simple, but it is more accurate to call them basic. They are lustrous with long and uninterrupted use. Though at first glance they might not be recognized, it is possible to see most of them today in their newest incarnations. They are beyond time, because they pertain not to the outside world but to the interior, to what goes on perpetually in the mind and heart.

The contemporary mood, temperament, force of habit, or even the elbow-nudge of a passing fashion can affect the way we see life but not the way we *know* it. This is personal and singular and obstinate and hard to kill. The novelist writes as his own person. And so he reads. In reading a novel, as in experiencing our own life, it is what people say and what they do and the way in which they say and do it that tells us the most about them. There is nothing in Jane Austen's work to let us imagine we have learned any more about human character and behavior than she knew; indeed, part of what we know today may well have come to us through reading and rereading her novels.

We have our own charts of the mind and diagnoses of the heart, but they are still the same dangerous territories that Jane Austen knew as well as the shrubbery at Steventon. And here it is their unchangeableness that gives us the shock of pleasure when we read her novels. How familiar, after all, and how inevitable is the motivation of man. His deeds by now may be numberless, but this is in contrast to the very small range of the feelings that drive him. He may fly to the moon at any moment, but at home on earth his motives can still be counted on his fingers. They have not increased or altered yet, and so, for some centuries to come, people may go on saying of Jane Austen, How really *modern* she is, after all.

What is the real secret of the novels' already long life? The answer seems to be: Life itself. The brightness of Jane Austen's eye simply does not grow dim, as have grown the outlines and colors of the scene she saw herself while she wrote—its actualities, like its customs and clothes, have receded from us forever. But she wrote, and her page is dazzlingly alive. Her world seems not only accessible but near, for under her authority and in her charge, all its animation is disclosure.

And toward this life is directed a point of view that is not quite like that of any other novelist at any time on earth. In this point of view she speaks to us, or a voice speaks: it is the author's, and possibly not the same voice that the family heard; but we cannot mistake it; it is her own. It must be the most personal expression of her own true and original mind. And it is inimitable, forever so.

Then will her novels not always catch up with her readers as the generations fly? To the farthest future, we might wonder if at least some of the characters might not safely travel—especially some of the great secondary characters: the eccentrics, like Mr. Woodhouse, but he is already feeling the draft; or the steady talkers, like Miss Bates, who has just recollected what she was talking *about,* her mother's spectacles. But it is already clear what Jane Austen's characters are made of: they are made of the novel they are in, and never can they come away from their context. Miss Bates, though always so ready to go anywhere, is not movable; she is part of *Emma.*

It might even be the case that the more original the work of imagination, the greater the danger of its succumbing to the violence of transportation. Insomuch as it is alive, it must remain fixed in its own time and place, whole and intact, inviolable as a diamond. It abides in its own element, and this of course is the mind.

No, Jane Austen cannot follow readers into any other time. She cannot go into the far future, and she never came to us. She is there forever where she wrote, immovable to the very degree of her magnitude. The readers of the future will have to do the same as we ourselves have done, and with the best equipment they can manage, make the move themselves. The reader is the only traveler. It is not her world or her time, but her art, that is approachable, today or tomorrow. The novels in their radiance are a destination.

Rebecca Mead

SIX REASONS TO READ JANE AUSTEN

Because we can't invite her to dinner, even though we'd like to

There exists, unfortunately enough, no league table of results for the popular parlor game of "Name Your Fantasy Dinner Party Guests," in which participants compile a list of the famous figures, living or dead, with whom it would be most fun to spend an evening. But if there were, Jane Austen would likely rank high on it. We imagine her sandwiched at table between Oscar Wilde on her left and William Shakespeare on her right, asking Cleopatra to pass the salt. There are some writers whose company, one can't help suspecting, might be less enjoyable than their literary works—Edgar Allan Poe, maybe, or Philip Larkin—but Austen, the thinking goes, would make excellent company. We imagine her offering acute observations on her fellow guests, *sotto voce,* of the sort we know she saved up for her letters to her sister, Cassandra: as she wrote after dining with one of her Hampshire neighbors, "Mrs Powlett was at once both expensively and nakedly dressed; we have had the satisfaction of estimating her Lace and Muslin."

Because she probably wouldn't want to come

Of course, though, it's entirely possible—let's admit it, entirely likely—that Austen would relish the prospect of dining with us far less than we would relish the prospect of doing so with her. "We are to have a tiny party here tonight," she wrote to Cassandra on another occasion. "I hate tiny parties—they force one into constant exertion." Devoted readers would not wish to force Jane Austen into anything, particularly not an activity that might interfere with her writerly concentration—although she regularly hid her pages under a blotting pad whenever a visitor called upon her, great literary works coming second to small social graces. Still, it wouldn't do to irritate her. As Lord David Cecil wrote, more than seventy years ago: "I should be seriously upset, I should worry for weeks and weeks, if I incurred the disapproval of Jane Austen."

Because the great recognized her greatness

Richard Sheridan, the most successful playwright of Austen's age, called *Pride and Prejudice* one of the cleverest things he had ever read; Sir Walter Scott, the preeminent novelist of his day, confided to his diary in 1825 that Austen "had a talent for describing the involvements and feelings and characters of ordinary life which is to me the most wonderful I have ever met with. The Big Bow-Wow strain I can do myself like any now going; but the exquisite touch, which renders ordinary commonplace things and characters interesting, from the truth of the description and the sentiment, is denied to me." When Marian Evans was readying herself mentally to try her hand for the first time at fiction—she would become George Eliot, the greatest novelist of the Victorian era—she undertook a trip to the Scilly Isles, off the tip of Cornwall, with her common-law husband, George Lewes. (Lewes, by the way, deserves the esteem of all who value literature, not just for his careful nurturing of George Eliot's talent in the face of her profound insecurity, but for his early, unstinting admiration of Austen, of whom he wrote in *Blackwood's Magazine* in 1859, "She will doubtless be read as long as English novels find readers.") What did the Leweses read aloud to each other every evening, in their lodgings upon the island of St. Mary's? The novels of Jane Austen.

Because we are made to in school

How old is old enough to read Jane Austen? They are books about young people—the immortal Emma Woodhouse is just twenty—written, at least in their earliest versions, by a girl no older than their heroines: Jane Austen was nineteen when she finished the first draft of *Sense and Sensibility,* and completed an early version of *Pride and Prejudice* at twenty-one. Even so, a too-early introduction to Austen may be a mistake. Austen is ironic; but sarcasm is the humor teenagers understand best. (That's why adolescents love *The Catcher in the Rye,* which—along with a taste for flavored cigarettes, cocktails composed of multiple liqueurs, and premature world-weariness—most readers grow out of, however impossible such a falling off of affection may seem when Salinger is first discovered.) Perhaps, instead of *Pride and Prejudice,* teens should be assigned what Austen herself produced at the age of fifteen: her witty, satirical *History of England.* Written in the guise of "a partial, prejudiced, & ignorant Historian," it briefly characterizes the successive monarchs of the realm in a voice already recognizably her own. Of Henry VIII, who established the Church of England in hitherto Catholic Britain, she makes the following marvelous observation: "Nothing can be said in his vindication, but that his abolishing Religious Houses & leaving them to the ruinous depredations of time has been of infinite use to the landscape of England in general."

Because no one understood better the heart's self-deceptions in matters of property

One of the most resonant lines in *Pride and Prejudice* is when Elizabeth Bennet is asked by her incredulous sister Jane when it was that she first fell in love with Mr. Darcy. "I believe I must date it from my first seeing his beautiful grounds at Pemberley," Elizabeth replies. Of course, she is joking: the reader has long realized her attraction to Mr. Darcy's intelligence, even as she is repelled by his air of apparent disdain. And yet— is she joking entirely? Modern-day visitors to the stately homes of England—including the splendid Chatsworth, in Derbyshire, thought to be one inspiration for Pemberley—might well understand how plausible a marriage to a master of the house far more unappealing than Mr. Darcy might suddenly seem. (With so many rooms, surely a husband might easily be avoided?) Perhaps sentiments of this kind were among those that led Austen to accept, at the belated age of twenty-seven, the marriage proposal of Harris Bigg-Wither, a family friend. Bigg-Wither, who was six years younger than his intended, was plain in looks, suffered a speech defect, and was conversationally inept. He was, however, heir to an estate that included Manydown, a handsome manor house recently enhanced by the addition of a new dining room and drawing room. Austen slept on her decision; the next day, she withdrew her acceptance. Beautiful grounds alone, she knew—as Elizabeth Bennet also knows—were not grounds enough for marriage.

Because it's possible to read everything she wrote

Six completed novels, three unfinished ones, three volumes of juvenilia, and some poems and letters: that's it. We may well wish there were more—we long to read those letters burned by her survivors, those un-written novels of her unlived middle age and later years. But, still, there's something satisfyingly manageable about the Austen oeuvre compared with, say, the work of Trollope, who produced forty-seven novels—enough to take a busy reader several lifetimes to complete. One of the greatest rewards of reading Jane Austen, by contrast, is that having done so, we get to reread Jane Austen on a later occasion. No one knew this better than the author, who liked to read her manuscript aloud to family as she was working on it, doubtless testing its effectiveness and tinkering with it thereafter. Even after publication—a point at which many authors withdraw from their work, with all its final, now ineradicable flaws—she liked to revisit her creations. When *Pride and Prejudice* finally appeared in print, she read chapters aloud to one Miss Benn, an impoverished gentlewoman neighbor. "She really does seem to admire Elizabeth," Austen wrote afterward in a letter to Cassandra. "I must confess that *I* think her as delightful a creature as ever appeared in print." Why do we read Jane Austen? Because Jane Austen read Jane Austen, and knew it was as close to perfection as any of us can hope for.

E. M. Forster

JANE AUSTEN: THE SIX NOVELS

I am a Jane Austenite, and therefore slightly imbecile about Jane Austen. My fatuous expression and airs of personal immunity—how ill they set on the face, say, of a Stevensonian! But Jane Austen is so different. She is my favorite author! I read and reread, the mouth open and the mind closed. Shut up in measureless content, I greet her by the name of most kind hostess, while criticism slumbers. The Jane Austenite possesses little of the brightness he ascribes so freely to his idol. Like all regular churchgoers, he scarcely notices what is being said. For instance, the grammar of the following sentence from *Mansfield Park* does not cause him the least uneasiness:

> And, alas! how always known no principle to supply as a duty what the heart was deficient in.

Nor does he notice any flatness in this dialogue from *Pride and Prejudice:*

> 'Kitty has no discretion in her coughs,' said her father; 'she times them ill.'
> 'I do not cough for my own amusement,' replied Kitty fretfully. 'When is your next ball to be, Lizzy?'

Why should Kitty ask what she must have known? And why does she say "your" ball when she was going to it herself? Fretfulness would never carry her to such lengths. No, something is amiss in the text; but the loyal adorer will never suspect it. He reads and rereads. And Mr. R. W. Chapman's fine new edition has, among its other merits, the advantage of waking the Jane Austenite up. After reading its notes and appendixes, after a single glance at its illustrations, he will never relapse again into the primal stupor. Without violence, the spell has been broken. The six princesses remain on their sofas, but their eyelids quiver and they move their hands. Their twelve suitors do likewise, and their subordinates stir on the perches to which humor or propriety assigned them. The novels continue to live their own wonderful internal life, but it has been freshened and enriched by contact with the life of facts. To promote this contact is the chief function of an editor, and Mr. Chapman fulfills it. All his erudition and taste contribute to this end—his extracts from Mrs. Radcliffe and Mrs. Inchbald, his disquisitions on punctuation and travel, his indexes. Even his textual criticism helps. Observe his brilliant solution of the second of the two difficulties quoted above. He has noticed that in the original edition of *Pride and Prejudice* the words "When is your next ball to be, Lizzy?" began a line, and he suggests that the printer failed to indent them, and, in consequence, they are not Kitty's words at all, but her father's. It is a tiny point, yet how it stirs the pools of complacency! Mr. Bennet, not Kitty, is speaking, and all these years one had never known! The dialogue lights up and sends a little spark of fire into the main mass of the novel. And so, to a lesser degree, with the shapeless sentence from *Mansfield Park*. Here we emend "how always known" into "now all was known"; and the sentence not only makes sense but illumines its surroundings. Fanny is meditating on the character of Crawford, and, now that all is known to her, she condemns it. And finally, what a light is thrown on Jane Austen's own character by an intelligent collation of the two editions of *Sense and Sensibility*! In the 1811 edition we read:

> Lady Middleton's delicacy was shocked; and in order to banish so improper a subject as the mention of a natural daughter, she actually took the trouble of saying something herself about the weather.

In the 1813 edition the sentence is omitted, in the interests of propriety: the authoress is moving away from the eighteenth century into the nineteenth, from *Love and Freindship* toward *Persuasion*.

Texts are mainly for scholars; the general attractions of Mr. Chapman's work lie elsewhere. His illustrations are beyond all praise. Selected from contemporary prints, from fashion plates, manuals of dancing and gardening, tradesmen's advertisements, views, plans, etc., they have the most wonderful power of stimulating the reader and causing him to forget he is in church; incidentally, they purge his mind of the lamentable Hugh Thompson. Never again will he tolerate illustrations which illustrate nothing except the obscurity of the artist. Here is the real right thing. Here is a mezzotint of "The Encampment at Brighton," where the desires of Lydia and Kitty mount as busbies into the ambient air. Here is the soul of Mrs. Rushworth in the form of a country house with a flap across it. Here is Jane Fairfax's Broadwood, standing in the corner of a print that carries us on to Poor Isabella, for its title is "Maternal Recreation." Here are Matlock and Dovedale as Elizabeth hoped they would be, and Lyme Regis as Anne saw it. Here is a Mona Marble Chimneypiece, radiating heat. Mr. Chapman could not have chosen such illustrations unless he, too, kindled a flame—they lie beyond the grasp of scholarship. And so with the rest of his work; again and again he achieves contact between the life of the novels and the life of facts—a timely contact, for Austen was getting just a trifle stuffy; our fault, not hers, but it was happening.

The edition is not perfect. Pedantry sometimes asserts itself; when *Persuasion* was published with *Northanger Abbey* in 1818 its title did not appear on the back of the volumes; but why should the inconvenience be perpetuated in 1923? And there is one really grave defect: *Love and Freindship, The Watsons,* and *Lady Susan* have all been ignored. Perhaps there may be difficulties of copyright that prevent a reprint of them, but this does not excuse their almost complete omission from the terminal essays. There are many points, both of diction and manners, that they would have illustrated. Their absence is a serious loss, both for the student and for the general reader, and it is to be hoped that Mr. Chapman will be able to issue a supplementary volume containing them and all the other scraps he can lay his hands on. There exist at least two manuscript-books of Jane Austen. The amazing *Love and Freindship* volume was extracted out of one of them; what else lies hidden? It is over a hundred years since the authoress died, and all the materials for a final estimate ought to be accessible by now, and to have been included in this edition.

Yet with all the help in the world how shall we drag these shy, proud books into the center of our minds? To be one with Jane Austen! It is a contradiction in terms, yet every Jane Austenite has made the attempt. When the humor has been absorbed and the cynicism and moral earnestness both discounted, something remains which is easily called Life, but does not thus become more approachable. It is the books rather than the author that seem to reject us—natural enough, since the books are literature and the author an aunt. As Miss Bates remarked, "Dear Jane, how shall we ever recollect half the dishes?"—for though the banquet was not long, it has never been assimilated to our minds. Miss Bates received no answer to her most apposite question; her dear Jane was thinking of something else. The dishes were carried back into the kitchen of the Crown before she could memorize them, and Heaven knows now what they contained!—strawberries from Donwell, perhaps, or apricots from Mansfield Rectory, or sugar-plums from Barton, or hothouse grapes from Pemberley, or melted butter from Woodston, or the hazel nut that Captain Wentworth once picked for Louisa Musgrove in a double hedgerow near Uppercross. Something has flashed past the faces of the guests and brushed their hearts—something as impalpable as stardust, yet it is part of the soil of England. Miss Austen herself, though she evoked it, cannot retain it any more than we can. When *Pride and Prejudice* is finished she goes up to London and searches in vain through the picture galleries for a portrait of Elizabeth Bennet. "I dare say she will be in yellow," she writes to Cassandra. But not in that nor in any color could she find her.

Brian Southam

A LIFE AMONG THE MANUSCRIPTS:
FOLLOWING IN THE STEPS OF DR. CHAPMAN

Looking back over the fifty years I have given to the study of Jane Austen's manuscripts, to this day I can remember the very moment when this academic preoccupation, until then an act of somewhat desiccated scholarship, was transformed into a living and lifelong devotion.

The place—the dining room of Cold Blow Farm—remains vividly before me: an oak-beamed room in an old farmhouse near the ancient town of Walmer, just south of Deal on the coast of East Kent. And placed at one end of that farmhouse table, a long polished table, was the object of my visit, a small quarto volume, measuring about six and a half inches by seven and a half—this treasure brought from its place of safekeeping in the local bank. The binding of white vellum, much handled over the years, was somewhat discolored, but the words "Volume the Second" could be clearly made out across the front cover and were written once again, in a cramped hand, across the spine. And the hand, cursive and graceful, as I saw at a glance, was Jane Austen's own. It was the sight of this book, my reading of it, and the conversations around it in the days that followed, that changed me from dutiful student into Janeite devotee, a transformation I have never regretted.

My journey to Cold Blow Farm in the spring of 1960 had brought me from Oxford, where I was studying under the guidance of Mary Lascelles of Somerville. It was to her that I owed my attention to the manuscripts. When I arrived in Oxford in 1958 as a graduate student, it had been with the aim of preparing a thesis on Jane Austen's style. Miss Lascelles gently detached me from that ambition, pointing to a job, as she put it, that really needed doing: a collective account of the literary manuscripts. Such a survey was needed, Miss Lascelles said, because while Dr. R. W. Chapman, the editor of the Oxford Jane Austen (1923)—an edition of the novels that has provided the bedrock for all subsequent scholarship—had also edited individual editions of the manuscript works, he had never produced such an overview. It was with this larger task in hand that I undertook my pilgrimage to Cold Blow Farm, for here was the only remaining manuscript that Chapman had never edited: *Volume the Second.*

The manuscript was, moreover, still in the hands of the family. Up to this point in my research, I had only been able to read the manuscripts in great institutional libraries: *Volume the First* in the Bodleian Library at Oxford, *Volume the Third* in the British Museum Library in London, *Sanditon* in King's College Library in Cambridge. *Lady Susan, Plan of a Novel,* and the opening pages of *The Watsons* were held at the Pierpont Morgan Library in New York and, as it was before the days of travel grants, I had to make do with microfilm. But here at Cold Blow Farm, for the first time I was able to encounter the real thing: Jane Austen's ink on the page, her fine copperplate hand before me. I was reading, furthermore, in an Austen home, the home of the manuscript's owner, Mrs. Rosemary Mowll, a great-great-niece of the author herself. It was an informal and homely setting, the very place for these little stories and hilarious "Scraps," entertainments that Jane Austen had collected and entered into this book to read aloud for the entertainment of the family circle. The intimacy of the scene was conjured up in the words of her brother Henry: "Her own works, probably, were never heard to so much advantage as from her own mouth; for she partook largely in all the best gifts of the comic muse."[1]

Most of all the contents of *Volume the Second,* I was looking forward to seeing Jane Austen's satire on the style of popular historical writing: her *History of England* "from the reign of Henry the 4th to the death of Charles the 1st." In this work "By a partial, prejudiced, & ignorant Historian," she tells us, "There will be very few Dates . . ." Her unconcealed partiality and prejudice are wholly on the side of the royal house of Stuart—this, a direct attack upon the many abridged versions of Oliver Goldsmith's *History of England* (1764), itself notoriously partial and prejudiced against the Stuart cause. Jane Austen's *History* provides pen portraits of her chosen monarchs, often including their wives, supporters, and enemies. The descriptions are casual and slangy, written in the manner of any hack novelist. Of Henry IV, "It is to be supposed that Henry was married, since he certainly had four sons"; of Henry VI, "I cannot say much for this Monarch's Sense"; of Henry VIII, "The Crimes & Cruelties of this Prince, were too numerous to be mentioned"; of Charles, "This amiable Monarch" whose enemies "would make too long a list to be written or read." Cassandra, too, contributed to the entertainment. Jane Austen's first and most sympathetic illustrator, she provided thirteen sharply drawn medallion portraits—some of them cartoon-like caricatures, all of them colored and captioned—to head each of the entries. These distant historical figures are garbed in the fashions of the 1790s: heroic and handsome, "Henry the 5th" is clad in the full dress of a young naval officer, a tribute to her sailor brothers Francis and Charles; the roguish and moustachioed "Henry the 8th" wears a *bonnet rouge*, the headgear of the revolutionary mob in France of this time; "Elizabeth," sharp-nosed and sharp-chinned, is elaborately begowned, and her elaborate fringe of curls is capped by a towering plume of feathers and flowers; and "Mary Q. of Scotts," sweet-looking and demure, is romantically swathed in a virginal white headdress and shawl. These graphic portraits catch the essential spirit of her sister's characters-in-prose.

I was also keen to see *Love and Freindship*, the other early masterpiece in *Volume the Second*. This was Jane Austen's burlesque on sentimental fiction—popular reading in the 1790s—with its cast of emotional heroines, their excessive sentiments and tender sensibilities flamboyantly displayed in a succession of hysterics, faintings, and torrents of tears. For the young children of the family Jane Austen conducted a vein of playful and hilarious nonsense; for the older children and grown-ups she provided an allusive and sophisticated satire.

But my purpose in coming to Cold Blow Farm was not just to enjoy reading these works in Jane Austen's own hand. At a more mundane level, the serious aim of my mission was to make an accurate transcription of the entire manuscript, 252 pages according to Jane Austen's own numbering, to establish a true text and record every one of Jane Austen's revisions, cancellations, and changes. In truth, of the 270 alterations I recorded many were trivial or of small significance: words cancelled, missing words inserted, spellings corrected, "too" changed to "two," "us go immediately" replaced by the more naturally colloquial "no time to be lost." Some, however, were of more importance. Sometimes Jane Austen had second thoughts during the process of copying, and passages were cancelled; and on the Contents page, the distinctive spelling of "Love and Freindship" had been altered to "Love and Friendship" (although, with the "ie" and "ei" spellings not yet stabilized, Jane Austen was happy to use both and to leave "ei" unchanged in the actual title of this piece).[2] That the manuscript was relatively clean came as no surprise to me. Like its companions, volumes the *First* and *Third, Volume the Second* was not a new composition. Instead, it was a gathering of her early writing, pieces dated and originally written between 1790 and 1793 (when Jane Austen was between fourteen and seventeen), which she entered later into this manuscript notebook as fair copies. Together with the other two notebooks, it made up a collected (and, we think, almost complete) edition of her juvenilia, their mock-pompous "Volume" titles a mild joke on the standard three-volume set in which contemporary novels were published.

My own somewhat mechanical task of transcription held me totally immersed. So it came as a great relief that from time to time during the day Mrs. Mowll would appear with a cup of coffee and a biscuit or a slice of cake. It was on these occasions that she told me something of the manuscript's history and its passage down through the family. Some of this was evident from the book itself. The very first words on the first page, *"Ex dono mei Patris"*—"A gift to me from my Father"—proudly announced the manuscript book's origin, while on the endpaper inside the front cover, many years later, Cassandra penciled "For my Brother Frank, C.E.A." (Admiral Francis Austen), an instruction repeated, this time in ink, on a scrap of paper pasted to the endpaper inside the back cover. This "ticketing,"[3] as Cassandra called it, ensured that at her own death, in 1845, its path within the family was already established. Mrs. Mowll explained to me that Francis Austen then left *Volume the Second* to his youngest daughter, Fanny (Frances-Sophia)—remembered rather ingloriously for having destroyed all Jane Austen's letters to her father's first wife, Mary Gibson, at the time of his death in 1865, a clearance she carried out without consulting anyone.

At the time of her own death, unmarried, in 1904, Fanny was living with her brother, Reverend Edward Thomas Austen, Mrs. Mowll's grandfather. Edward—the ninth of Francis's eleven children—was the rector of Barfrestone, a village only ten miles or so inland from Walmer.

The longest-lived of his generation, Edward Austen survived into the twentieth century, dying in 1908 at the age of eighty-eight. *Volume the Second,* which he had inherited from his sister Fanny, passed to his eldest daughter, Janet Rose Austen (Mrs. Sanders). As Mrs. Sanders's younger sister Mary Jane Austen (Mrs. Spanton) predeceased Mrs. Sanders, who died in 1946 at the age of ninety, the manuscript then came directly to Mrs. Spanton's daughter, Mrs. Mowll. Thus, kept securely within this strict line of inheritance, the manuscript, regarded as a precious family heirloom, had remained throughout in Austen hands.

The secure provenance also helped dissolve a mystery: of the original 264 pages, each numbered by Jane Austen, it was obvious from the jagged stubs remaining that twelve had been cut out with scissors. This weighed on my mind as I recalled that in the nineteenth century misguided acts of generosity had led to Jane Austen's signature, cut from letters, ending up in autograph albums. These pages must have been blank, since no items were missing from the contents list. Furthermore, since the manuscript had remained secure in the family guardianship since the day it left Jane Austen's hands, I could feel satisfied that it had remained intact.

The manuscript had been kept secure at the price of accessibility. It was a guardianship that the Austens did not take lightly: For many years a quasi embargo had been maintained on the publication of the juvenilia. In the *Memoir of Jane Austen* (1870), James Edward Austen-Leigh judged "it would be as unfair to expose preliminary processes to the world, as it would be to display all that goes on behind the curtain of the theatre" and let it be known that "The family have, rightly, I think, declined to let these early works be published,"[4] although this position was relaxed very slightly in the expanded *Memoir* (1871), where Austen-Leigh presented *The Mystery,* a comic playlet from *Volume the First* alongside other material from the later manuscripts.

With the passage of time and the rebirth of interest in Jane Austen following the Great War, these sensibilities faded and Mrs. Sanders decided it would be right for *Volume the Second* to see the light of day. With the help of London's leading literary agents, A. P. Watt & Son, arrangements were made for its publication in 1922 by the Chatto & Windus publishing house.[5] The title page was highly descriptive: *Love & Freindship and Other Early Works Now First Printed From the Original MS. By Jane Austen.* It was an elegant little book, decoratively bound. Facing the title page, beneath a tissue interleaving, was a frontispiece reproduction of the manuscript title page for *The History of England*. This showed to good effect the full flourish and cursive elegance of Jane Austen's penmanship. Also on that page was Jane's dedication, "To Miss Austen, eldest daughter of the Revd George Austen." This tribute to her sister was particularly appropriate, for twelve of Cassandra's thirteen medallion portraits for *The History of England* were reproduced in full color on the endpapers.

Also mentioned on the title page was the "Preface by G. K. Chesterton." Chesterton had already announced himself a fervent admirer of Jane Austen, opening his famous clerihew "The novels of Jane Austen / Are the ones to get lost in."[6] In his preface, Chesterton seized upon the essential value of this material, placing the young Jane Austen in a comic tradition running from Cervantes to Dickens. He greeted the title work, *Love and Freindship,* as a literary extravaganza "to laugh over again and again as one laughs over the great burlesques of Peacock or Max Beerbohm." The discovery of the manuscript was, he wrote, "more than the discovery of a document; it is the discovery of an inspiration," revealing "the psychology of the artistic vocation," the young writer possessing an "instinct for the intelligent criticism of life." He saw this as "the first of reasons that justify a study of her juvenile works."[7]

Not surprisingly, the book was an instant success. In America the book occupied lead position on the front page of *The New York Times Book Review,* where Zona Gale opened with a ringing declaration: that "Henceforth" the book was "a part of literary experience."[8] In the *New Statesman* Virginia Woolf celebrated the presence of a true writer: "She is writing for everybody, for nobody, for our age, for her own; she, in short, is writing"; and she heard snatches "of music," the sound of Jane Austen "trying over a few bars of the music for *Pride and Prejudice* and *Emma.*"[9] The following year, Woolf returned to *Love and Freindship.* She found the title work "astonishing and unchildish," an "incredible" work for a girl of fifteen, in whose style she again hailed a true writer: "One hears it in the rhythm and shapeliness and severity of the sentences."[10]

In his review for *The Times Literary Supplement,* however, R. W. Chapman greeted the 1922 Chatto volume sourly, describing it as "the present act of espionage or exhumation"; and he added—with a hint (for those in the know) toward his professional standpoint—"We should be sorry to have been responsible for this publication."[11]

This takes me to the second strand in this story. For beyond my personal encounter at Cold Blow Farm, there lie the outlines of a wider drama, involving Chapman's pursuit of the manuscript—an engagement going back a further thirty years, into the 1920s, and leading eventually to his own visit to Cold Blow. This common interest was the link that brought the two of us together: he as the doyen of Austen studies, myself as an eager student seeking his advice and setting forth.

In the 1920s, Chapman was engaged in establishing his reputation as the world's leading Austen scholar. His own complete Oxford edition of the novels was far advanced and it was soon in his mind to add a further volume, a volume six to include all the surviving manuscript works[12]— in short, he wanted to publish his own authorized version of *Volume the Second* along with the other works of juvenilia, and to do this he needed to consult the original manuscript. With volume six on his mind he opened his inquiries into the copyright status of the 1922 Chatto text of *Volume the Second.* He sought the opinion of a certain F. D. MacKinnon, who, unaware of Cassandra's note that assigned the manuscript to Francis, instead followed the wording of her will and gave his opinion that Chatto possessed no copyright, and that the right to publish rested with the line of Charles Austen, to whom Cassandra had left the body of the manuscripts. As a consequence, Chapman and MacKinnon seem to have gone off on a wild goose chase, seeking the line of descent from "the last surviving of Cassandra's three executors (Edward Knight, Junior),"[13] a turn of events that Jane Austen, and after her, Trollope, would have turned into high comedy.

In the autumn of 1931, while he was gathering copies of Jane Austen's letters, Chapman returned again to his planned volume six, what he described as "a volume of the Fragments and Minor Pieces."[14] On the question of including the text of *Volume the Second,* he wrote to the agent of the first 1922 edition, Watt, to ask "if the MS would be available for verification? It is I think the only Jane Austen MS which I have not examined with these eyes."[15] After consulting Mrs. Sanders, there came a dusty answer communicated by Watt in Mrs. Sanders's own words:

> The MS. "LOVE AND FREINDSHIP" is too frail to be used, some of the pages being almost loose from the binding and the paper is in a very delicate state, this is my first reason, there would have been others, such as insurance.
>
> I am sorry to disappoint Dr. Chapman.[16]

Indeed, Chapman was disappointed. He would be willing, he answered, to agree to a royalty, "if I could be sure of my text—which one can only be, by ocular demonstration." He concluded his letter with what could be understood to be a lightly veiled threat, that unless he had "an opportunity of verifying the text" his "desire to include it in a collection is very much weakened."[17] But Mrs. Sanders stood firm. Watt informed Chapman that while regretting to disappoint him, "she has quite definitely decided that she cannot allow you to collate the original MS." Did he still want to include *Love and Freindship* in his volume six?[18]

Chapman was piqued by this response. Hitherto, other members of the family had seemed only too happy to grant him access to their Austen papers and to allow publication by Oxford. Now he was meeting what he described in his brief reply to Watt as "Mrs. Sanders's obduracy," leaving "the plan of a collection very much less attractive to me than it was."[19] At this point, Chapman faced frustration on another front. He was left nursing the suspicion that his plans for volume six were in danger of being scuppered. There was news of the publication of a rival *Minor Works* volume ahead of his own, to be published by J. M. Dent & Sons, and to be edited by Reginald Brimley Johnson, an enthusiastic and enormously prolific scholar-amateur. This impending threat, he wrote to R. A. Austen-Leigh, "Stung" him "to fury . . . "[20]

Whatever Dent and Brimley Johnson had in planning, the volume that eventually appeared, in 1934—*Sanditon and Other Miscellanea* (*The Watsons, Lady Susan,* and one of the "cancelled" chapters of *Persuasion*)— was no threat. Hence the field remained open for Chapman's volume six, a project that was revived in 1948 at the suggestion of Geoffrey Cumberlege, Oxford's London publisher. He renewed his search for the manuscript of *Volume the Second,* which he believed, wrongly as it turned out, to be in America.[21] Accordingly, the press approached Harvard, Yale, and Princeton universities on his behalf. Then the press got the idea that the family had sold the manuscript. In point of fact, with the death of Mrs. Sanders it had passed on directly to her niece, Mrs. Mowll, and remained securely in England.

And so it was with Mrs. Mowll's agreement that, at long last, in 1951, Chapman was able to see the manuscript for himself at Cold Blow, visiting the farm on a winter's afternoon and leaving in a snowstorm. With so brief a visit, Chapman confessed that he was able to do no more than carry out "a necessarily cursory collation" of the manuscript and he "detected little more in the edition of 1922 than a few trifling misprints."[22]

He made these corrections to the 1922 text, thus completing his own edition of the so-called *Minor Works,* the long-delayed volume six, published by Oxford in 1954.[23]

It was five years after this, only a few months before his death in April 1960, that I consulted Dr. Chapman on a number of manuscript questions. With great kindness and patience he answered me from his hospital bed. Regarding the manuscript of *Volume the Second,* he referred to Mrs. Mowll's hospitality in giving him and his sister lunch and leaving them alone with the manuscript "for a long afternoon"; and he suggested that I not bother Mrs. Mowll, "who has taken trouble enough."[24] Rightly or wrongly, as readers will have gathered, I went against this advice, and it was as a result of Mrs. Mowll's kindness that I was able to finally supply Oxford with the fully collated text first envisioned by Chapman, one that recorded all the changes to the manuscript and described its principal features. This was duly published by Oxford in 1963. I was also able to treat *Volume the Second* thoroughly in my thesis, published by Oxford in 1964 under the title *Jane Austen's Literary Manuscripts: A Study of the Novelist's Development through the Surviving Papers.* And I felt that my debt of gratitude to Dr. Chapman, the founding father of Austen scholarship, could be repaid, if only belatedly and in part, when the press invited me to revise his edition of the *Minor Works* volume, his beloved volume six. In this new edition, 1969, the original, faulty 1922 Chatto text of *Love and Freindship* was replaced—now employing Jane Austen's own designation—by *Volume the Second.*

It only remains to say that on Mrs. Mowll's death in 1973, the manuscript passed to her brother, Colonel E. J. C. Spanton. It then appeared in the Sotheby's London book sale catalogue for July 6, 1977, as lot number 298, "*The Property of a descendant of Jane Austen.*" On behalf of the British Library, the manuscript was purchased by Bernard Quaritch Antiquarian Booksellers for £40,000, and is now to be found in the Library's Manuscript Catalogue as Add MS 59874. Fifteen years later, *Volume the Third* too made its final appearance at auction, at Sotheby's New York, the property of the British Rail Pension Fund. On September 28, 1988, it was bought, after some fierce bidding, on behalf of the British Library for $224,000.[25] It was a purchase that sharpened Britain's sense of its precious yet dwindling literary heritage. That the manuscript was now destined to stay on this side of the Atlantic was an occasion for national celebration—a mood of thanksgiving captured in the words of Michael Borrie, the British Library's Keeper of Western Manuscripts: "It is particularly gratifying that all three volumes of Jane Austen's 'Juvenilia' are now preserved in this country."[26] Assuredly, Jane Austen would have said "Amen" to that.[27]

Susannah Carson

READING *NORTHANGER ABBEY*

The recent BBC–Masterpiece Theatre production of *Northanger Abbey* is perhaps the best film version possible of a literary work that almost violently resists translation into anything other than itself. The set designer resurrects "Austen's world," the costumer makes certain that the bonnets are not worn too high, and the director pulls the words off the page and shines them onto the screen—most felicitously in the vivid portrayal of Catherine's wild fancies. But none of these achievements can resolve the central predicament of the film: it is based on a fundamentally unfilmable work of literature.

In 1803, *Northanger Abbey* was the first novel Jane Austen sold, but it was not published until after her death, late in 1817.[1] When it finally appeared after a twenty-three-year lapse, it was bound with her last novel, *Persuasion.* The two novels span Austen's career, and the pairing of her starting point and her ending point accentuates the great distance she traveled as a novelist. *Persuasion* is often described as having an "autumnal" cast; the term does much to express the mood of the novel, which is otherwise difficult to characterize. It is melancholic without being morose, it has a certain measured pace which is not slow, and it is full of a sense of loss which is never without hope. When the longing of Anne and Wentworth finally turns to fully realized love, we are moved to a tearful smile rather than to open laughter. Sir Walter Scott praised the author of *Emma* for her "knowledge of the human heart": in *Persuasion,* this knowledge has become subtler, shrewder, and altogether richer. Not only does *Persuasion* claim a place in the Western canon, but it can with justice be proposed as one of the finest examples of the novel in the English language.

I have always felt that *Northanger Abbey,* in contrast, rings of spring: the tone is lighthearted, the portraits are sketched in pastels, and the story stands on wobbly legs. This literary toddler holds only a tenuous place, even in Austen's own corpus. There are the five major novels, *Sense and Sensibility, Pride and Prejudice, Mansfield Park, Emma,* and *Persuasion;* on the other side of the canonical divide lie the truncated epistolary novel *Lady Susan,* the unfinished novels *The Watsons* and *Sanditon,* and the juvenilia, consisting notably of the outrageous novella *Love and Freindship* and the comic *History of England.* Any attempt to set *Northanger Abbey* on one side or the other will necessarily make it into something it is not. To compare it to *Love and Freindship* is to recognize the central parodic intent, but also to dismiss it as spoof. *Northanger Abbey* is more mature in terms of talent, complexity, and scope than any of Austen's earlier or partial attempts, and yet to class it with the major novels and compare it to *Pride and Prejudice* is to charge it with a burden it simply cannot carry. The perfect novel, as Austen defines it in her famous defense of the novel in Chapter 5 of *Northanger Abbey,* is a "work in which the greatest powers of the mind are displayed, in which the most thorough knowledge of human nature, the happiest delineation of its varieties, the liveliest effusions of wit and humour, are conveyed to the world in the best-chosen language." Austen will meet her own requirements in her later novels, but in *Northanger Abbey* she's not there yet.

The romance between Catherine Morland and Henry Tilney, to give the most obvious example of where *Northanger Abbey* lacks literary maturity, is highly and conspicuously unconvincing. In the five major novels, Austen seems to believe that one of the tasks of a novel is to color in a romance that, for better or worse, could be a real relationship enjoyed by individuals in the non-fictional world. What happens to Austen's lovers after their novels end? We can imagine Anne sailing the high seas with Wentworth—the model for their relationship is already provided in the novel by the Admiral and Mrs. Croft. We can imagine Fanny and Edmund Bertram happy in the parsonage of Mansfield, and Elinor and Edward Ferrars happy in the parsonage of Delaford. In the great house of Delaford proper, Marianne and Colonel Brandon will lead a different sort of happy life: what she has lost in sentimental sparkle, he will make up for in pure admiration. Emma and George Knightley will need to overcome a similar gap in age and mood, but their equally strong wills will make for a livelier household. Sparks are also bound to fly at Pemberley, where Elizabeth and Fitzwilliam Darcy will no doubt feed their passion with the occasional quarrel. None of Austen's couples are so well matched as Jane and Charles Bingley. Mr. Bennet predicts their curious compatibility: "I have not a doubt of your doing very well together. Your tempers are by no means unlike. You are each of you so complying, that nothing will ever be resolved on; so easy, that every servant will cheat you; and so generous, that you will always exceed your income."

But what of Catherine Morland and Henry Tilney? It is difficult to see what will happen after their marriage, since it is difficult to see why they marry in the first place. Catherine is affectionate, unaffected, and attracted to Henry, which is a good start. Unfortunately, however, she is also ignorant, gullible, and therefore unable to appreciate Henry's main character trait—his wit—and so it is doubtful that she will ever be able to appreciate him for who he truly is. Austen describes her lovers' first meeting: "He talked with fluency and spirit—and there was an archness and pleasantry in his manner which interested, though it was hardly understood by her." When Henry humors Mrs. Allen by idly chatting about muslins, Catherine understands just enough of the uneven dynamics to fear, "as she listened to their discourse, that he indulged himself a little too much with the foibles of others." Although she is dimly aware that there is something different about Henry's conversation, not once does she fully engage with his ironic repartee.

Most of the time, in fact, Catherine is oblivious to the very existence of multiple levels of meaning. Catherine's supposed best-friend-forever, Isabella Thorpe, has just traded in one fiancé for a richer one, Catherine's brother for Henry's. Catherine hopes that a full explanation will exculpate her friend. In a response directed to his sister, Eleanor, Henry pretends to concur, but instead paints a sarcastic portrait of Isabella and a true portrait of Catherine.

> "Prepare for your sister-in-law, Eleanor, and such a sister-in-law as you must delight in! Open, candid, artless, guileless, with affections strong but simple, forming no pretensions, and knowing no disguise."
>
> "Such a sister-in-law, Henry, I should delight in," said Eleanor with a smile.
>
> "But perhaps," observed Catherine, "though she has behaved so ill by our family, she may behave better by yours."

Henry teases Catherine, for he is endeared by her simplicity. He then suggests that Catherine must be greatly afflicted by the loss of her friend, as most young women would claim to be, and when Catherine responds that she is only moderately afflicted he comments, "You feel, as you always do, what is most to the credit of human nature."

And yet, how long can the marriage of innocence and irony last? The young lovers might continue to complement each other in an ideal, fictional world, but were they to be transplanted into the real world, we might cynically predict that Henry would feel frustrated at not being loved for all of himself and that this would only increase his acerbic bent. His ironic remarks have already been purchased at Catherine's expense, and it is possible that she would become a main source of fun. She would not understand this but she would feel it, and so she would be filled with sadness and resentment—bitter feelings that would never lead to any deeper insights into herself or her husband since she is, as Austen tells us, not very bright. Catherine is supposed to be the opposite of all the dissembling, superficial, fortune-hunting Isabella Thorpes of the world. Although Catherine shares Jane Bennet's innocence and amiability, she is uninformed; although Henry shares Charles Bingley's unprepossessing playfulness, he also possesses a superior intellect and would never be satisfied with an intellectually inferior wife. One would expect Henry Tilney to foresee all or at least part of this, and it is one of the wonders of the book that he carries on and concludes a romance which is bound to leave him unfulfilled.

Austen is aware that her hero and heroine are not ideally compatible, and so ascribes Henry's affection to "gratitude." She jumps into the text to explain:

> [Catherine] was assured of his affection; and that heart in return was solicited, which, perhaps, they pretty equally knew was already entirely his own; for, though Henry was now sincerely attached to her, though he felt and delighted in all the excellencies of her character and truly loved her society, I must confess that his affection originated in nothing better than gratitude, or, in other words, that a persuasion of her partiality for him had been the only cause of giving her a serious thought.

Austen's intervention here is reminiscent of her tidy prose conclusion of the epistolary work *Lady Susan,* in which she saves herself the trouble of writing the second half of a novel by giving a summary of the subsequent pairings. Similarly, what she has not shown or will not show in the course of *Northanger Abbey,* she simply appends: Austen appears as a *dea ex machina* waving the wand of gratitude.

The problem with the romance, however, is not that gratitude is the source of Henry's affection: elsewhere, Austen proves that it is possible to bind two people together with the glue of gratitude. In *Sense and Sensibility,* Marianne's affection for Colonel Brandon begins with gratitude for his patience and admiration. Even though the relationship is perhaps not ideal, at least it is plausible. The problem is not, then, gratitude itself, but rather that it is implausible that such a small debt of gratitude could lead to affection strong enough to outweigh Catherine and Henry's disparate temperaments. Such a deep, saving relationship has not been prepared for throughout the course of the novel. Just because Austen enters the text to tell us that it is indeed strong enough does not save us from our doubts. We are left with the lingering suspicion that their marriage is a mistake—not quite as great, but of the same variety of mistake as that made by Mr. and Mrs. Bennet in their youth.

This is the case against the romance plot of *Northanger Abbey.* I have stated it as strongly as possible, and I have done so with some misgivings, for it seems ungrateful to point out such an apparent flaw. And yet there is no getting around it: the romance plot is, at best, shaky. Many Janeites express a sort of discomfort with respect to *Northanger Abbey,* for it seems that at some point one is bound to have to admit what one would rather not admit: that an author as great as Austen wrote less than great works.

But what if Austen really is just as great as we want her to be—and *Northanger Abbey* is great in a different way? What if Austen actually intended the romance plot to be unconvincing? There is a case to be made *for* the romance plot too, or, to be exact, for its very awkwardness. According to the principle of critical charity, we should assume that Austen did, in fact, know what she was about. Although *Northanger Abbey* was the first novel she drafted, she revised it and sent it out for publication after she had written initial versions of *Sense and Sensibility* and *Pride and Prejudice*—that is, after she had become the novelist whose skills and judgment are now considered exemplary. It is probable, then, that Austen intended the failure of the romance plot, not to sabotage her own work, but to make a point about romance plots in general. Her point, it seems to me, is that romance plots are inherently artificial.

It is a truth universally acknowledged that Austen's novels are about marriage: they all end with at least one successful match, and sometimes as many as three. Dating guidebooks have been compiled from advice culled from her novels, suggesting that much of Austen's current appeal lies in her treatment of the romance plot. If we read Austen, will we improve our chances of finding the right mate? Perhaps, but such instruction is incidental: Austen does not set out to describe ideal relationships. Her interest is in flawed characters who achieve a greater level of self-understanding throughout the course of each novel and who are rewarded at the end with relationships which, although never entirely perfect, are perfect for them. Elizabeth will always be a bit too cynical, Emma a bit too full of herself, and Anne a bit too reserved for some. Imagine, for instance, Elizabeth with Knightley, Emma with Wentworth, and Anne with Darcy, and you will see that although they might all get along together at a dinner party, the pairings just don't work. No, it is Elizabeth and Darcy, Emma and Knightley, and Anne and Wentworth: what Austen hath joined together, let no man put asunder.

These couples strike us as natural and perhaps even inevitable, and yet the coupling itself is entirely contrived. Austen uses basic literary techniques and tropes to explore human nature: the development of one individual in relation to another is perhaps the most essential technique of literature generally, and the conjugal dénouement is the key trope of romantic comedy. The romance plot is a narrative trick as old as story. In the hands of the best authors, however, it can be made vibrantly new. In Austen's canonical novels, the trick is executed with such art that we do not see it as a trick at all, even when we watch her perform the same sleight of pen five times in a row.

In *Northanger Abbey,* on the other hand, the trick is exposed: instead of artfully concealing her art, Austen calls our attention to its artificiality by insisting that a marriage will work which we suspect might not. The romance between Catherine and Henry is not secured by real compatibility, but by the whim of an omnipotent, ludic author who imposes her imaginative will on real-life probability. Austen seems to revel in her unlimited control of the literary world she has created.

Once we perceive the artificiality of the romance plot, we see that the rest of the novel is a series of similarly artful techniques. There is something strange, for instance, about the heroine herself. Harold Bloom asks whether "Austen's heroines, like Shakespeare's in the comedies, imaginatively speaking, marry down?"[2] Although heroes such as "dazzling Darcy" and "the benign Mr. Knightley" rise to meet their heroines more than many of Shakespeare's heroes, they still fall short of their heroines. This is a sad fate for the plucky heroines, but inevitable as their heroes are their inferiors in character, intelligence, and wit. In *Northanger Abbey* it is the hero who marries down: although the heroine has made some progress, at the end of the novel she is still very young and she is not the strong woman she would need to be to match Henry. She has become more aware of her silliness and better able to control her imagination, but she is still a surface being and has nothing like Anne Elliot's depth of soul.

But this is only to be expected, since Catherine is not a study of human nature but a study of the literary heroine. The novel begins: "No one who had ever seen Catherine Morland in her infancy would have supposed her born to be an heroine." After an unpromising childhood, however, "she was in training for a heroine; she read all such works as heroines must read." Austen introduces her famous apology of the novel, which appears as an authorial interjection in Chapter 5, by reporting that Catherine and Isabella read novels.

> Yes, novels; for I will not adopt that ungenerous and impolitic custom so common with novel-writers, of degrading by their contemptuous censure the very performances; to the number of which they are themselves adding—joining with their greatest enemies in bestowing the harshest epithets on such works, and scarcely ever permitting them to be read by their own heroine, who, if she accidentally take up a novel, is sure to turn over its insipid pages with disgust. Alas! If the heroine of one novel be not patronized by the heroine of another, from whom can she expect protection and regard?

Northanger Abbey is not simply about a young girl's overfondness for gothic romances; it is rather about the construction of a heroine from other heroines. Within the novel, Catherine attempts to fashion herself as a heroine and Austen plays with her self-fashioning heroine from without. Catherine is a paper creation through and through, and for this reason cannot quite round out the costumes of film. The great irony of *Northanger Abbey* is that Catherine is right in suspecting that she is a heroine—her only mistake is genre. She thinks she is in a gothic romance, and then a love story, but in fact she is wandering through a literary labyrinth.

The same is true of *Northanger Abbey* in its entirety. Austen turns her own novel inside out to show the seams. All novels, of course, are variations on received techniques and tropes, but some novels use these inherited tools to dissect the great world beyond, and some use them to take themselves apart. *Northanger Abbey* is somewhat clumsily constructed of three parts—social satire, gothic pastiche, and romance. The unusual juxtaposition of genres calls attention to the conventions of each; consequently, the whole presents itself as a literary exercise rather than as a faithful representation of reality.

Northanger Abbey is a special sort of novel that is highly self-conscious of itself as a special sort of novel: in theme it evokes *Don Quixote,* and in detail it borrows from contemporary gothic and sentimental romances. Throughout, the novel establishes itself in counterpoint by calling attention to all that it is *not.* Catherine's father was "a very respectable man, though his name was Richard," who "was not in the least addicted to locking up his daughters": a reference to Richard Lovelace of Richardson's *Clarissa,* as well as to all the villainous fathers and stepfathers of Ann Radcliffe's novels. When Catherine goes with the Allens to Bath, "Neither robbers nor tempests befriended them, nor one lucky overturn to introduce them to the hero": these plot twists are present in the earliest novels of classical Greece as well as in the contemporaneous gothic novels, and are even echoed by Austen herself in the later scene of Marianne's tumble and Willoughby's rescue.

Austen mentions missing story elements not just for play, as in these quick asides, but also to heighten the effect of her own writing:

> A heroine returning, at the close of her career, to her native village, in all the triumph of recovered reputation, and all the dignity of a countess, with a long train of noble relations in their several phaetons, and three waiting-maids in a travelling chaise and four, behind her, is an event on which the pen of the contriver may well delight to dwell; it gives credit to every conclusion, and the author must share in the glory she so liberally bestows. But my affair is widely different; I bring back my heroine to her home in solitude and disgrace; and no sweet elation of spirits can lead me into minuteness. A heroine in a hack post-chaise is such a blow upon sentiment, as no attempt at grandeur or pathos can withstand.

On the contrary, the contrast only heightens the pathos of Catherine's storyless homecoming—as surely Austen is aware. Not only does

Northanger Abbey set itself against previous novels to call out the absurdities of the old clichés, but it does so to call attention to its own innovations in plot and portraiture: her "affair is widely different." Although Austen mocks novels for comic effect, she does so with great affection— much in the manner in which Henry mocks Catherine.

Northanger Abbey is caught in a literary web from which it cannot and does not want to escape. The great joy of the novel is found in the generic gallimaufry, the excessive intertextual references, and Austen's playful, peekaboo authorial interventions. In this pen-and-ink world, all things are indeed possible: even the marriage of Catherine Morland and Henry Tilney. Austen simply says that it will work, and whereas this reassurance would be insufficient in a more realistic novel, in this supremely literary novel her pronouncement is authoritatively and indisputably prophetic.

Throughout the twenty-three years spanning Austen's first and last novels, popular taste and Austen's own interests and talents evolved. In *Northanger Abbey,* the young novelist refines and reflects on the process of artful creation that will last her through her greatest novels. More practiced in her art, in her later novels Austen will then turn the seams of narrative construction right side in. While we can also enjoy these later, more realistic novels in film format, to fully appreciate the special, self-consciously literary qualities of *Northanger Abbey,* we must simply sit down and read it through.

Ian Watt

ON *SENSE AND SENSIBILITY*

The basic conflict in *Sense and Sensibility* is by no means as remote from us as the society in which it is set. Many of Jane Austen's admirers, it is true, read her novels as a means of escape into a cozy sort of Old English nirvana, but they find this escape in her pages only because, as E. M. Forster has written, the devout "Janeite" "like all regular churchgoers . . . scarcely notices what is being said."

An appreciation of what Jane Austen is really saying obviously involves, in the first place, some understanding of the very different social, literary, and linguistic conventions of her time.

We cannot, for example, see the characters clearly until we make allowances for the social order in which they are rooted. Even after their fall in the world the Dashwoods still keep two maids and a manservant; and when Jane Austen refers to the "work" of Elinor or Marianne, she only means elegant needlework. But we should not assume that the Dashwoods were self-pitying in thinking of themselves as poor; they really were, by the standards of their class; and what we would now be inclined to condemn as laziness or frivolity was then a universally accepted part of the leisure-class code. Similarly, it would be wrong to regard Edward Ferrars as an irresponsible sponger; in the reign of George the Third, young gentlemen with expectations of inherited wealth were not supposed to work. If they took up a profession, it was usually only as a matter of social convenience or prestige, and so Ferrars's concern about his vocation deserves much more credit than it would today. Nor is he hypocritical in deciding upon holy orders: his modest degree of religious commitment was certainly as great as, if not greater than, that normally found among the Anglican clergy of the period.

Even the code of Regency manners has some bearing on our interpretation of the characters and the plot. When Elinor is addressed as Miss Dashwood, for example, it is not because the speaker is being unduly formal in omitting her given name, but only because "Miss" and the surname was the correct appellation for the eldest daughter. Nor is Elinor herself to be regarded as a suspicious prude when she assumes, merely from Willoughby's "addressing her sister by her christian name alone," that he and Marianne must be engaged. This was a fair deduction in the more formal society of Jane Austen's England, and Mrs. Dashwood's failure to clarify the position was, she later admits, a serious breach of her duties as a mother.

The form of *Sense and Sensibility* is not in itself particularly remote from us, since domestic comedy is a characteristically English literary genre, although somewhat out of fashion today. The danger here is rather that the novel's lightness of manner may lead us to underestimate its real scope. Jane Austen restricted her means very consciously. She always "kept to her own style," a style which, as she described it, "dealt in pictures of domestic life in country villages"; and each of these pictures were painted "on to the little bit (two inches wide) of ivory on which I work with so fine a brush, as produces little effect after much labour." But the effect is not really so little, at least not for the kind of reader she laughingly envisaged in a jingle (which is itself a parody of Sir Walter Scott): "I do not write for such dull elves / As have not a great deal of ingenuity themselves." Nor do we need such a great deal of ingenuity to see that all, or nearly all, the great issues in human life make their appearance on Jane Austen's narrow stage. True, it is only the stage of petty domestic circumstance; but that, after all, is the only stage where most of us are likely to meet them.

Jane Austen's stage, then, is narrow; it is also devoted to entertainment; and we may fail to recognize the great issues of life in their humorous garb unless we are prepared to view the comic mode as an entertainment which can be both intellectually and morally serious. Jane Austen's comedy belongs to the general category of what, in his essay "On the Artificial Comedy of the Past Century" (1822), Charles Lamb was to call "Comedy of Manners," referring to Restoration comedy and its successors. *Sense and Sensibility* is certainly a narrative form of what Meredith called "High Comedy"—the kind of comedy which arouses "thoughtful laughter" at human weakness, folly, and affectation, usually presented in their more sophisticated forms. Our attitude to such comedy must be appropriately sophisticated and thoughtful; we must try to see all the characters sufficiently objectively to be able to build up from their follies and mistakes a coherent pattern of the positive norms from which the characters have deviated.

Today we are less accustomed to look for universal norms in what we read: partly because there is so much less common agreement about intellectual, moral, and social standards, and partly because we tend to see life, and therefore literature, mainly in terms of individual experience. Jane Austen's own standards—always present in her use of such abstract terms as "reason," "civility," "respectability," and "taste"—were, like those of her age, much more absolute; and as a novelist she presented all her characters in terms of their relation to a fixed code of values. It follows that our attitude to her characters and their actions should be rather detached, both emotionally and intellectually; we must not be so bound up with the fate of Jane Austen's two heroines that we are blind to the emerging general pattern of values in the novel as a whole; if we confine all our attention to what is going to happen next to Elinor and Marianne, a great deal in the novel will seem redundant.

The most direct clue to the scheme of values which underlies *Sense and Sensibility* is its language. Jane Austen never bettered, and perhaps never equaled, the force and the brilliance of her verbal ironies in such scenes as those of John Dashwood and his wife discussing his father's dying wishes, or the grand dinner at which the Dashwoods entertain the Middletons, and where "no poverty of any kind, except of conversation, appeared." These ironies often depend on the power of abstract terms, as, for example, when Elinor smiles to see Mrs. Ferrars and her daughter being gracious to Lucy Steele "whom, of all others, had they known as much as she did, they would have been most anxious to mortify; while she herself, who had comparatively no power to wound them, sat pointedly slighted by both." Mark Schorer has finely observed that "there are none but verbal brutalities" in Jane Austen's novels. The brutalities are not gratuitous; they are the means whereby Jane Austen shocks us into seeing the disparity between proper norms of conduct and the actualities of human behavior, as in this case we are shocked into seeing the cruelty that underlies social pride.

The speech habits of the characters are also a means not only of psychological description but of placing each individual in Jane Austen's total scheme. The pretentious illiteracies of Lucy Steele, for instance, are less glaring than her sister's lamentably arch vulgarity; but they are nevertheless the means whereby the Dashwood sisters, and the reader, are enabled both to diagnose Lucy's sly and unscrupulous exploitation of the forms of intimacy, and to judge it in intellectual, social, and moral terms. Similarly, Marianne's proclaimed dislike of cliché is a sign of her genuine sense as well as of her verbal sensibility; and we must therefore balance her occasional lapses into the modish extravagancies of the sentimental novel against the genuine intellectual power suggested by the simple force of her language on such occasions as when, after Willoughby's desertion, she so grandly exclaims to Elinor: "The Middletons and Palmers—how am I to bear their pity?"

The very words of Jane Austen's title require some explanation. In modern usage, *Sense and Sensibility* can be paraphrased as meaning something like "Common Sense and Sensitiveness"; and its original reviewer in *The British Critic* interpreted it fairly enough: "The object of the work is to represent the effects on the conduct of life, of discreet quiet good sense on the one hand, and an over-refined and excessive susceptibility on the other." Yet behind the two terms there is also a complex historical and literary tradition which helps us to understand both why Jane Austen thought the problem important and why she presented it in the way she did.

Some forty years ago T. S. Eliot gave wide currency to the phrase "the dissociation of sensibility," and, through the phrase, to the idea that since the end of the metaphysical school of Donne and Herbert English poetry had suffered from a growing divorce between feeling and intellect. The very term "sensibility," however, is itself a product of the process he deplores; and this process has much to do, not only with the background of *Sense and Sensibility,* but with the development of the novel in general.

In the seventeenth century, no doubt because the Renaissance had begun to undermine the traditional order in man's social, intellectual, and religious outlook, philosophers became much preoccupied with the problem of whether man is a wholly self-centered and self-seeking being. Hobbes argued that he was; and this also seemed to be a possible consequence of Locke's theory of the *tabula rasa,* the notion that at birth the individual had no innate propensities, and that his moral and social being must therefore be regarded merely as the result of the impressions inscribed by the external environment on the originally "clean slate" of his mind during the process of growing up. As a result a great deal of attention in the eighteenth century was focused on the problem of how the sensations in man's mind were connected with the people and the world outside it; and since these sensations involved the feelings as well as the intellect, great attention was paid to the process of emotional identification, or sympathy. One very influential group of philosophers, headed by Lord Shaftesbury and Francis Hutcheson, maintained that Hobbes and Locke were wrong, and that man was naturally benevolent; that he had an innate moral sense, in the meaning of a specific ethical faculty, and that this faculty spontaneously led the individual to satisfy his impulses of sympathetic goodwill through his personal relationships.

This doctrine of natural benevolence, and of the innate moral sense, was taken up by many of the writers of the eighteenth century. It had important political implications: if man was naturally good, then society must be at fault, and this idea led toward Rousseau and the French Revolution. The revolt against Hobbes also had other and more directly literary consequences. For one thing, man's outgoing impulses obviously included the sensations of imaginative and aesthetic pleasure; these also were unselfish feelings, and as a result an intense love both of nature and art somehow became indicators of the individual's moral superiority in general. Eventually, with the Romantic movement, "sensibility" became one of the terms which reflected a radical change in the view of man's essential nature by embodying a historically new emphasis on the domain of feeling and imagination, as opposed to that of reason, will, and fact.

Jane Austen's particular target was one of the extreme literary consequences of the doctrine of benevolence—the sentimental novel. Its most characteristic emphasis was on the sympathetic tear. Hobbes had said we enjoyed the misfortune of others; but Henry Mackenzie's *Man of Feeling* (1771) so completely identified himself with the sentiments of others that he spent his whole life weeping at them—and so did nearly two generations of popular heroes and heroines. The word "sentimental," as in the title of Sterne's *The Sentimental Journey* (1768), was originally used in a wholly favorable sense; like "sensibility" it denoted a strong capacity for sympathetic identification; but since the staple form of fiction during the last decades of the eighteenth century set out to portray intense emotional reactions to situations, reactions that demonstrated the depth of the character's "sensibility," the novels of the school of sensibility inevitably tended to be "sentimental" in the modern sense of "showing feeling in excess of the demands of the situation."

Many of Jane Austen's youthful writings were parodies of the popular sentimental fiction of the day; and *Sense and Sensibility* contains some evidence that it was originally prompted by a primarily satiric, as opposed to novelistic, impulse. The quality of Marianne's sensibility in general is shown by the intensity of her feeling for poetry and landscape. She rejoices that she does not love Edward Ferrars, for example, when she hears him read Cowper because "it would have broke *my* heart had I loved him, to hear him read with so little sensibility." Later, Jane Austen is obviously parodying the sentimental heroine's stock reactions to places that remind her of lost love when she writes: "in such moments of precious, of invaluable misery, [Marianne] rejoiced in tears of agony to be at Cleveland."

For the most part, however, Jane Austen takes Marianne more seriously, and makes her a study of a person who lives according to the general tenets of the Moral Sense philosophers, with their idea of an innate and spontaneous ethical sense. When, for example, Elinor reproves her for accepting the horse from Willoughby, Marianne retorts: "If there had been any real impropriety in what I did, I should have been sensible of it at the time, for we always know when we are acting wrong, and with such a conviction I could have had no pleasure."

Jane Austen, of course, does not agree. A more traditional school of moralists had taught her that we must beware of how our moral judgment, and indeed our whole consciousness, can be colored by our self-regarding impulses; even pride in one's own sensibility might well be a form of selfishness. This criticism is found in one of her hilarious early parodies, *Love and Freindship,* where Jane Austen's heroine Laura proudly confesses that "a sensibility too tremblingly alive to every affliction of my friends, my acquaintance and particularly to every affliction of my own, was my only fault, if a fault it could be called." The cooing note of self-approving pleasure at one's susceptibility to the afflictions of others had in fact been rather conspicuous both in the Moral Sense philosophers and in their literary analogues, the sentimental novelists: Sterne, for example, proudly exclaimed: "Praised be God for my sensibility!" Jane Austen, on the other hand, makes us observe that Marianne's selfish indulgence of her own sufferings makes her insensitive to Elinor's; and indeed the criticism goes deeper, since the narrative shows such indulgence resulting in a parasitical exploitation of others. Marianne forces Elinor to take over all the unpleasant tasks of practical life, while at the same time scorning her sister's steady self-command because it demonstrates the inferiority of her sensibility.

Sensibility is also shown to be self-interested in a more directly economic sense. Marianne thinks no more than her mother about the need for economy, and despises Elinor for allowing herself to worry about such gross practical matters. But just as in *Love and Freindship* Laura's lover, Augustus, assumes an innate right to the material goods he despises, and "gracefully purloins" money "from his unworthy father's escritoire," so Marianne is made to attack Elinor for holding that "wealth has much to do with happiness," although she herself assumes that "a family cannot very well be maintained" on less than two thousand pounds a year—twice what Elinor sees as the prerequisite of happiness. This point, of course, is later underlined by the plot; Marianne marries Colonel Brandon who indeed has two thousand a year, while Elinor marries Edward Ferrars, who has a third of that income. Not only so: Marianne's first love, Willoughby, whose taste and spirit in everything from poetry to passion was of the requisite intensity, actually relinquishes Marianne for a mercenary marriage merely because it is the price of continued self-indulgence; while Edward, whose defective sensibility has been exhaustively diagnosed by Marianne, is now called "unfeeling" by John Dashwood because he unhesitatingly endures disinheritance so that he can marry for love.

The case against the various sorts of selfishness associated with sensibility is pushed home relentlessly—too relentlessly, certainly, unless we appreciate that Jane Austen does not do this merely to build up a case for its opposite quality, "sense." Actually, the manifestations of "sense" in the novel are equally varied and ambiguous. Elinor's "sense," for example, obviously includes a prudent regard for economic reality; but it is soon made clear that not all kinds of economic "sense" are laudable. Elinor, for example, "soon allowed" the Steele girls "credit for some kind of sense when she saw with what constant and judicious attentions they were making themselves agreeable to Lady Middleton." We must, therefore, abandon any attempt to view the book as based on an unqualified and diametrical opposition between sense and sensibility, and see instead that Jane Austen requires us to make much more complex discriminations between the two terms.

The opening scene, with the John Dashwoods' coolly disengaging themselves from their solemn family obligations to support Mrs. Dashwood and her daughters, begins the book, it must be noted, with an attack on the abuses, not of sensibility, but of sense, in its prudential economic meaning. John Dashwood is much more a caricature of a narrow view of sense than Marianne is of sensibility; while his wife, as Jane Austen tells us, is a "strong caricature" of him. When we come to the Middletons, however, we have a less obvious thematic contrast. Sir John is a caricature of some aspects of sensibility—he is prompt in relieving the distress of his homeless female relatives, and his whole nature is an epitome of man as a benevolent social animal. His wife, on the other hand, is a parallel case of Fanny Dashwood's conventional "sense." "There was a kind of cold hearted selfishness on both sides," we are told, "which mutually attracted them; and they sympathised with each other in an insipid propriety of demeanour, and a general want of understanding."

The Middleton duality is repeated, in turn, by the Palmers: Mrs. Palmer is a ludicrously optimistic expression of her brother-in-law's jovial gregariousness, while her husband flaunts his rudeness as if it were an emblem of social distinction, a masculine variant of Lady Middleton's inarticulate and insensitive elegance.

The similarity between the two villains completes the picture, since Lucy Steele's pretense at sensibility, though less convincing than Willoughby's, is a mere surface veneer to hide her basic cruelty and selfishness. We are thus in a position to see almost the whole of Jane Austen's *dramatis personae* as highly unsatisfactory representatives of the two concepts which she has aligned against each other. Her moral judgment of their relative merits, however, becomes fairly clear when we consider that the characters on the side of sensibility, as equated with unselfish benevolence, are obviously superior to the protagonists of sense, in its selfish prudential form.

Thus Sir John Middleton clearly lacks sense in the finer meaning of judgment; he is easily taken in by the surface politeness of the Misses Steele. He is also deficient in the finer aspects of sensibility; quite apart from his lack of aesthetic interests, he completely fails to understand the importance of emotional and intellectual rapport in personal relationships, thinking nothing "more [is] required" for intimacy between people than "sitting an hour or two together in the same room almost every day." Still, Middleton is much closer to a desirable human norm than his wife, and only the intransigent perfectionism of youth would take violent offense at the promiscuity of his benevolence; and this "irritable refinement" of the adolescent sensibility, which Elinor diagnoses in Marianne, but which she herself partly shares, is eventually humbled.

Interestingly enough, the main agent of this educative process is the vulgar Mrs. Jennings. She has all Sir John's indiscriminate cheerfulness; her tactless curiosity and thoughtless gossip begin by offending Elinor and Marianne even more deeply; yet by the end of the novel they have learned that the uncultivated Mrs. Jennings has the essence of what really matters as regards both sense and sensibility. Once her intellectual judgments are made, and her benevolent feelings are engaged, she acts disinterestedly and energetically, siding with Elinor and Marianne against the wealth and the family connections of the Dashwoods and the Ferrarses. Even before then her "naturalness" and her "blunt sincerity" have implicitly corrected Marianne's erroneous assumptions about the proper relationship between marriage and money, for she at once assumes that the very modest income of Edward Ferrars's living at Delaford will not and should not be any obstacle to the marriage of lovers: her head and her heart combine to point out that the lovers must merely make do with less.

Elinor and Marianne, of course, come to look back with shame on their early superciliousness about Mrs. Jennings; indeed they even learn to be grateful to the later kindness of the Palmers. This is part of a general softening of the thematic oppositions between sense and sensibility in the last chapters; even Willoughby's rather stagy confession to Elinor underlines the suffering that comes from letting economic sense dominate the dictates of sensibility; reason and experience have brought him, by a devious route, toward a sorrowful understanding of the need to reconcile the two claims. The fact that Elinor responds to him with great sympathy also serves to remind us that just as Jane Austen does not intend any flat opposition between sense and sensibility, so she does not intend any diametrical opposition between her heroines either, since one major emphasis in the narrative is on how differences between them are eventually removed.

. . . It would not have been easy to make Elinor as attractive as her sister. For it is not only in this book, and it is not only in Jane Austen, that grave difficulties arise in making sensible characters vivid and attractive. Every novelist, surely, must feelingly echo the old prayer that the bad may be made good, the good nice, and the nice—interesting.

Elinor is good and nice, but she is only intermittently interesting. Yet her general functions in the narrative are clear enough, and some of them have occasionally been overlooked. For, just as it is evident that Marianne has sense, has an excellent "understanding both natural and improved," so Elinor is by no means deficient in sensibility. She shares all the tastes of her sister, if with a lesser intensity, but, perhaps because she is older, she consistently tries to relate her imagination and her feelings to her judgment and to the moral and social tradition on which the order of society is based. Almost the whole course of the book, in fact, presents us with a picture of the everyday heroism of Elinor struggling to control the anguish of disappointed love so that she can fulfill her obligations as a daughter, a sister, and member of society. For this, of course, she is rewarded; and, in no very oblique criticism of the tearful tendency of the cult of sensibility, Jane Austen shows Elinor nearly overcome by joyful emotion when she hears that Edward Ferrars is, after all, going to be free to marry her: she "almost ran out of the room, and as soon as the door was closed, burst into tears of joy."

The joy was not less intense because Elinor remembered that ladies do not run, and that they always shut the door. But Elinor's sense involves much more than prudent reticence and a regard for the forms of social decorum; these may be its surface expression, but its essence is fidelity to the inward discriminations of both the head and the heart. As Jane Austen so assuredly puts it, after the lovers have at last been united Edward is "the happiest of men . . . not only in the rapturous profession of the lover, but in the reality of reason and truth."

Edward Ferrars and Colonel Brandon have found even fewer admirers than Elinor. It is clear that both heroes are intended to combine the prudence, responsibility, and practical intelligence of sense with the good-heartedness and emotional delicacy of sensibility. That they are also both rather dull fellows is perhaps in accord with the sad truth that in real life the attempt to combine the qualities of sense and sensibility often leads to a certain timidity in speech and action, presumably because the pressure of the dual set of considerations tends to inhibit or at least retard full intellectual or emotional commitment. Even so, there is certainly an unconvincing quality about Brandon, especially when he tells all to Elinor; and the final marriage to Marianne is hurriedly presented and psychologically unconvincing. One of the best of Jane Austen's modern critics, Marvin Mudrick, indeed goes much further, and charges that "Marianne, the life and center of the novel, has been betrayed; and not by Willoughby."

This position, however, depends upon our accepting Marianne as an admirable example of the gallant struggle of the individual sensibility against a hostile world. But, as we have seen, that was not Jane Austen's view of the matter. Like T. S. Eliot, she was, in her own way, an opponent of the dissociation of sensibility: she knew very well that in life both the heart and the mind often came up against all but insurmountable obstacles; and, charming as she found Marianne, she thought her tactics unwise. Silent rather than open suffering sometimes seemed both the more prudent and the more dignified course; society often had to be met with its own despicable weapons, since it was idle to pretend and futile to expect that the "realities of reason and truth" could be widely shared. With the complacent loquacity of the Robert Ferrarses of this world, for example, Jane Austen certainly endorsed Elinor's tactics when she merely "agreed to it all, for she did not think he deserved the compliment of rational opposition."

It is an immortal phrase for a perennial predicament—and before we condemn such venial dishonesties we must consider the alternatives. When Marianne, for example, was asked a boring or awkward question in company, "she was silent; it was impossible for her to say what she did not feel, however trivial the occasion." But the consequence was instructive: "Upon Elinor, therefore, the whole task of telling lies when politeness required it, always fell."

Jane Austen, one may hazard, thought that in life sensibility would founder if it were not directed by sense, because its course would take no account of what she thought were the actual, and assumed to be the unalterable, configurations of society. Marianne had been lucky, not only to find Colonel Brandon waiting to take her in, but also to have a sister like Elinor who took a more realistic view of what the individual can concede without losing his integrity. When Marianne accused her of advocating being "subservient to the judgments of our neighbours," Elinor replied, "My doctrine has never aimed at the subjection of understanding." The question is how far one can afford to be either intellectually or emotionally sincere, and under what conditions. There will always be many views about this, and Jane Austen was perhaps essentially closer than she would have cared to the position of Joyce's Stephen Dedalus who, a century later, thought the price of individual integrity not less than "silence, exile, and cunning." With this difference, that, unlike Marianne—or Dedalus—Jane Austen was not a Romantic; she did not visualize the course of the individual life as a process of climbing to higher and yet higher planes of aesthetic perfection and moral insight. More classical, and more pessimistic, she saw the individual life less as a series of pinnacles to be scaled than as, and in many senses, a set position to be maintained against the forces of selfishness, unreason, and emotional excess;

nor, all things considered, were silence and cunning too high a price to pay for maintaining it at home.

As regards her treatment of Marianne, then, we can, with R. W. Chapman, say of Jane Austen that "the hostile criticism amounts to . . . little more than this, that she was not a poet." Jane Austen was, indeed, the inheritor of the eighteenth century, the age of Prose and Reason, as Matthew Arnold called it. But that was only one side of her age, and she learned from the other side too, the side which has been labeled sentimental and pre-Romantic, and which, after all, gave us much of our modern way of looking at the individual's consciousness of himself and of his personal and social relationships. The primary importance of *Sense and Sensibility* in the history of the novel—and for us—is that in it Jane Austen developed for the first time a narrative form which fully articulated the conflict between the contrary tendencies of her age: between reason and rapture, between the observing mind and the feeling heart, between being sensible and being sensitive. The dissociation of sensibility may or may not have been all but mortal for poetry, but in splitting the human mind into its component parts, and so making them available for inspection, both in themselves and in relation to the outside world, it brought life to the novel. So, in addition to the timeless relevance of its general theme, great historical importance attaches to the novel in which, despite a certain amount of awkwardly obtrusive manipulation, Jane Austen nevertheless brought off her supreme coup as a matchmaker, and triumphantly introduced Sense to Sensibility.

Lionel Trilling

My subject is of a speculative kind and as it develops it will lead us away from Jane Austen and toward the consideration of certain aspects and functions of literature and art generally. It did not have its origin in reflections upon our author's canon of work in itself but was proposed by a phenomenon of our contemporary high culture, the large and ever-growing admiration which Jane Austen's work is being given. This phenomenon may be thought the more significant because, contrary to what would have been the case at an earlier time, young people have a salient part in it, and what I shall begin by talking about is the intensity of feeling which students at my university directed to Jane Austen when I gave a course in her novels two years ago.

An account of the incident I refer to must touch upon some dull scholastic details. As I envisaged my course, it was not to be given in lectures but as a "class." That is to say, each of its two meetings a week would start with my remarking on some significant aspect of the novel that was being considered and to this the members of the class would address themselves, developing or disagreeing with what I and then their fellow students had said. This method of instruction is likely to be held in greater regard than it deserves. In any class there will be students who cannot be induced to say anything at all, and there will be those who cannot be kept from trying to say everything, and of course even a measured articulateness does not ensure the cogency of what is said. But if through luck or cunning one can get the method working at all well, it has a quite special pedagogic value.

For this way of teaching, the optimum number of students would seem to be twenty and a practicable maximum probably cannot be higher than thirty. To my amazement and distress the number of students who attended the first meeting of the course was something like 150. Although there was no clear principle by which I could choose among such a number, I was determined to stay with the method of instruction I had originally proposed to myself. I addressed my little multitude and said that the course as I had planned it could not accommodate nearly as many students as were now gathered, and that beginning at once and going on for as long as was necessary, I would interview students in my office and post a list of those who might register. There were the conventional student sounds of dismay but no polemical challenge was offered to my decision and by the time I reached my office a long line had formed outside it.

All through that afternoon, through the whole of the next day and the day after I conducted interviews, and with each one the absurdity of the procedure became more apparent. As I have said, there was no reasonable criterion by which I might judge the applicants. I had to see that the comments I jotted down about each student were subjective and in some sense discriminatory; they expressed my estimate of the applicant's intellectual aptitude, range of knowledge, and—inevitably—personal interestingness. Yet despite my growing discomfort, I continued as I had begun, feeling that I had made my decision for good reason.

The reason deserves some notice. It had to do with my ambiguous feelings about the position Jane Austen had come to occupy in our literary culture and about the nature of the esteem and the degree of attention she was being given by scholars and critics. If I looked back over the period of my life during which I was at all aware of Jane Austen, I had of course to recognize that a decisive change had taken place in the way she was being thought about. One could not adequately describe this change by saying that she stood now in higher esteem than formerly. A glance through Chapman's critical bibliography makes plain to what heights the esteem had long ago ascended, how grand were the terms in which admiration had been expressed, including comparison with Shakespeare. Indeed, when it came to the question of how much praise she deserved, a personage no less authoritative than Henry James could say that she was given too much of it, or at least that it was of the wrong sort and given by people of the wrong sort. And as if at the instance of Henry James's little burst of temper over this state of affairs, the regard in which

Jane Austen was held began to change its nature in a radical way—she ceased to be a darling and a pet, she ceased to be what James deplored her being, "dear Jane." She became ever less the property of people who, through being nice people, were excluded from the redemptive strenu- osities of the intellectual life. One was the less disposed to share the views of this order of her admirers because it had been shown that Jane Austen herself actually hated such people. And now having been deliv- ered from their deplorable adulation, she was safe and presumably happy in the charge of scholars and critics of the most enlightened and ener- getic kind.

Instructed and lively intellects do not make pets and darlings and dears out of the writers they admire but they do make them into what can be called "figures"—that is to say, creative spirits whose work re- quires an especially conscientious study because in it are to be discerned significances, even mysteries, even powers, which carry it beyond what in a loose and general sense we call literature, beyond even what we think of as very good literature, and bring it to as close an approximation of a sacred wisdom as can be achieved in our culture. Flaubert is of course a figure *par excellence;* Stendhal somewhat less of one; Balzac, though cer- tainly much admired, remains a writer. Dickens became a figure quite some time back; there has been a large increase in the admiration we now give Trollope, but it is unlikely that he will ever become a figure. Kafka was a figure from the first; Gide was a figure twenty-five years ago but seems now to have lost much of his figurative ground.

The making of Jane Austen into a figure has of recent years been ac- celerated, probably in part by the contemporary demand for female fig- ures, though certainly not for that reason alone. I find it difficult to say why I am not on comfortable terms with the figurative process generally and as it touches Jane Austen in particular, but a chief reason for my not wanting to give the course as lectures was that lectures would almost cer- tainly have to take account of the enormous elaboration of articulate sen- sibility which has developed around Jane Austen and would put me under the obligation of trying to add to it. Perhaps because I somewhere held the primitive belief that there really was such a thing as life itself, which I did not want interfered with by literature or by the ingenuities of academic criticism, I did not wish either to encompass or to augment the abundant, the superabundant, the ever more urgent intellectual activity that was being directed toward a body of work whose value I would be the first to assert.

How, then, did I want my students to think of Jane Austen? Was she perhaps to be thought of as nothing more than a good read? I do not accept that my purpose can be thus described, though now that we have before us that British locution, which Americans have lately taken to using, the question might be asked why the phrase should have come to express so much force of irony and condescension, why a good read should necessarily imply a descent into mere creature comfort, into downright coziness. As my case stood, I would have granted that we must get beyond the unexamined pleasure with which we read in childhood and be prepared to say why and how it is that pleasure comes to us from stories; we keep it in mind here that some of my students were in graduate school and going on to the teaching of literature as their profession. But it seemed to me that the enterprise of consciousness could best be forwarded, could best be kept direct and downright, by the colloquial give-and-take of class discussion rather than by lectures.

As the interviews got under way, however, I found myself becoming doubtful that the directness and downrightness I hoped for could actually be achieved, for such qualities of literary discourse did not consort well with the prevailing emotional tone of the interviews. Many of these did of course proceed in, if I may put it so, a normal enough way. An undergraduate had read *Pride and Prejudice,* had liked it and wanted more of the same; a graduate student concentrating in the Romantic period might naturally wish to give close attention to the six novels. But most of the students had no special scholarly reason for reading Jane Austen and yet displayed a degree of anxiety about their admission to the course which seemed to say that their motive was something other than that of ordinary literary interest. There was something they wanted, not from me, as was soon apparent, but from Jane Austen, something that was making for an intensity in their application for the course such as I had no preparation for in all my teaching career. So far as I could make out, they did not think it absurd that they should be required to formulate reasons why they should be allowed to take the course—why should not the sincerity of their vocation be tested? Several of them, after their interviews, wrote me pleading notes. Several sought out colleagues of mine with whom they were in good repute and asked them to intercede with me. Two messages came from friends who taught in other colleges in the city telling me that certain graduate students who had worked with them as undergraduates deserved my most thoughtful consideration.

When at last I posted my roster, with all due misgiving and such com-

punction as led me to revise upward to forty my notion of what is a feasible number for classroom discussion, there were appeals made to me to
reconsider my decisions. There were even expressions of bitterness.

The course as it was given must have gone well enough, for I recall
that I enjoyed giving it. The bizarre show of almost hysterical moral ur-
gency which marked its beginning disappeared as soon as we got down
to business. Although there might have been some pedagogic value in
my doing so, I did not revert to that uncanny episode to try to explain it.
But the occurrence deserves some effort of explanation.

One line of understanding which inevitably proposes itself is that the
students were so especially eager to take the course because they had
formed the impression that Jane Austen's novels presented a mode of life
which brought into question the life they themselves lived and because
it offered itself to their fantasy as an alternative to their own mode of life.
If this was indeed the case, nothing could have been more characteristic
of our high culture—we have built into the structure of our thought
about society the concept of *Gemeinschaft* in its standing criticism of
Gesellschaft and we can readily suppose that the young men and women
who so much wanted to study Jane Austen believed that by doing so they
could in some way transcend our sad contemporary existence, that, from
the world of our present weariness and desiccation, they might reach
back to a world which, as it appears to the mind's eye, is so much more
abundantly provided with trees than with people, a world in whose green
shade life for a moment might be a green thought.

The use of social-political terms to explain the literary predilection I
was dealing with is lent a degree of substantiation by the circumstance
that five years before there had been given to another English literary figure a devotion which, though of a different kind, was as intense as that
which was now being given to Jane Austen and which clearly received its
impetus from feelings about social existence. American undergraduates
seem to be ever more alienated from the general body of English literature, but they had for some time made an exception of William Blake,
pledging him their unquestioning allegiance, and in 1968, when the large
majority of the students at my university were either committed to or ac-
quiescent in its disruption, they found him uniquely relevant to their
spiritual aspirations. It might seem that, no less than Blake, Jane Austen
offered a position from which to scrutinize modern life with adverse intention. The style phases of our culture are notoriously short; it was not
to be thought anomalous that at one moment disgust with modern life

should be expressed through devotion to a figure proposing impulse, excess, and the annihilation of authority, and then a scant five years later through devotion to the presiding genius of measure, decorum, and irony.

It is not hard to say what are the attributes of the world of Jane Austen's novels which might make it congenial to the modern person who feels himself ill accommodated by his own time. I have referred in passing to an aspect of the visual character of that world, its abundance of trees as compared with the number of people who come into our or each other's ken; and in general it is a thing taken for granted by readers that the novels represent a world which is distinctly, even though implicitly, gratifying to the eye and to the whole sensory and cognitive system. We are seldom required by Jane Austen to envision a displeasing scene, such as Fanny Price's parental home, and almost all places, even those that are not particularly described, seem to have some degree of pleasantness imputed to them. Notable among the elements of visuality which lead to the effect of amenity is that of *scale,* the relation in size between human beings and the components of their environment. No one needs to be reminded that the dialectic over what sort of scale is to be preferred is ancient and ceaseless—sometimes the hygiene of the soul is thought to be best served by spaces and objects whose magnitude overawes and quiets the will, or, alternatively, challenges it to heroic assertion; sometimes the judgment goes that the most salubrious situation is one in which moderate though generous size conveys the idea of happy accommodation. At the present time the sensibility of educated persons is likely to set particular store by this latter sort of scale as it is represented in Jane Austen's novels.

But it is plain that the charming visual quality of Jane Austen's "world," even when we grant it all the moral significance it can in fact have, will not of itself account for the present appeal that the novels make. If it could do so, we might expect that William Morris's *News from Nowhere* would rival the Austen novels in interest, for no one ever gave so much moral weight as Morris did to the *look* of human existence, especially to the question of scale, making it one of the traits of his redeemed Londoners of the future that they should hold in contempt the dimensions of St. Paul's and the coarseness of the mind of Christopher Wren in having fixed upon them. But of course to the modern taste Morris's utopian romance is little more than a pleasing curiosity. It is a tribute to Morris's honesty that we can so easily perceive why this is so, for

Morris is explicit in saying that the one discontent that at least a few of the inhabitants of Nowhere might be expected to feel is that being a person is not interesting in the way that novelists had shown it to be in the old unregenerate time.

It might be said that Morris, for his own reasons, adumbrates the programmatic negation of character which increasingly marks the novel of our day, the contemporary novelist finding it ever more beside the point to deal with destinies as if they were actually personal, or at least to do so in any other way than that of pastiche and parody. Surely one obvious reason why the students turned so eagerly to Jane Austen is that they felt the need to see persons represented as novels once typically represented them; that, without formulating their need, they were in effect making a stand against the novel in its contemporary mode. We should never take it for granted that young people inevitably respond affirmatively to what is innovative and antitraditional in the high artistic culture of their time; there is the distinct possibility that the students with whom I was dealing saw the contemporary novel as being of a piece with those elements of the modern dispensation which they judged to be maleficent, such as industrialism, urbanization, the multiversity. This maleficence would have to do with the reduction of their selfhood, and presumably it could be neutralized by acquaintance with the characters of Jane Austen's novels, an association that was indeed licensed by the aesthetic of the works. That is, these fictive persons would be experienced as if they had actual existence, as if their "values" were available to assessment, as if their destinies bore upon one's own, and as if their styles of behavior and feeling must inevitably have a consequence in one's own behavior and feeling.

If this was really what the students felt in reading Jane Austen, they were of course fulfilling the aim of traditional humanistic education. In reading about the conduct of other people as presented by a writer highly endowed with moral imagination and in consenting to see this conduct as relevant to their own, they had undertaken an activity which humanism holds to be precious, in that it redeems the individual from moral torpor; its communal effect is often said to be decisive in human existence.

Humanism does not in the least question the good effect of reading about the conduct of other people of one's own time, but it does put a special value upon ranging backward in time to find in a past culture the paradigms by which our own moral lives are put to test. In its predilection for the moral instructiveness of past cultures, humanism is resolute in the belief that there is very little in this transaction that is problematic; it is confident that the paradigms will be properly derived and that the judgments made on the basis they offer will be valid. Humanism takes for granted that any culture of the past out of which has come a work of art that commands our interest must be the product, and also, of course, the shaping condition, of minds which are essentially the same as our own.

Perhaps this is so, but after the Jane Austen course had gone on for a time, the enormous qualifying power of that word "essentially" became manifest to me. Essentially like our own that past culture and those minds, or selves, which created it and were created by it doubtless were, but between them and us there stretched a great range of existential differences.

The word "code" has a traditional place in discourse about society, but in our day it has acquired a new force which isn't quite continuous with what used to be intended by such phrases as "the social code" or "the code of honor." The question I tried to raise with my class was the extent to which any of us who delighted in Jane Austen's novels and found them so charged with moral significance could comprehend the elaborately encoded values of the society they depicted and read accurately the signals being sent out.

A certain amount of difficulty was produced by the question of what kind of society was being represented by the novels. There was a general readiness among the students to say that the society was "aristocratic," but one young man remarked that it was an aristocracy without any nobles—he actually used that by now oddly vulgar word. This observation had the effect of somewhat relaxing the inhibition which American students are likely to feel about taking note of social gradations and we managed to achieve a reasonably complicated view of the system of status and deference on which the novels are based. I had the sense, however, that the students were never quite easy with it and didn't finally believe in its actuality.

Then, following my observation that Jane Austen does not find the relation between servants and their masters or mistresses as interesting as many English novelists do and therefore gives but little help to the modern reader in understanding the part servants played in the life of her time, I had to particularize for the students such matters as what it was that servants were needed for and how many were required for one or another kind of domestic establishment. It turned out that most of the students, though of the middle class, had no real conception of what a servant was or did and could not imagine what the existence of a servant class might imply for a culture—to take a simple example, what effect, for good or ill, their relationships with servants might have upon the children of the house.

We gave some attention to the nature of familial and personal relationships. In the fall of 1973, when my course was being given, the debate in *The Times Literary Supplement* over how brothers and sisters might naturally have felt toward each other early in the nineteenth century had not yet begun, but we remarked the relations between sister and sister in Jane Austen's novels and agreed that this relation was represented as having the possibility of greater closeness than is now likely. And at a moment when notions of youthful solidarity and community were strong, we came to the conclusion that the ideal of friendship had become considerably less vivid than it once was.

We remarked on the circumstance that no one in the novels sought personal definition through achievement. For instance, to none of her heroines and to none of her male characters does Jane Austen attribute her own impulse to literary composition. In 1973 the "work ethic" was still under a cloud, yet I could not fail to see that for all their readiness to be wry about "performance" and "roles," the students expected the interest of life to be maintained by some enterprise requiring effort. But although they could perceive that the idea of vocation lent dignity to Mr. Gardiner or Edmund Bertram or Captain Wentworth, it did not occur to them to find alien to their conception a society in which most persons naturally thought that life consisted not of doing but only of being.

And then there was the question of the way and the degree in which a person might be morally conscious. The students were not in the least inclined to cynicism but they were gently amused when Elinor Dashwood, in response to Marianne's question, says that what had sustained her in a bad time was the consciousness that she was doing her duty. They thought it downright quaint of Anne Elliot to say to Captain Wentworth that she had been right in submitting to Lady Russell because a "strong sense of duty is no bad part of a woman's portion," and we did what we could to take account of the cultural implications of that highly charged word "portion."

Inevitably we went into manners in its several meanings, including, of course, the one that Hobbes assigns to it when he says that manners are small morals. I sought to elicit an explanation of the legendary propriety of the novels in relation to what might be concluded about the sexual mores of the age and about those curious moments in the author's published letters which E. M. Forster speaks of as the "deplorable lapses of taste over carnality."

All this might well suggest that the direction of the discussion was toward subverting the basic assumption of humanistic literary pedagogy: so far from wishing to bring about the realization of how similar to ourselves are the persons of a past society, it was actually the dissimilarity between them and us that I pressed upon. At the time, I was conscious of no reason why I inclined to cast doubt upon the procedure by which humanism puts literature at the service of our moral lives, but my more or less random undertaking has since been given a measure of rationalization by certain formulations which have been put forward by a distinguished anthropologist.

I refer to the lecture, delivered in the spring of 1974, in which Professor Clifford Geertz examines the epistemology of cultures, asking what knowledge we can have of cultures unlike our own and what are the means by which we gain this knowledge.[1] The chief intention of the lecture is to say that, contrary to common belief, the faculty of empathy plays but a minimal part in the knowledge an anthropologist gains of unfamiliar cultures and to describe the means by which reliable understanding actually is achieved. Drawing upon his own experience, Mr. Geertz puts the matter thus:

> In all three of the societies I have studied intensively, Javanese, Balinese, and Moroccan, I have been concerned, among other things, with attempting to determine how the people who live there define themselves as persons, what enters into the idea they have (but . . . only half realize they have) of what a self, Javanese, Balinese, or Moroccan style, is.

He goes on:

> In each case I have tried to arrive at this most intimate of notions not by imagining myself as someone else—a rice peasant or a tribal sheikh, and then seeing what I thought—but by searching out and analyzing the symbolic forms—words, images, institutions, behaviors—in terms of

which, in each place, people actually represent themselves to themselves and to one another.

Mr. Geertz then specifies the method by which these symbolic forms are to be induced to yield up their meaning: he tells us that one follows "what Dilthey called the hermeneutic circle," in which a conceived whole is referred to its particularities and then the particularities are referred to the conceived whole, and so on in ceaseless alternation.

Mr. Geertz cites two examples of the hermeneutic circle, or, as it sometimes appears, the hermeneutic spiral. One of these is the process by which we comprehend a baseball game. "In order to follow a baseball game, one must understand what a bat, a hit, an inning, a left fielder, a squeeze play, a hanging curve, or a tightened infield are, and what the game in which these 'things' are elements is all about." The second example of the hermeneutic circle or spiral is the attempt of "an *explication de texte* critic like Leo Spitzer" to interpret Keats's "Ode on a Grecian Urn." The attempt, Mr. Geertz says, will involve the critic in "repetitiously asking himself the alternating questions, 'What is the whole poem about?' and 'What exactly has Keats seen (or chosen to show us) depicted on the urn he is describing?'; at the end of an advancing spiral of general observations and specific remarks he emerges with a reading of the poem as an assertion of the aesthetic mode of perception over the historical."

With reference to the two examples of the hermeneutic process which Mr. Geertz considers appropriate to ethnology, he says, "In the same way, when a meanings-and-symbols ethnographer like myself attempts to find out what some pack of natives conceives a person to be, he moves back and forth between asking himself, 'What is the general form of this life?' and 'What exactly are the vehicles in which that form is embodied?' emerging at the end of a similar sort of spiral with the notion that they see the self as a composite, or a persona, or a point in a pattern."

No student of literature can read Mr. Geertz's lecture without having it borne in upon him that anthropologists conceive unfamiliar cultures to be much more difficult to comprehend than do humanist scholars or the ordinary readers they instruct. Mr. Geertz spends years trying to discover the concepts on which the members of one or another unfamiliar culture base their sense of being persons or selves, and eventually, by following the hermeneutic circle or spiral, he is able to tell us what these concepts are. By and large, the humanist way of dealing with alien cultures feels itself to be under no such necessity. I recently read for the first time the well-known Icelandic story called "Audun and the Bear," which tells about a rather poorly-off man from the Westfirths who takes ship for Greenland and there buys a bear, said to be "an absolute treasure," which he wants to present as a gift to King Svein of Denmark; King Harald of Norway, Svein's enemy, would like to have this treasure of a bear for himself but behaves very well about it, and there follows a series of incidents in which Audun and the two kings adumbrate a transcendent ethos of magnanimity and munificence. I had no difficulty in "understanding" this story. I did exactly what Mr. Geertz says he does not do when he wants to arrive at the understanding of what a self is in an alien culture: I made use of empathy, I imagined myself someone else, a not very well-off man from the Westfirths, and this seemed to suit my purpose admirably, leading me to know all that I felt I needed to know about bears and their excellence, and kings, and gift giving.

But actually, of course, if Mr. Geertz is right, I don't know anything at all about Audun and his bear and his two kings, or at best I know something that merely approximates the cultural fact—and it was in this pleasant but wholly imprecise way of empathy that my students knew the culture represented in Jane Austen's novels. Humanism brushes aside the imprecision, and doubtless would brush aside gross error if it were proved; humanism takes the line that we are to be confident of our intuitive understanding of behavior in Iceland a thousand years ago; we understand it because it is part of "Western" culture and as such pretty directly continuous with our own culture of the present time. Just so, we know all about Abraham or Achilles because of what we call the "Judaeo-Hellenic tradition," which constitutes a considerable part of the tradition we conceive ourselves to be in. Of course neither the Jews nor the Greeks thought like humanists—they believed that nothing could be, or should be, more incomprehensible than alien cultures, the ways that *goyim* or *barbaroi* chose to go about being persons or selves.

In thinking about the cultures of the past which are presumably continuous with our own, humanists of our time do of course acknowledge one striking and quite invincible alienation—they know that we of the present time may not do certain things that were done in the cultures of the past even though they are things upon which we bestow the very highest praise. For example, although we are of course enlightened and exalted and generally made better by the art of, say, Giotto or Michelangelo, we know that we must not make use of the idioms of their art or of the art of their epochs in our own creative enterprises. When we bring into conjunction with each other the certitude that great spiritual good is to be derived from the art of the past and the no less firmly held belief that an artistic style cannot be validly used in any age other than that in which it was invented, we confront what is surely one of the significant mysteries of man's life in culture.

W. Somerset Maugham

JANE AUSTEN AND *PRIDE AND PREJUDICE*

The events of Jane Austen's life can be told very briefly. The Austens were an old family whose fortunes, like those of many of the greatest families in England, had been founded on the wool trade, which was at one time the country's staple industry; having made money, again like others of more importance, they bought land and so in time joined the ranks of the country gentry. Jane was born in 1775 at Steventon, a village in Hampshire, of which her father, the Reverend George Austen, was rector. She was the youngest of seven children.[1] When she was sixteen her father resigned his living, and with his wife and his two girls, Cassandra and Jane, for his sons were already out in the world, moved to Bath. He died in 1805, and his widow and daughters settled at Southampton. Not long afterward one of Jane's brothers inherited estates in Kent and in Hampshire, and offered his mother a cottage on either of them. She chose to go to Chawton in Hampshire—this was in 1809—and there, with occasional visits to friends and relations, Jane remained till illness obliged her to go to Winchester in order to put herself in the hands of better doctors than could be found in a village, and there she died in 1817. She was buried in the cathedral.

She is said to have been in person very attractive; "her figure was rather tall and slender, her step light and firm, and her whole appearance expressive of health and animation. In complexion she was a clear brunette with a rich color; she had full round cheeks with mouth and nose small and well-formed, bright hazel eyes, and brown hair forming natural curls close round her face." The only portrait of her I have seen shows a fat-faced young woman with undistinguished features, large round eyes and an obtrusive bust; but it may be that the artist did her less than justice. She had a rare and racy sense of humor, and since she says that her conversation was exactly like her letters, and her letters are full of witty, ironical and malicious remarks, it is impossible to doubt that her conversation was brilliant.

Most of the letters that have remained were written to her sister Cassandra. She was greatly attached to her. As girls and women they were constantly together, and indeed shared the same bedroom till Jane's death. When Cassandra was sent to school Jane went with her because, though too young to profit by such instruction as the seminary for young ladies provided, she would have been wretched without her. "If Cassandra were going to have her head cut off," said her mother, "Jane would insist on sharing her fate." Cassandra was handsomer than Jane, of a colder and calmer disposition, less demonstrative and of a less sunny nature; she had "the merit of always having her temper under command, but Jane had the happiness of a temper that never required to be commanded." Many of Jane Austen's warmest admirers have found her letters disappointing, and have thought they showed that she was cold and unfeeling and that her interests were trivial. I am surprised. They are very natural. Jane Austen never imagined that anyone but Cassandra would read them, and she told her exactly the sort of things she knew would interest her. She told her what people were wearing and how much she had paid for the flowered muslin she had bought, what acquaintances she had made, what old friends she had met and the gossip she had heard.

Of late years several collections of letters by eminent authors have been published, and for my part, when I read them, I am now and then disposed to suspect that the writers had at the back of their minds the notion that one day they might find their way into print. They give me not seldom the impression that they might have been used just as they were in the columns of a literary journal. In order not to annoy the devotees of the recently deceased I will not mention their names, but Dickens has been dead a long time and it is possible to say what one likes of him without offense. Whenever he went on a journey he wrote long letters to his friends in which he described eloquently the sights he had seen and which, as his biographer justly observes, might well have been printed without the alteration of a single word. People were more patient in those days; still one would have thought it a disappointment to receive a letter from a friend who gave you word pictures of mountains and monuments when you wanted to know whether he had come across anyone interesting, what parties he had been to and whether he had been able to get you the books or ties or handkerchiefs you had asked him to bring back.

Jane Austen hardly ever wrote a letter that had not a smile or a laugh in it, and for the delectation of the reader I will give a few examples of her manner. I can only regret that I have not space for more.

"Single women have a dreadful propensity for being poor, which is one very strong argument in favor of matrimony."

"Only think of Mrs. Holder being dead! Poor woman, she has done the only thing in the world she could possibly do to make one cease to abuse her."

"Mrs. Hall, of Sherborne, was brought to bed yesterday of a dead child, some weeks before she expected, owing to a fright. I suppose she happened unawares to look at her husband."

"The death of Mrs. W. K. we had seen. I had no idea that anybody liked her, and therefore felt nothing for any survivor, but I am now feeling away on her husband's account, and think he had better marry Miss Sharpe."

"I respect Mrs. Chamberlayne for doing her hair well, but cannot feel a more tender sentiment. Miss Langley is like any other short girl with a broad nose and wide mouth, fashionable dress and exposed bosom. Admiral Stanhope is a gentlemanlike man, but then his legs are too short and his tail too long."

Jane Austen was fond of dancing. Here are a few comments connected with balls she went to.

"There were only twelve dances, of which I danced nine, and was merely prevented from dancing the rest by want of a partner."

"There was one gentleman, an officer of the Cheshire, a very good-looking young man, who, I was told, wanted very much to be introduced to me; but as he did not want it quite enough to take much trouble in effecting it, we never could bring it about."

"There were few beauties, and such as there were, were not very handsome. Miss Iremonger did not look well and Mrs. Blunt was the only one much admired. She appeared exactly as she did in September, with the same broad face, diamond bandeau, white shoes, pink husband and fat neck."

"Charles Powlett gave a dance on Thursday to the great disturbance of all his neighbours, of course, who you know take a most lively interest in the state of his finances, and live in hopes of his being soon ruined. His wife is discovered to be everything that the neighbourhood would wish her to be, silly and cross as well as extravagant."

"Mrs. Richard Harvey is going to be married, but as it is a great secret, and only known to half the neighbourhood, you must not mention it."

"Dr. Hall is in such very deep mourning that either his mother, his wife or himself must be dead."

When Miss Austen was living with her mother at Southampton they paid a call and this is what she wrote to Cassandra:

We found only Mrs. Lance at home, and whether she boasts any offspring besides a grand pianoforte did not appear . . . They live in a handsome style and are rich, and she seems to like to be rich; we gave her to understand that we were far from being so; she will soon feel therefore that we are not worth her acquaintance.

A relation of Jane's seems to have given occasion to gossip owing to the behavior of a certain Dr. Mant, behavior such that his wife retired to her mother's, whereupon Jane wrote: "But as Dr. M. is a clergyman their attachment, however immoral, has a decorous air." She had a sharp tongue and a prodigious sense of humor. She liked to laugh and she liked to make others laugh. It is asking too much of the humorist to expect him—or her—to keep a good thing to himself when he thinks of it. And, heaven knows, it is hard to be funny without being sometimes a trifle malicious. There is not much kick in the milk of human kindness. Jane had a keen appreciation of the absurdity of others, their pretentiousness, their affectations and their insincerities; and it is to her credit that they amused rather than annoyed her. She was too amiable to say things to people that would pain them, but she certainly saw no harm in amusing herself at their expense with Cassandra. I find no ill nature in even the most biting and witty of her remarks; her humor was based, as humor should be, on accurate observation and frankness.

It has been remarked that though she lived through some of the most stirring events of the world's history, the French Revolution, the Terror, the rise and fall of Napoleon, she made no reference to them in her novels. She has on this account been blamed for an undue detachment. It should be remembered that in her day it was not polite for women to occupy themselves with politics, that was a matter for men to deal with; they did not even read the newspapers; but there is no reason to suppose that because she did not write about these events she was not affected by them. She was fond of her family, two of her brothers were in the navy, often enough in danger, and her letters show that they were much on her mind. But did she not show her good sense in not writing about such matters? She was too modest ever to suppose that her novels would be read long after her death, but if that had been her aim she could not have acted more wisely than she did in avoiding to deal with affairs which from the literary standpoint were of passing interest. Already the novels concerned with the Great War that have been written in the last few years are as dead as mutton. They were as ephemeral as the newspapers that day by day told us what was happening.

There is a passage in Austen-Leigh's *Life* from which, by the exercise of a little imagination, one can get an idea of the sort of existence Miss Austen must have led during those long quiet years in the country. "It may be asserted as a general truth, that less was left to the charge and discretion of servants, and more was done, or superintended by the masters and mistresses. With regard to the mistresses, it is, I believe, generally understood that . . . they took a personal part in the higher branches of cookery, as well as in the concoction of home-made wines, and distilling of herbs for domestic medicines . . . Ladies did not disdain to spin the thread out of which the household linen was woven. Some ladies liked to wash with their own hands their choice china after breakfast or tea." Miss Austen took a healthy interest in gowns, bonnets, and scarves; and she was a fine needlewoman, both plain and ornamental. She very properly liked young men to be good-looking and had no objection to flirting with them. She loved not only dancing, but theatricals, card games, and other more simple amusements. She was "successful in everything that she attempted with her fingers. None of us could throw spillikins in so perfect a circle, or take them off with so steady a hand. Her performances with a cup and ball were marvellous. The one used at Chawton was an easy one, and she has been known to catch it on the point an hundred times in succession, till her hand was weary." It is not surprising to learn that she was a favorite with children; they liked her playful ways with them and her long circumstantial stories.

No one could describe Jane Austen as a bluestocking (a type with which she had no sympathy) but it is plain that she was a cultivated woman. R. W. Chapman, the great authority on her novels, made a list of the books she is known to have read and it is an imposing one. Of course she read novels, Fanny Burney's, Maria Edgeworth's and Mrs. Radcliffe's (*The Mysteries of Udolpho*); and she read novels translated from the French and German (among others Goethe's *Sorrows of Young Werther*); and whatever others she could get from the circulating library at Bath and Southampton. She knew her Shakespeare well, and among the moderns she read Scott and Byron, but her favorite poet seems to have been Cowper. It is not hard to see why his cool, elegant and sensible verse appealed to her. She read Dr. Johnson and Boswell, a good deal of history and not a few sermons.

This brings me to what is obviously the most important thing about her, the books she wrote. She began writing at a very early age. When she was dying at Winchester she sent a niece who had taken to writing a message to the effect that if she would take her advice she would cease doing so till she was sixteen, and that she had herself often wished that she had read more and written less in the corresponding years (twelve to sixteen) of her own life. At that time it was thought far from ladylike for a woman to write books. Monk Lewis wrote: "I have an aversion, a pity and contempt for all female scribblers. The needle, not the pen, is the instrument they should handle, and the only one they ever use dexterously." The novel was a form held in low esteem, and Jane Austen was herself not a little shocked that Sir Walter Scott, a poet, should write fiction. She was "careful that her occupation should not be suspected by servants, or visitors, or any person beyond her family party. She wrote upon small sheets of paper which could easily be put away, or covered with a piece of blotting paper. There was between the front door and the offices, a swing door which creaked when it was opened; but she objected to having this little inconvenience remedied, because it gave her notice when anyone was coming." Her eldest brother, James, never even told his son, then a boy at school, that the books he read with delight were by his aunt Jane; and her brother Henry in his memoir states: "No accumulation of fame would have induced her, had she lived, to affix her name to any productions of her pen." So her first book to be published, *Sense and Sensibility,* was described on the title page as "by a Lady."

It was not the first she wrote. That was a novel called *First Impressions.* Her brother George Austen wrote to a publisher offering for publication, at the author's expense or otherwise, a "manuscript novel, comprising three volumes; about the length of Miss Burney's *Evelina.*" The offer was refused by return of post. *First Impressions* was begun during the winter of 1796 and finished in August 1797; it is generally supposed to have been substantially the same book as sixteen years later was issued as *Pride and Prejudice.* Then, in quick succession, she wrote *Sense and Sensibility* and *Northanger Abbey,* but had no better luck with them, though after five years a Mr. Richard Crosby bought the latter, then called *Susan,* for ten pounds. He never published it and eventually sold it back for what he had paid. Since Miss Austen's novels had been published anonymously he had no notion that the book he parted with for so small a sum was by the successful and popular author of *Pride and Prejudice.*

She seems to have written nothing but a fragment called *The Watsons* between 1798 when she finished *Northanger Abbey* and 1809. It is a long interval for a writer of such gifts to wait, and it has been suggested that her silence was due to a love affair that occupied her to the exclusion of other interests. But this is mere surmise. She was young in 1798—twenty-four—and it is likely enough that she fell in love more than once, but she was hard to please, and it is equally likely that she fell out again without any great perturbation of spirit. The most probable explanation of her long silence is that she was discouraged by her inability to find a publisher. Her close relations, to whom she read them, were charmed with them, but she was as sensible as she was modest, and she may well have concluded that their appeal was only to persons who were fond of her and had, it may be, a shrewd idea who the models of her characters were.

Anyhow in 1809, in which year she settled with her mother and sister in the quiet of Chawton, she set about revising her old manuscripts, and in 1811 *Sense and Sensibility* at last appeared. By then it was no longer outrageous for a woman to write. Professor Spurgeon in a lecture on Jane Austen delivered to the Royal Society of Literature quotes a preface to *Original Letters from India* by Eliza Fay. This lady had been urged to publish them in 1782, but public opinion was so averse "to female authorship" that she declined. But writing in 1816, she said: "Since then a considerable change has gradually taken place in public sentiment, and its development; we have now not only as in former days a number of women who do honour to their sex as literary characters, but many unpretending females, who fearless of the critical perils that once attended the voyage, venture to launch their little barks on the vast ocean through which amusement or instruction is conveyed to a reading public."

Pride and Prejudice was published in 1813. Jane Austen sold the copyright for ten pounds.

Besides the three novels already mentioned she wrote three more, *Mansfield Park, Emma,* and *Persuasion.* On these few books her fame rests, and her fame is secure. She had to wait a long time to get a book published, but she no sooner did than her charming gifts were recognized. Since then the most eminent persons have agreed to praise her. I will only quote what Sir Walter Scott had to say; it is characteristically generous:

> That young lady had a talent for describing the involvements, feelings and characters of ordinary life which is to me the most wonderful I have ever met with. The big bow-wow I can do myself like anyone going; but the exquisite touch which renders commonplace things and characters interesting from the truth of the description and the sentiment is denied to me.

It is odd that Scott should have omitted to make mention of the young lady's most precious talent: her observation was searching and her sentiment edifying, but it was her humor that gave point to her observation and a kind of prim liveliness to her sentiment. Her range was narrow. She wrote very much the same sort of story in all her books, and there is no great variety in her characters. They are very much the same persons seen from a somewhat different point of view. She had common sense in a high degree, and no one knew better than she her limitations. Her experience of life was confined to a small circle of provincial society, and that is what she was content to deal with.

She wrote only of what she knew; and it has been noticed that she never attempted to reproduce a conversation of men when by themselves, which in the nature of things she could never have heard.

She shared the opinions common in her day and, so far as one can tell from her books and letters, was quite satisfied with the conditions that prevailed. She had no doubt that social distinctions were important, and she found it natural that there should be rich and poor. A gentleman's younger son was properly provided for by taking orders and being given a fat family living; young men obtained advancement in the service of the King by the influence of powerful relations; a woman's business was to marry, for love certainly, but in satisfactory financial circumstances. All this was in the order of things, and there is no sign that Miss Austen saw anything objectionable in it. Her family was connected with the clergy and the landed gentry, and her novels are concerned with no other class.

It is difficult to decide which is the best of them because they are all so good, and each one has its devoted, and even fanatic, admirers. Macaulay thought *Mansfield Park* her greatest achievement; other critics, equally illustrious, have preferred *Emma;* Disraeli read *Pride and Prejudice* seventeen times; today many look upon *Persuasion* as her most exquisite and finished work. The great mass of readers, I believe, has accepted *Pride and Prejudice* as her masterpiece, and in such a case I think it well to accept their judgment. What makes a classic is not that it is praised by critics, expounded by professors and studied in college classes, but that the great mass of readers, generation after generation, have found pleasure and spiritual profit in reading it.

My own opinion, for what it is worth, is that *Pride and Prejudice* is on the whole the most satisfactory of all the novels. *Emma* offends me by the snobbishness of the heroine; she is really too patronizing to the persons she looks upon as her social inferiors, and I can take no particular interest in the love affair of Frank Churchill and Jane Fairfax. It is the only one of Miss Austen's novels that I find long-winded. In *Mansfield Park* the hero and heroine, Fanny and Edmund, are intolerable prigs, and all my sympathies go out to the unscrupulous, sprightly, and charming Henry and Mary Crawford. *Persuasion* has a rare charm, and except for the incident on the Cobb at Lyme Regis I should be forced to look upon it as the most perfect of the six. Jane Austen had no great gift for inventing incident of an unusual character, and this one seems to me a very clumsy contrivance. Louisa Musgrove runs up some steep steps, and is "jumped down" by her admirer Captain Wentworth. He misses her, she falls on her head and is stunned. If he was going to give her his hands, as we are told he had been in the habit of doing in "jumping her off" a stile, she could not have been more than six feet up, and as she was jumping down it is impossible that she should have fallen on her head. In any case she would have fallen against the stalwart sailor, and though perhaps shaken and frightened could hardly have hurt herself. Anyhow, she was unconscious, and the fuss that was made is unbelievable. Everybody loses his head. Captain Wentworth, who has seen action and made a fortune out of prize money, is paralyzed with horror. The immediately subsequent behavior of all concerned is so idiotic that I find it hard to believe that Miss Austen, who was able to take the illnesses and deaths of her friends and relations with considerable fortitude, did not look upon it as uncommonly foolish.

Professor Garrod, a learned and witty critic, has said that Jane Austen was incapable of writing a story, by which, he explains, he means a sequence of happenings, either romantic or uncommon. But that is not what Jane Austen had a talent for, and not what she tried to do. She had too much common sense and too sprightly a humor to be romantic, and she was not interested in the uncommon, but in the common. She made it uncommon by the keenness of her observation, her irony and her playful wit. By a story most of us mean a connected and coherent narrative with a beginning, a middle, and an end. *Pride and Prejudice* begins in the right place, with the arrival on the scene of the two young men whose love for Elizabeth Bennet and her sister Jane is the main theme of the novel, and it ends in the right place with their marriage. It is the traditional happy ending. This sort of ending has excited the scorn of the sophisticated, and of course it is true that many, perhaps most, marriages are not happy, and further, that marriage concludes nothing; it is merely an entry upon another order of experience. Many authors have in consequence started their novels with marriage and dealt with its outcome. It is their right. But I have a notion that there is something to be said for the simple people who look upon marriage as a satisfactory conclusion to a work of fiction. I think they do so because they have a deep, instinctive feeling that by mating, a man and a woman have fulfilled their biological function; the interest which it is natural to feel in the steps that have led to this consummation, the birth of love, the obstacles, the misunderstandings, the avowals, now yields to its result, their issue, which is the generation that will succeed them. To nature each couple is but a link in a chain, and the only importance of the link is that another link may be added to it. This is the novelist's justification for the happy ending. In Jane Austen's books the reader's satisfaction is considerably enhanced by the knowledge that the bridegroom has a substantial income from real estate and will take his bride to a fine house, surrounded by a park, and furnished throughout with expensive and elegant furniture.

Pride and Prejudice seems to me a very well-constructed book. The incidents follow one another naturally, and one's sense of probability is nowhere outraged. It is, perhaps, odd that Elizabeth and Jane should be so well-bred and well-behaved, whereas their mother and three younger sisters should be so ordinary; but that this should be so was essential to the story Miss Austen had to tell. I have allowed myself to wonder why she did not avoid this stumbling block by making Elizabeth and Jane the daughters of a first marriage of Mr. Bennet and making the Mrs. Bennet of the novel his second wife and the mother of the three younger daughters. Jane Austen liked Elizabeth best of all her heroines. "I must confess," she wrote, "that I think her as delightful a creature as ever appeared in print." If, as some have thought, she was herself the original for her portrait of Elizabeth; and she has certainly given her her own gaiety, high spirit and courage, wit and readiness, good sense and right feeling; it is perhaps not rash to suppose that when she drew the placid, kindly, and beautiful Jane Bennet she had in mind her sister Cassandra. Darcy has been generally regarded as a fearful cad. His first offense was his refusal to dance with people he didn't know and didn't want to know at a public ball to which he had gone with a party. Not a very heinous one. It is true that when he proposes to Elizabeth it is with an unpardonable insolence, but pride, pride of birth and wealth, was the predominant trait of his character, and without it there would have been no story to tell. The manner of his proposal, moreover, gave Jane Austen opportunity for the most dramatic scene in the book; it is conceivable that with the experience she gained later she might have been able to indicate Darcy's feelings in such a way as to antagonize Elizabeth without putting into his mouth speeches so improbable as to shock the reader. There is perhaps some exaggeration in the drawing of Lady Catherine and Mr. Collins, but to my mind little more than comedy allows. Comedy sees life in a light more sparkling, but colder than that of common day, and a touch of exaggeration, that is of farce, is often no disadvantage. A discreet admixture of farce, like a sprinkle of sugar on strawberries, may well make comedy more palatable. With regard to Lady Catherine one must remember that in Jane Austen's day rank gave its possessors a sense of immense superiority over persons of inferior station, and not only expected to be treated by them with the utmost deference, but were. If Lady Catherine looked upon Elizabeth as so much white trash, let us not forget that Elizabeth looked upon her aunt Phillips, because she was the wife of an attorney, as very little better. In my own youth, a hundred years after Jane Austen wrote, I knew great ladies whose sense of importance, though not quite so blatant, was not far removed from Lady Catherine's. And as for Mr. Collins, who has not known even today men with that combination of pomposity and sycophancy?

No one has ever looked upon Jane Austen as a great stylist. Her spelling was peculiar and her grammar often shaky, but she had a good ear. I think the influence of Dr. Johnson can be discerned in the structure of her sentences. She is apt to use the word of Latin origin rather than the plain English one, the abstract rather than the concrete. It gives her phrase a slight formality which is far from unpleasant; indeed it often adds point to a witty remark and a demure savor to a malicious one. Her dialogue is probably as natural as dialogue can ever be. To set down on paper speech as it is spoken would be very tedious, and some arrangement of it is necessary. Since so many of the speeches are worded exactly as they would be today we must suppose that at the end of the eighteenth century young girls in conversation did express themselves in a manner which would now seem stilted. Jane Bennet, speaking of her lover's sisters, remarks: "They were certainly no friends to his acquaintance with me, which I cannot wonder at, since he might have chosen so much more advantageously in many respects." I am willing to believe that this is just how she put it, but I admit, it requires an effort.

I have said nothing yet of what to my mind is the greatest merit of this charming book: it is wonderfully readable—more readable than some greater and more famous novels. As Scott said, Miss Austen deals with commonplace things, the involvements, feelings, and characters of ordinary life; nothing very much happens and yet when you reach the bottom of a page you eagerly turn it in order to know what will happen next; nothing very much does and again you turn the page with the same eagerness.

After I had finished this essay I happened one evening to be sitting at dinner next to a lady who was related to a descendant of Jane Austen's brother. This brother, the reader will remember, was left large properties in Kent and Hampshire by a cousin, and by the testator's will had to adopt the name of Knight. He had daughters, one of whom, Fanny, was Jane Austen's favorite niece. She grew up, and by her marriage became Lady Knatchbull. Our conversation at dinner turned upon Jane Austen, and my neighbor told me that this relation of hers had an unpublished letter from Lady Knatchbull to her younger sister, Mrs. Rice, in which she spoke of her famous aunt. I was of course all eagerness to see it, and shortly afterward the kind lady sent me a copy of it. It was so surprising, so characteristic of the period in which it was written, and in its own way so diverting that I felt it should be published. By permission of Lord Brabourne, a direct descendant of Lady Knatchbull, I am now enabled to do so. The italics mark the words she underlined.

It may be surmised from the way the letter begins that Mrs. Rice was uneasy about some things she had heard that reflected on her aunt Jane's gentility, and had written to inquire if they were by any frightful chance true. Lady Knatchbull replied as follows:

Yes my love it is very true that Aunt Jane from various circumstances was not so *refined* as she ought to have been from her *talent,* & if she had lived 50 years later she would have been in many respects more suitable to our more refined tastes. They were not rich & the people around with whom they chiefly mixed, were not at all high bred, or in short anything more than *mediocre* & *they* of course tho' superior in *mental powers* & *cultivation* were on the same level as far as *refinement* goes—but I think in later life their intercourse with Mrs. Knight (who was very fond of & kind to them) improved them both & Aunt Jane was too clever not to put aside all possible signs of 'common-ness' (if such an expression is allowable) & teach herself to be more refined, at least in intercourse with people in general. Both the Aunts (Cassandra & Jane) were brought up in the most complete ignorance of the World & its ways (I mean as to fashion etc) & if it had not been for Papa's marriage which brought them into Kent, & the kindness of Mrs. Knight, who used often to have one or the other of the sisters staying with her, they would have been, tho' not less clever and agreeable in themselves, very much below par as to good Society and its ways. If you hate all this I beg yr. pardon, but I felt it at my *pen's end* & it chose to come along & speak the truth. It is now nearly dressing time . . .

. . . I am ever beloved Sister yours most affec.

F.C.K.

It just shows that you may make a great stir in the world and yet sadly fail to impress the members of your own family.

Martin Amis

FORCE OF LOVE: *PRIDE AND PREJUDICE*
BY JANE AUSTEN

The first challenge you face when writing about *Pride and Prejudice* is to get through your first sentence without saying, "it is a truth universally acknowledged . . . " With that accomplished (with *that* out of the way), you can move on to more testing questions. For example: why does the reader yearn with such helpless fervor for the marriage of Elizabeth Bennet and Mr. Darcy? Why does the reader crow and flinch with almost equal concern over the ups and downs of Jane Bennet and Mr. Bingley? Jane and Elizabeth's mother, Mrs. Bennet (stupid, prattling, coarse, greedy), is one of the greatest comic nightmares in all literature, yet we are scarcely less restrained than she in our fretful ambition for her daughters. Jane Austen makes Mrs. Bennets of us all. How?

And, even more mysteriously, this tizzy of zealous suspense actually survives repeated readings. Finishing the book for perhaps the fifth or sixth time, the present writer felt all the old gratitude and relief: an undiminished catharsis. These days, true, I wouldn't have minded a rather more detailed conclusion—say, a twenty-page sex scene featuring the two principals, with Mr. Darcy, furthermore, acquitting himself uncommonly well. (Such a scene would take place, of course, not in a country inn or a louche lodging house in town but amid all the comfort and elegance of Pemberley, with its parklands and its vistas and its ten thousand a year.) Jane Austen, with her divine comedies of love, has always effortlessly renewed herself for each generation of readers (and critics, too: moralists, Marxists, myth-panners, deconstructors—all are kept happy). One may wonder what she has to say to the current crop of twenty-year-olds, for whom "love" is not quite what it was. Today love faces new struggles: against literalism, futurelessness, practicality, and nationwide condom campaigns. But maybe the old opposition, of passion and prudence, never really changes; it just sways on its axis.

Let us begin by pinpointing the moment at which love blooms—for Mr. Darcy, and for every male reader on earth. It blooms on page 33 of my edition (the *Oxford Illustrated Jane Austen,* 1923). We have had the Meryton assembly, the straitlaced *thé dansant,* at which the local community thrills to the entrance of the eligible gents and their entourage, and we have protectively endured Mr. Darcy's audible humiliation of our heroine: "She is tolerable; but not handsome enough to tempt *me . . .* " Soon afterward Jane Bennet—meek, sweet, uncomplicated—is invited to dine with the fashionable newcomers. "Can I have the carriage?" she asks her mother. "No, my dear, you had better go on horseback, because it seems likely to rain, and then you must stay all night." Jane rides, it rains, she falls ill—and cannot be moved. Elizabeth's anxiety is one we can easily share: experienced in the ways of nineteenth-century fiction, we know that these frail beauties can fall apart more or less overnight. So, the next morning, impelled by sibling love, Elizabeth strides off through the November mud to Netherfield, that fortress of privilege and disdain. She arrives unannounced, and scandalously unaccompanied, "with weary ancles, dirty stockings, and a face glowing with the warmth of exercise." By now the male reader's heart is secure (indeed, he is down on one knee). But Darcy's palpitations are just beginning.

As for female susceptibilities—as for falling in love with *him*—Mr. Darcy, I think, ravishes the entire gender on his very first appearance:

> Mr Darcy soon drew the attention of the room by his fine, tall person, handsome features, noble mien; and the report which was in general circulation within five minutes after his entrance, of his having ten thousand a year.

That, plus this—

> 'You have a house in town, I conclude?'
> Mr Darcy bowed.

—will about do it. Auden, among many others, was shocked by Jane Austen's celebration of "the amorous effects of brass": that is, of money, and *old* money, too. Money is a vital substance in her world; the moment you enter it you feel the frank horror of moneylessness, as intense as the tacit horror of spinsterhood. Funnily enough, our hopes for Elizabeth and Darcy are egalitarian, and not avaricious, in tendency. We want love to bring about the redistribution of wealth. To inspire such a man to *disinterested* desire, non-profit-making desire: this is the romantic hinge.

Elizabeth Bennet is Jane Austen with added spirit, with subversive passion, and, above all, with looks. Although writers' lives are no more than optional extras in the consideration of their work, the dull fact of Jane Austen's spinsterhood—her plainness, her childlessness, her virgin death—invests her comedies with disappointment, and with a sense of thwarted homing. It also confirms one's sense of the diminishing physicality of her later heroines: inconspicuous, undetectable Fanny Price; the regal Emma (with her avuncular Mr. Knightley); the poignant staidness of Anne Elliot. Incredibly, Jane Austen was about the same age as Elizabeth when she began *Pride and Prejudice* ("I am not one and twenty"), and Elizabeth remains her only convincingly sexual heroine. Even her father, indolent Mr. Bennet, is sufficiently aware of her passionate nature to deliver an exceptional warning: "discredit and misery" would await her, she "could be neither happy nor respectable," in a loveless marriage. *His* marriage is loveless, and so is everybody else's; and they have all settled for it. But he knows that Elizabeth would never settle for anything less than love.

How do we get a sense of this society, this universe, with its inhibition, its formality, its echelonized emotions? It comes to us most clearly, perhaps, in its language. Mr. Darcy's first name is Fitzwilliam, which is a nice name—but Elizabeth will never use it. She will call him "Mr Darcy" or, occasionally, "My dear Mr Darcy." You call your mother "Madam" and your dad "Sir." When the dance floor is "crouded," young ladies may get a "headach." You may "teaze" a gentleman, should you "chuse," and should he consent to be "laught" at. If it be the sixth of October, then "Michaelmas" will have been celebrated "yesterday se'nnight." "La," what "extacies" we were in! Everyone is much "incumbered" by "secresy" and the need to watch their "expences." A rich man must marry a rich girl, to avoid "degradation" or even "pollution." But a poor man must marry a rich girl too, in order to achieve a "tolerable independence." So who is to marry all the *poor* girls—the poor girls, how will they find "an husband"? How will they swerve between passion and prudence, between sensibility and sense, between love and money?

Two extreme cases are explored in *Pride and Prejudice*. Or, rather, they are unexplored, unexamined; they define the limitations of Jane Austen's candor and, perhaps, the limitations of her art. First is the marriage that is all sense, all money (and not very much money either): the marriage of Mr. Collins and Charlotte Lucas. Charlotte is Elizabeth's neighbor and her closest friend. Mr. Collins is, of course, a world-class grotesque; he has a slimy vigilance that Mr. Podsnap might have envied. "Can he be a sensible man, sir?" Elizabeth asks her father, having acquainted herself with Mr. Collins's introductory letter. Mr. Bennet responds with typically droll and fateful laxity:

> No, my dear: I think not. I have great hopes of finding him quite the reverse. There is a mixture of servility and self-importance in his letter, which promises well. I am impatient to see him.

Mr. Collins comes to stay. Because of the famous "entail" in Mr. Bennet's estate, the girls will be bypassed, and cousin Collins is next in line to inherit. He therefore feels obliged to marry one of the many Bennet daughters. His gaze first alights on Jane, then (one day later) on Elizabeth, to whom (eight days later) he unsuccessfully proposes before fixing on Charlotte Lucas (one day later). He proposes to *her* one day later. And she accepts him.

Jane Austen expends little energy on physical description. Her characters are "handsome" or "pleasing" or "not at all handsome." The feature-by-feature inventory she leaves to the hags and harpies (this is Miss Bingley on Elizabeth: "Her face is too thin . . . Her nose wants character . . . Her teeth are tolerable, but not out of the common way"). She deals in auras, in presences; her creations fill a certain space with a certain personal style, and they are shaped by their idiolects. Of the Reverend William Collins we are told only this: "He was a tall, heavy looking young man of five and twenty." But his immense physical dreariness is nonetheless fully summoned. (The twenty-page sex scene is in this case not sorely missed. "I crave your indulgence, my dear Mrs Collins, if, at this early juncture . . . ")

Anyway, Charlotte repairs to what Collins calls his humble abode. And that's her life gone. Jane Austen interprets the matter with a kind of worldly savagery: Charlotte accepts Collins "from the pure and disinterested desire of an establishment"; marriage is "the only honourable provision" for women so placed, and "must be their pleasantest preservative from want." Elizabeth is not so hard-barked about it, but her "astonishment" at her closest friend's expediency soon modulates into the quiet conviction "that no real confidence could ever subsist between them again." And by the time she pays a visit to the newlyweds, she has decided that "all the comfort of intimacy was over." Isolation, then, is part of the price Charlotte pays, and expects to pay. Elizabeth feels she can discuss her best friend's situation with Mr. Darcy, whom at this stage she thoroughly dislikes ("[Mr. Collins's] friends may well rejoice in his having met with one of the very few sensible women who would have accepted him"); but she doesn't feel she can discuss her best friend's situation with her best friend. Why not? Well, people didn't, then. There is no reason why it should occur to Elizabeth to question this miserable silence. But perhaps it ought to have occurred to Jane Austen. Elizabeth is quick to find rueful humor in the business, and Jane Austen is even quicker to find non-rueful humor in it (we hear Charlotte's mother inquiring "after the welfare and poultry of her eldest daughter"). The marriage is pitiful and creepy; but it is routinely pitiful and creepy. It is everyday.

The other escape from the love-money, passion-prudence axis is the escape undertaken by Elizabeth's youngest sister, Lydia: all love, or at least all passion, or at any rate no prudence (and certainly no money). Little Lydia elopes with the feckless Lieutenant Wickham. Now, in Jane Austen's universe, elopement is a tractable delinquency, provided the absconders marry very soon, preferably before nightfall. Should she neglect the wedlock end of it, however, the woman will face an isolation far more thoroughgoing than Charlotte Lucas's: "irremediable infamy," ostracism, demimondainedom. Lydia languishes for two whole weeks with Wickham before the affair is patched and pelfed together (largely by Mr. Darcy, it transpires); thus Lydia's virtue is precariously and, as it were, retroactively preserved. Wickham consents to make an honest woman of her, after heavy bribes.

So what are we meant to feel about Lydia? Slimeball Mr. Collins writes to Mr. Bennet, at an early stage in the scandal, "The death of your daughter would have been a blessing in comparison of this." In a later letter, having "rejoiced" that the "sad business has been so well hushed up," Collins adds,

> I must not . . . refrain from declaring my amazement, at hearing that
> you received the young couple into your house as soon as they were

married. It was an encouragement of vice . . . You ought certainly to forgive them as a christian, but never to admit them in your sight or allow
their names to be mentioned in your hearing.

"*That,*" says Mr. Bennet, "is his notion of christian forgiveness!" But
what is Jane Austen's notion of it? We may well believe that as a Christian she forgives Lydia. But we will want to know whether as an *artist* she
forgives her.

Installed in "all the comfort and elegance" of Pemberley, Elizabeth
sends the Wickhams odd bits of spare cash, and "occasionally" receives
her sister there. Lydia, so to speak, is wheeled off onto a siding, lost to her
sister. And this despite the following mitigations (which gallantry, as well
as conscience, obliges one to list): that Lydia's fall was precisely and
vividly foretold by Elizabeth; that its likelihood was blamed on parental
and familial laxity; that Elizabeth was at one point entirely gulled by
Wickham's charms and lies; and that Lydia, during the course of the
novel, only just turns sixteen. Calling on her privilege as the local omniscient, Jane Austen consigns Lydia's marriage to the communal grave
("His affection for her soon sunk into indifference; hers lasted a little
longer"), underlining her exclusion from the circumambient happy ending. Lydia, so beautifully evoked (brawny, selfish, clumsy, wholly trans-
parent: after the ball at Netherfield "even Lydia was too much fatigued to
utter more than the occasional exclamation of 'Lord, how tired I am!' accompanied by a violent yawn"), is now summarily written out. And here,
I think, the reader begins to feel that artists should know better than that;
we expect them to know better than that. We expect artists to stand as
critics not just of their particular milieu but of their society, and of their
age. They shouldn't lose sight of their creations at exactly the same point
that "respectability"—or stock response—loses sight of them.

For all its little smugnesses and blind spots, despite something airless
and narrow, *Pride and Prejudice* is Jane Austen's most sociable book—and,
strangely, her most socially idealistic. The impulse is in fact strongly present. And because this is a romantic comedy, the impulse expresses itself
through the unlikely personage of Fitzwilliam Darcy. Darcy doesn't account for the novel's eternal humor and élan, but he does account for its
recurrent and remorseless power to move. Elizabeth's prejudice is easily
dealt with: all she needs is the facts before her. Yet the melting of Darcy's
pride demands radical change, the difference between his first declaration ("In vain have I struggled") and his second ("You are too generous

to trifle with me"). The patching-up of the Lydia business involves Darcy in some expense, but it also forces him to descend into the chaos of unrestrained dreads and desires—an area where Jane Austen fears to linger, even in her imagination. The final paragraph gives us the extraordinary spectacle of Darcy opening his house, and his arms, to Elizabeth's aunt and uncle, who make what money they have through *trade*. Darcy, Jane Austen writes, "really loved them." This is the wildest romantic extravagance in the entire corpus: a man like Mr. Darcy, chastened, deepened, and finally democratized by the force of love.

Benjamin Nugent

THE NERDS OF *PRIDE AND PREJUDICE*

In Chapter 47 of *Pride and Prejudice,* Elizabeth Bennet's sister Mary tries to commiserate with her on the public disgrace of their younger sister Lydia. At this point, Lydia has run off with Wickham, who has not yet agreed to marry her. If Wickham doesn't ask for Lydia's hand, Lydia will be ruined for other men, destined to live sequestered from society or to fall into prostitution. Says Mary:

> "This is a most unfortunate affair; and will probably be much talked of. But we must stem the tide of malice, and pour into the wounded bosoms of each other, the balm of sisterly consolation."
>
> Then perceiving in Elizabeth no inclination of replying, she added, "Unhappy as the event must be for Lydia, we may draw from it this useful lesson; that loss of virtue in a female is irretrievable—that one false step involves her in endless ruin—that her reputation is no less brittle than it is beautiful,—and that she cannot be too much guarded in her behaviour toward the undeserving of the other sex."
>
> Elizabeth lifted up her eyes in amazement, but was too much oppressed to make any reply.

Pride and Prejudice is consistently funny and insightful, but this is one of the few scenes in the novel that achieves tragedy. Mary's overtures are just too lame for Elizabeth to acknowledge, even in the Bennet family's bleakest hour. Austen's ear for dialogue is perfect as usual; pouring sisterly balm into wounds is exactly the inept metaphor for sharing feelings that Mary Bennet would construct. At the moment when the sisters need each other the most, Elizabeth finds Mary so ridiculous she can't even respond to her offer of sympathy. It's not that Mary's ignorant; she's always retreating to her room to read, the most literate of the Bennet sisters. And yet she can't earn Elizabeth's respect, because Elizabeth, herself so charmingly sneaky in conversation, finds Mary's awkwardness insufferable. In other words, Mary's a nerd, one of the earliest examples of a nerd in a famous work of literature.

Austen dramatizes the contrast between Mary and Elizabeth early on, in Chapter 4. Elizabeth is, in contemporary terms, a cool person. The difference between the two sisters emerges in the way they play piano.

> Mary had neither genius nor taste; and though vanity had given her application, it had given her likewise a pedantic air and conceited manner, which would have injured a higher degree of excellence than she had reached. Elizabeth, easy and unaffected, had been listened to with much more pleasure, though not playing half so well . . .

In speech as well as music, Mary is studious but clumsy. She can be relied upon to poison a casual conversation with pedantry and formality:

> "Pride," observed Mary, who piqued herself upon the solidity of her reflections, "is a very common failing I believe. By all that I have ever read, I am convinced that it is very common indeed, that human nature is particularly prone to it, and that there are very few of us who do not cherish a feeling of self-complacency on the score of some quality or other, real or imaginary."

She goes on like this, spooning out cant at such length as to suggest she believes it's a great gift to her audience. Elizabeth and Darcy both engage in the same kind of psychological dissections, as when Darcy explains to his friend Bingley that Bingley mentions how quickly he makes decisions in order to appear self-deprecating while actually boasting of his own spontaneity and daring. Elizabeth constantly analyzes Darcy's pride to her deferential older sister Jane. What makes Mary's analysis repellent to Elizabeth is the way it suggests a lack of emotional engagement with its subject. Just as Mary cannot imbue her skillful piano playing with romance, she cannot imbue her speeches with a convincingly empathetic tone.

The one man in Meryton who seems a plausible match for Mary is Mr. Collins, whom Elizabeth also disdains. What makes Mr. Collins so annoying to Elizabeth is his failure to *feel* correctly. He believes himself in love with Jane, but when Mrs. Bennet informs him that Jane is unavailable, he transfers his love to Elizabeth with no visible effort. When Elizabeth rejects his proposal repeatedly he blithely shifts his affections to Charlotte Lucas, the plain twenty-eight-year-old of modest means who is one of the few women in Meryton's bourgeois society desperate enough to settle for him.

The reason Mary and Mr. Collins irritate Elizabeth while Darcy ultimately attracts her is that their pride is of a different type than Darcy's. Mary speaks of pride as if it's a disease that afflicts every patient the same way, but Austen makes clear that it takes multiple forms. Mary and Mr. Collins grasp for validation and show off; they puff out their chests because they so badly want to impress and to be liked. Mr. Collins, Austen tells us, has never in his life been paid much attention to, and now wants everybody to know exactly how intimately acquainted he is with Lady Catherine, zealous in his belief that her approval bequeaths authority. Mary hopes that if she shows off her learning—both her piano technique and her knowledge of books—it will make up for her plainness. In the argot of our own time, they are majorly compensating. Darcy is different because he knows his distinguishing qualities are innate. He was born into the aristocracy with a lot of money, and he's really good-looking. Across the Channel, people like him have been put to the guillotine; the reason all those soldiers are patrolling the countryside, tantalizing Kitty and Lydia, is to defend the realm should Bonaparte get any ideas. But in England Darcy's status is safe, unconditional, so he has no problem admitting to being a slow letter-writer when Elizabeth first hangs out with him at Bingley's house. Mary and Mr. Collins have, in their affectations, lost their ability to express themselves honestly, to know their hearts and speak plainly. Their form of pride kills romance; Darcy's doesn't.

In this way, Mary and Mr. Collins both give the appearance of being like Mary Shelley's unfeeling scientist, Dr. Victor Frankenstein, a character created at about the same time they were. (*Frankenstein* was published in 1818, *Pride and Prejudice* in 1813). Victor's great problem is that while he possesses the academic drive to create another person out of corpse parts, he lacks the ability to emotionally connect with that being.

So when the "monster" he creates comes to life, he flees from it in terror and refuses to father it. The monster becomes more fully human than the scientist.

Similarly, Darcy, an unproductive aristocrat, is a more fully realized human being than Mr. Collins, who applies himself rigorously to study and upward mobility, reading aloud Fordyce's sermons to the Bennets and heaping praise upon his noble benefactor, Lady Catherine. Just as Elizabeth, also, in some sense, useless, is a more fully realized human being than Mary. It's not that Elizabeth is utterly devoid of social ambition; she experiences a longing for Pemberley, Darcy's ancestral home, when she visits it as a tourist, and this is one of the moments she realizes she's beginning to fall in love with him. But Elizabeth's means of upward mobility is accidental—she just expresses her emotions around Darcy, and one of the emotions she expresses, contempt for his prideful character, makes him fall in love with her. The two of them connect through candor and spontaneity, and this grants them happiness that sycophants like Mr. Collins will never experience.

I dislike the implied lesson: that being a sparkling, emotionally open conversationalist is a good way to marry up, that being "accomplished" in the sense of book learning is not. Austen's world is a hell, if you believe in meritocracy. How can Elizabeth Bennet, I scream into the void, fall for a brat like Darcy? He has no right to cast aspersions on anyone, because casting aspersions is all he actually does. He's an aggressively judgmental trust-fund kid who, by his own confession, loves Elizabeth because she's the only person in the whole of his experience who hasn't treated him like a superior by birthright. I begin the novel sympathetic toward the widely beloved Lizzy, but when she falls in love, I turn my back on her and sulk through the rest of the book.

And yet, Austen's obsession with conversation as it's actually spoken, with tone and cadences, and the way these things can set the course of lives—this was the obsession I needed to acquire when I was a nerdy teenager. When I was fourteen, I was like Mary Bennet, which is to say I paid attention to the way poets and philosophers expressed themselves on the page but not the way the people around me expressed themselves with their mouths. The first writers who showed me that the ways people reached out for each other with their casual remarks—flirtatiously, aggressively—were screenwriters. Whit Stillman's movie *Metropolitan,* in which the characters actually discuss *Mansfield Park,* was the first film to obsess me—when I was seventeen years old, I watched it between ten and twenty times. All anyone did was sit around and talk, and the way the movie put the nuances of conversation before all else showed me a new mode of observation. Eric Rohmer's films, like Stillman's, were Austen-like, in that nothing happened but a series of conversations between upper-middle-class characters in the country. *Claire's Knee* moves forward only through the way the vacationing Frenchmen attract and repulse each other with their voices. When I finally got around to reading Austen, she seemed like the original source, the ultimate talky French movie.

Austen's protagonists, young women of marrying age, living around the beginning of the nineteenth century, had no choice but to listen intently to conversation; barred from becoming, say, engineers, there was no other way for them to seize control over fate. The awful thing about the place and time Austen wrote of was that young women like Mary Bennet stood no chance, their inclinations toward mechanical reasoning squandered because of their sex. But for contemporary nerds, young people disposed to think like Mary, it's helpful to be thrown temporarily into a world in which one's gifts are disregarded. If you read sci-fi novels, you'll generally read about worlds in which scientists and the technologies they create drive the plot; if you read Austen, you'll read about a world in which technology means nothing and the triumphs and failures of conversational agility drive everything. Young nerds should read Austen because she'll force them to hear dissonant notes in their own speech they might otherwise miss, and open their eyes to defeats and victories they otherwise wouldn't even have noticed. Like almost all worthwhile adolescent experience, it can be depressing, but it can also feel like waking up.

J. B. Priestley

AUSTEN PORTRAYS A SMALL WORLD
WITH HUMOR AND DETACHMENT

Pride and Prejudice was first begun as early as 1796, when Jane Austen was only twenty-one, and was then called *First Impressions*. In this form it was refused by the publisher, and afterward it was considerably revised, being published in its present form in 1813. It is worth remembering that at this time, Napoleon was still master of most of Western Europe, and that the England of Jane Austen was still engaged in a life-and-death struggle with him. The fact that her novel completely ignores all this is significant. Jane Austen was a great artist, and she knew very well that her fiction could only be effective if it were kept within certain definite limits. It is all a question of proportion and scale. If we are made aware of the fact that nations are at war and thousands of men dying on battlefields, then we cannot bring ourselves to take any interest, for example, in one silly young girl's elopement. So Jane Austen, who knew exactly what she was doing, deliberately left out of her picture nine tenths of life—war and politics and commerce and violent deaths and madness and terrible illnesses and ruin and starvation—and made all her characters reasonably cozy and comfortable, in a tiny world in which a canceled dinner party or a shower of rain is an important event, so that we could attend to and enjoy her delicate and subtle comedy. It is, I repeat, all quite deliberate. She was, above all else, a highly self-conscious artist, who knew exactly what she was doing.

The English Social World Treated with a Balanced View

Now the social world she described so minutely was that of the Regency, a period, partly in the eighteenth, partly in the nineteenth century, that had its own particular characteristics. It was a time when the rigid class system of the earlier eighteenth century in England was breaking down, especially in the middle, between the top ruling class of the wealthy and influential landowning aristocrats and the working classes. Now when you have a rigid class system, with everybody more or less fixed on one social level or another, there is very little snobbery, just because people know exactly where they are and it is no use pretending. It is precisely when the system is breaking down, without completely disappearing, that there is most snobbery, most pretense of social importance and grandeur. So it is not surprising that the novels of Jane Austen, a member of the middle class during this period, should be, among other things, comedies of snobbery, social pretense, and prejudice. Because these attitudes existed, because they continually influenced people, Jane Austen dealt with them largely, and with infinite irony, in her novels, as we can see from *Pride and Prejudice,* in which nine tenths of the action is really concerned with snobbery and social climbing and their various by-products. But notice that she herself is quite detached from them, though she takes for granted a social system far removed from the social democracy that America has, to some extent, achieved. But before we decide that the little world she shows us is absurdly antiquated, we had better take a good look at the social life we know, which still contains plenty of snobbery, pretense, and prejudice. We all know people who violently condemn the local country club because, in fact, they have not been asked to join it. And if you are no longer snobbish about titles and estates, you can be snobbish about automobiles. Superficially, in *Pride and Prejudice,* Jane Austen is describing a world that has vanished. Go below the surface, however, and she is coming close to people, with their absurd hopes and fears, their little meannesses and acts of generosity, as they still are today. Consider carefully Mr. and Mrs. Bennet, Elizabeth, Jane and Lydia, Darcy and Bingley and Wickham, Lady Catherine and Mr. Collins, and you will soon discover people not unlike them all round you . . .

Unlike so many later women novelists, Jane Austen was not a romantic. What does that mean? It means chiefly that she did not believe that it is worthwhile sacrificing everything for the sake of one tremendous passion. Her attitude toward life was essentially the classical one, holding a balance, not asking for too much of anything, insisting upon moderation. This attitude is of immense help to the writer of ironic comedy. It provides a sort of measuring rod of common sense, with which to test the motives, actions, and pretensions of his or her characters. Jane Austen never stops using this measuring rod. So as soon as we begin reading *Pride and Prejudice,* we know that Mrs. Bennet, a rather foolish, amiable woman, is too eager and anxious to marry off her daughters, while Mr. Bennet, an intelligent but rather lazy and selfish man, is really not sufficiently concerned about his daughters' futures. Mrs. Bennet goes too far one way, Mr. Bennet too far the other way. And throughout the whole tangle of events that follow, the motives, actions, and pretensions of the characters are always being judged. But this does not result in heavy moralizing on the part of the author, as it was to do later, for example, in the novels of Thackeray. Jane Austen does not keep digging us in the ribs. She directs on people and events a keen but quick light glance, and, following her, we have to have our wits about us, or we are liable to miss point after point, flashing stroke after stroke. If we can appreciate to the full all these points, these tiny but effective strokes, the result can be exhilarating, like listening to a brilliant conversationalist. But we must remember that her favorite weapon is irony. This irony is there in the very first sentence of *Pride and Prejudice:* "It is a truth universally acknowledged, that a single man in possession of a good fortune, must be in want of a wife." Read this sentence aloud, and immediately you catch the undertone of irony. It tells us at once that we are about to meet an anxious matchmaking mother and some girls longing to get married.

Social Bores Made Comic: Elizabeth Made Real

In real life the kind of people Jane Austen writes about, and the sort of existence they lead, so uneventful that an invitation to a ball may be discussed for a month, would bore us to desperation. But only stupid readers will be bored by her account of such people and their existence. By selection, emphasis, and the constant sparkle of her own mind, she brings about a magical transformation. Boring types, from whom we would run in real life, are transformed into enchanting comic characters. A wonderful example in this novel—and there are plenty in her other novels—is Mr. Collins, whose idiotic solemnity and snobbery and naïve conceit of himself would make him unbearable as a real acquaintance, whereas in these pages we have just enough of him to enjoy him as a monumental ass. Not that Jane Austen is equally good with everybody. No novelist can be. Obviously she knows a great deal more about her young women than she does about her young men. Characters like Darcy and Bingley and Wickham are not falsely drawn—and in places are very shrewdly observed—but they are always seen against a feminine background, not a masculine one; and we cannot help feeling that Jane Austen has little idea how they talk and behave when they are away from the ladies. Nevertheless, though Darcy is seen rather girlishly, all very imposing and splendid, the thoughtless selfishness of such a spoiled young man, as he himself finally has to confess, is brought out into the open. Jane Austen never loses her head over anybody. That cool though sparkling glance of hers always reveals the truth.

But of course the key figure in *Pride and Prejudice* is its heroine, Elizabeth Bennet, into whom Jane Austen undoubtedly put a great deal of herself. She is, to my mind, one of the most delightful girls in the whole wide range of English fiction. Oddly enough—for we never associate Jane Austen with Shakespeare, and superficially no two writers could be less alike—Elizabeth has much in common with Shakespeare's heroines, not the ultraromantic misses like Juliet and Desdemona and Ophelia but the heroines of the comedies, like Rosalind and Viola and Beatrice. Like them—and unlike nearly all the heroines of fiction and drama between Shakespeare and Jane Austen—she is lively and sensible, practical and affectionate, humorous and independent-minded. She is a real girl, a person in her own right, with a will of her own, instead of the beautiful dummy that so many romantic men writers bring into their fiction. Literature is crowded with mere dream figures we are asked to accept as heroines. But real women are much better, altogether more satisfying, than dream figures; and Elizabeth Bennet is one of the first and best of them in fiction, not only English but all fiction. And she comes closest, in motive and action, tone and style, not only of the characters in this novel but perhaps in all of Jane Austen's works, to representing Jane Austen's own attitude of mind and point of view. Even so, however, though her creator's sympathy with and affection for Elizabeth are obvious, Jane Austen still does not entirely lose her detachment.

Lasting Qualities in Austen's Art

It is this detachment, together with her power of selection and emphasis and her constant unforced social and moral criticism, that makes Jane

Austen a great novelist. That she was a great novelist, and remains one, there can be no doubt whatever. She is not great in the sense of being huge, expansive, overwhelming, as novelists like Tolstoy and Dickens and Balzac are. She created for her own use, as we have seen, a tiny world of her own, but no novelist before or since has succeeded better than she did in bringing close to perfection what she set out to do. While her characters may be merely gossiping and chattering about some small social event, their creator is coolly and exquisitely presenting us with her version of the perpetual human comedy, in which we all have to play our parts. And to watch her making one delicate but sure stroke after another is a most engrossing and rewarding pastime, and one that, so long as we begin to appreciate it, we shall enjoy all the more the older and wiser we are. Jane Austen is in fact one of the most lasting of English novelists: she "wears well," as they say in England. Make friends with this quiet but brilliant woman, this superb artist in fiction, and you have made a friend for life.

Anna Quindlen

PRIDE AND PREJUDICE
AND THE MYSTERIES OF LIFE

"It is a truth universally acknowledged, that a single man in possession of a good fortune, must be in want of a wife." So begins one of the finest novels written in the English language, *Pride and Prejudice*. Yet it was published anonymously, its author described on the title page only as "a lady." The writing of novels was a disreputable profession in the early part of the nineteenth century; when her family composed the inscription for her tomb in Winchester Cathedral shortly after her death in 1817, Jane Austen was described as daughter, as Christian, but not as writer. In a memoir of his aunt, J. E. Austen-Leigh wrote of the verger at the cathedral who asked a visitor to the grave, "Pray, sir, can you tell me whether there was anything particular about that lady; so many people want to know where she was buried."

She wrote not of war and peace, but of men, money, and marriage, the battlefield for women of her day and, surely, of our own. She set both theme and tone in that tartly aphoristic first sentence. This is a world in which personal relationships are based more often on gain than on love and respect. It is the world of the five Bennet sisters, growing up in the English countryside as the eighteenth century gives way to the nineteenth, who must find husbands if they are to make their way in the world. And it is about the dance of attraction between two brilliant, handsome human beings who teach each other, through trial and considerable error, the folly of their greatest faults.

But *Pride and Prejudice* is also about that thing that all great novels consider, the search for self. And it is the first great novel to teach us that that search is as surely undertaken in the drawing room making small talk as in the pursuit of a great white whale or the public punishment of adultery. "And Jane Austen," Somerset Maugham once wrote, "the daughter of a rather dull and perfectly respectable father, a clergyman, and a rather silly mother. How did she come to write *Pride and Prejudice*? The whole thing is a mystery." Maugham misses the point. What was true of Austen is true of many other women throughout history; she was educated in human nature by her friends, family, and neighbors, and it was to that circle of polite society that she turned in her fiction. She is the standard-bearer for what we now sometimes, condescendingly, call domestic drama, a writer who believed the clash of personalities was as meaningful as—perhaps more meaningful than—the clash of sabers. For those of us who suspect that all the mysteries of life are contained in the microcosm of the family, that personal relationships prefigure all else, the work of Jane Austen is the Rosetta stone of literature. We can only hope that when she described her first novel as "rather too light and bright," she was being ironic rather than self-deprecating.

Serious literary discussions of *Pride and Prejudice* threaten to obscure the most important thing about it: it is a pure joy to read. Part of that is because its central character is so alive, so riveting, so much one of us, only better. Elizabeth Bennet is a witty and jaded observer of her milieu, wise enough to decline a marriage offer from a man she finds odious but foolish enough to be taken in temporarily by a seductive scoundrel. Although she is contemptuous of the ways of the world in which she lives, a world in which accomplishment for a woman means being able to "paint tables, cover screens and net purses," she is reconciled to conforming to those ways. She is capable of pleading with one man who believes her refusal of his proposal must be a female ploy: "Do not consider me now as an elegant female intending to plague you, but as a rational creature speaking the truth from her heart." And she is just as capable of concluding without much regret, when another with whom she has had a flirtation moves on, "The sudden acquisition of ten thousand pounds was the most remarkable charm of the young lady to whom he was now rendering himself agreeable." At once cynical and idealistic, she is finally terribly real.

The action of the novel revolves around Elizabeth and her sister, the sweet-tempered Jane, sugar to Elizabeth's lemonade. (This polar approach to the female character will appear later in nineteenth-century English literature, more broadly and unforgivingly drawn, in Dorothea

Casaubon and Celia Brooke of *Middlemarch*.) Jane falls in love with a well-to-do young man named Bingley, while Elizabeth takes an instant dislike to Bingley's closest friend, the wealthy Fitzwilliam Darcy. For much of the book these two spar verbally, contentiously, delightfully; as Elizabeth says, "We are each of an unsocial, taciturn disposition, unwilling to speak, unless we expect to say something that will amaze the whole room, and be handed down to posterity with the eclat of a proverb."

The tale that follows is, as John Halperin writes in his biography of Austen, "about true and false moral values" in a society that sometimes seems to find value only in great fortune and high position. Darcy learns to trust his heart and mute his arrogance, Elizabeth not to make hasty judgments: hence the pride and the prejudice of the title. (Austen originally named the book *First Impressions;* thank God for second thoughts!) The novel explores matches of uncomplicated attraction, deadening practicality, and frivolous concupiscence. And it is filled with minor characters as broad, ridiculous, and entertaining as any in Dickens: the haughty Lady Catherine de Bourgh, the pompous Mr. Collins, and Mr. and Mrs. Bennet, the oddest and most ill-matched of parents. The breeding of the well-bred is revealed as every bit as bad as that of the low-born, and the judgment of the intelligent as sometimes stupid indeed. The assessment of human nature is acute, unforgiving, even cruel. "You could not shock her more than she shocks me; / Beside her Joyce seems innocent as grass," wrote the poet W. H. Auden of Austen.

In many ways *Pride and Prejudice* is a nearly perfect novel: the wry ironic tone is unwavering, the pace remarkably lively without feeling excessively plotted. The sole exception to this is the ending. Austen is temperamentally unsuited to happily-ever-afters; the dénouements of all six of her novels feel hastily wrapped. But many of the other scenes are so fine—the ball at which Darcy first notices Elizabeth, the proposal by Mr. Collins and Mrs. Bennet's hysterical response, the unexpected meeting between Darcy and Elizabeth at Pemberley, the verbal dueling match between Elizabeth and Lady Catherine de Bourgh—that that is easily forgiven. The biggest problem with the ending of *Pride and Prejudice* is that it means this marvelous book is over.

Why has a story of the marrying off of young women in Regency England endured where most other novels of its time have sunk into obscurity? Ironically the answer is perhaps best found in those who have been, over two centuries, Austen's detractors. Critics have complained that her books are devoid of the politics of her era, the tumult of the French and American revolutions. Yet it is precisely because she chose to investigate and illuminate the enduring issues of social pressures and gender politics that *Pride and Prejudice* seems as vital today as ever, the most modern of nineteenth-century novels.

C. S. Lewis

A NOTE ON JANE AUSTEN

I begin by laying together four passages from the novels of Jane Austen.

(1) Catherine was completely awakened . . . Most grievously was she humbled. Most bitterly did she cry. It was not only with herself that she was sunk, but with Henry. Her folly, which now seemed even criminal, was all exposed to him, and he must despise her for ever. The liberty which her imagination had dared to take with the character of his father, would he ever forgive it? The absurdity of her curiosity and her fears, could they ever be forgotten? She hated herself more than she could express . . . Nothing could be clearer than that it had been all a voluntary, self-created delusion, each trifle receiving importance from an imagination resolved on alarm, and everything forced to bend to one purpose by a mind which, before she entered the Abbey, had been craving to be frightened . . . She saw that the infatuation had been created, the mischief settled, before her quitting Bath . . . Her mind made up on these several points, and her resolution formed, of always judging and acting in future with the greatest good sense, she had nothing to do but forgive herself and be happier than ever.

(*Northanger Abbey*, Chapter 25)

(2) "Oh! Elinor, you have made me hate myself forever. How barbarous have I been to you!—you, who have been my only comfort, who have borne with me in all my misery, who have seemed to be suffering only for me!" . . . Marianne's courage soon failed her, in trying to con-

verse upon a topic which always left her more dissatisfied with herself than ever, by the contrast it necessarily produced between Elinor's conduct and her own. She felt all the force of that comparison; but not as her sister had hoped, to urge her to exertion now; she felt it with all the pain of continual self-reproach, regretted most bitterly that she had never exerted herself before; but it brought only the torture of penitence, without the hope of amendment . . . [Elinor later saw in Marianne] an apparent composure of mind which, in being the result, as she trusted, of serious reflection, must eventually lead her to contentment and cheerfulness . . . "My illness has made me think . . . I considered the past: I saw in my own behaviour nothing but a series of imprudence towards myself, and want of kindness to others. I saw that my own feelings had prepared my sufferings, and that my want of fortitude under them had almost led me to the grave. My illness, I well knew, had been entirely brought on by myself, by such negligence of my own health as I felt even at the time to be wrong. Had I died, it would have been self-destruction. I wonder . . . that the very eagerness of my desire to live, to have time for atonement to my God and to you all, did not kill me at once . . . I cannot express my own abhorrence of myself."

(*Sense and Sensibility,* Chapters 37, 38, 46)

(3) As to his real character, had information been in her power, she had never felt a wish of inquiring. His countenance, voice, and manner had established him at once in the possession of every virtue . . . She perfectly remembered everything that had passed in conversation between Wickham and herself, in their first evening at Mr. Philip's . . . She was *now* struck with the impropriety of such communications to a stranger, and wondered that it had escaped her before. She saw the indelicacy of putting himself forward as he had done, and the inconsistency of his professions with his conduct . . . She grew absolutely ashamed of herself . . . "How despicably have I acted!" she cried; "I, who have prided myself on my discernment! . . . who have often disdained the generous candour of my sister, and gratified my vanity in useless or blamable distrust. How humiliating is this discovery! yet, how just a humiliation! Had I been in love, I could not have been more wretchedly blind. But vanity, not love, has been my folly . . . I have courted prepossession and ignorance, and driven reason away . . . Till this moment I never knew myself."

(*Pride and Prejudice,* Chapter 36)

(4) Her own conduct, as well as her own heart, was before her in the same few minutes . . . How improperly had she been acting by Harriet! How inconsiderate, how indelicate, how irrational, how unfeeling, had been her conduct! What blindness, what madness, had led her on! It struck her with dreadful force, and she was ready to give it every bad name in the world . . . Every moment had brought a fresh surprise, and every surprise must be matter of humiliation to her. How to understand it all? How to understand the deceptions she had been thus practising on herself, and living under! The blunders, the blindness, of her own head and heart! She perceived that she had acted most weakly; that she had been imposed on by others in a most mortifying degree.

(*Emma,* Chapter 47)

Between these four passages there are, no doubt, important distinctions. The first is on a level of comedy which approximates to burlesque. The delusion from which Catherine Morland has been awakened was an innocent one, which owed at least as much to girlish ignorance of the world as to folly. And, being imaginative, it was a delusion from which an entirely commonplace or self-centered mind would hardly have suffered. Accordingly, the expiation, though painful while it lasts, is brief, and Catherine's recovery and good resolutions are treated with affectionate irony. The awakening of Marianne Dashwood is at the opposite pole. The situation has come near to tragedy; moral, as well as, or more than, intellectual deficiency has been involved in Marianne's errors. Hence the very vocabulary of the passage strikes a note unfamiliar in Jane Austen's style. It makes explicit, for once, the religious background of the author's ethical position. Hence such theological or nearly theological words as "penitence," even the "torture of penitence," "amendment," "self-destruction," "my God." And though not all younger readers may at once recognize it, the words "serious reflection" belong to the same region. In times which men now in their fifties can remember, the adjective "serious" ("serious reading," "Does he ever think about serious matters?") had indisputably religious overtones. The title of Law's *Serious Call* is characteristic. Between these two extracts, those from *Pride and Prejudice* and *Emma* occupy a middle position. Both occur in a context of high comedy, but neither is merely laughable.

Despite these important differences, however, no one will dispute that all four passages present the same kind of process. "Disillusionment," which might by etymology be the correct name for it, has acquired cynical overtones which put it out of court. We shall have to call it "undeception" or "awakening." All four heroines painfully, though with varying degrees of pain, discover that they have been making mistakes both about themselves and about the world in which they live. All their *data* have to be reinterpreted. Indeed, considering the differences of their situations and characters, the similarity of the process in all four is strongly marked. All realize that the cause of the deception lay within; Catherine, that she had brought to the Abbey a mind "craving to be frightened," Marianne, that her own feelings had prepared her sufferings, Elizabeth, that she has "courted ignorance" and "driven reason away," Emma, that she has been practicing deceptions on herself. Self-hatred or self-contempt, though (once more) in different degrees, are common to all. Catherine "hated herself"; Marianne abhors herself; Elizabeth finds her conduct "despicable"; Emma gives hers "every bad name in the world." Tardy and surprising self-knowledge is presented in all four, and mentioned by name in the last two. "I never knew myself," says Elizabeth; Emma's conduct and "her own heart" appear to her, unwelcome strangers both, "in the same few minutes."

If Jane Austen were an author as copious as Tolstoy, and if these passages played different parts in the novels from which they are taken, the common element would not, perhaps, be very important. After all, undeception is a common enough event in real life, and therefore, in a vast tract of fiction, might be expected to occur more than once. But that is not the position. We are dealing with only four books, none of them long; and in all four the undeception, structurally considered, is the very pivot or watershed of the story. In *Northanger Abbey* and *Emma*, it precipitates the happy ending. In *Sense and Sensibility* it renders it possible. In *Pride and Prejudice* it initiates that revaluation of Darcy, both in Elizabeth's mind and in our minds, which is completed by the visit to Pemberley. We are thus entitled to speak of a common pattern in Jane Austen's four most characteristic novels. They have "one plot" in a more important sense than Professor Garrod suspected.[1] This is not so clearly true of *Sense and Sensibility*, but then it has really two plots or two "actions" in the Aristotelian sense; it is true about one of them.

It is perhaps worth emphasizing what may be called the hardness—at least the firmness—of Jane Austen's thought exhibited in all these undeceptions. The great abstract nouns of the classical English moralists are unblushingly and uncompromisingly used: *good sense, courage, contentment, fortitude,* "some duty neglected, some failing indulged," *impropriety, indel-*

icacy, generous candor, blamable distrust, just humiliation, vanity, folly, ignorance, reason. These are the concepts by which Jane Austen grasps the world. In her we still breathe the air of the *Rambler* and *Idler.* All is hard, clear, definable; by some modern standards, even naïvely so. The hardness is, of course, for oneself, not for one's neighbors. It reveals to Marianne her "want of kindness" and shows Emma that her behavior has been "unfeeling." Contrasted with the world of modern fiction, Jane Austen's is at once less soft and less cruel.

It may be added, though this is far less important, that in these four novels, self-deception and awakening are not confined to the heroines. General Tilney makes as big a mistake about Catherine as she has made about him. Mrs. Ferrars misjudges her son. Mr. Bennet is forced at last to see his errors as a father. But perhaps all this does not go beyond what might be expected from the general nature of human life and the general exigencies of a novelistic plot.

The central pattern of these four has much in common with that of a comedy by Molière.

Two novels remain. In *Mansfield Park* and *Persuasion* the heroine falls into no such self-deception and passes through no such awakening. We are, it is true, given to understand that Anne Elliot regards the breaking off of her early engagement to Wentworth as a mistake. If any young person now applied to her for advice in such circumstances, "they would never receive any of such certain immediate wretchedness and uncertain future good." For Anne in her maturity did not hold the view which Lord David Cecil attributes to Jane Austen,[2] that "it was wrong to marry for money, but it was silly to marry without it." She was now fully "on the side of early warm attachment, and a cheerful confidence in futurity, against that over-anxious caution which seems to insult exertion and distrust Providence." (Notice, in passing, the Johnsonian cadence of a sentence which expresses a view that Johnson in one of his countless moods might have supported.) But though Anne thinks a mistake has been made, she does not think it was she that made it. She declares that she was perfectly right in being guided by Lady Russell who was to her "in the place of a parent." It was Lady Russell who had erred. There is no true parallel here between Anne and the heroines we have been considering. Anne, like Fanny Price, commits no errors.

Having placed these two novels apart from the rest because they do not use the pattern of "undeception," we can hardly fail to notice that they share another common distinction. They are the novels of the solitary heroines.

Catherine Morland is hardly ever alone except on her journey from Northanger Abbey, and she is soon back among her affectionate, if placid, family. Elinor Dashwood bears her own painful secret without a confidant for a time; but her isolation, besides being temporary, is incomplete; she is surrounded by affection and respect. Elizabeth always has Jane, the Gardiners, or (to some extent) her father. Emma is positively spoiled; the acknowledged center of her own social world. Of all these heroines we may say, as Jane Austen says of some other young women, "they were of consequence at home and favourites abroad."

But Fanny Price and Anne are of no "consequence." The consciousness of "mattering" which is so necessary even to the humblest women, is denied them. Anne has no place in the family councils at Kellynch Hall; "she was only Anne." She is exploited by her married sister, but not valued; just as Fanny is exploited, but not valued, by Mrs. Norris. Neither has a confidant; or if Edmund had once been a confidant as well as a hero to Fanny, he progressively ceases to be so. Some confidence, flawed by one vast forbidden topic, we may presume between Anne and Lady Russell; but this is almost entirely offstage and within the novel we rarely see them together. Both heroines come within easy reach of one of the great archetypes—Cinderella, Electra. Fanny, no doubt, more so. She is almost a Jane Austen heroine condemned to a Charlotte Brontë situation. We do not even believe in what Jane Austen tells us of her good looks; whenever we are looking at the action through Fanny's eyes, we feel ourselves sharing the consciousness of a plain woman.

Even physically, we see them alone; Fanny perpetually in the East Room with its fireless grate and its touching, ridiculous array of petty treasures (what Cinderella, what Electra, is without them?) or Anne, alone beside the hedge, an unwilling eavesdropper, Anne alone with her sick nephew, Anne alone in the empty house waiting for the sound of Lady Russell's carriage. And in their solitude both heroines suffer; far more deeply than Catherine, Elizabeth, and Emma, far more innocently than Marianne. Even Elinor suffers less. These two novels, we might almost say, stand to the others as Shakespeare's "dark" comedies to his comedies in general. The difference in the lot of the heroines goes with a difference in the "character parts." Mrs. Norris is almost alone among Jane Austen's vulgar old women in being genuinely evil, nor are her greed and cruelty painted with the high spirits which make us not so much hate as rejoice in Lady Catherine de Bourgh.

These solitary heroines who make no mistakes have, I believe—or had while she was writing—the author's complete approbation. This is connected with the unusual pattern of *Mansfield Park* and *Persuasion*. The heroines stand almost outside, certainly a little apart from, the world which the action of the novel depicts. It is in it, not in them, that self-deception occurs. They see it, but its victims do not. They do not of course stand voluntarily apart, nor do they willingly accept the role of observers and critics. They are shut out and are compelled to observe: for what they observe, they disapprove.

It is this disapproval which, though shared both by Fanny and Anne, has perhaps drawn on Fanny, from some readers, the charge of being a prig. I am far from suggesting that Fanny is a successful heroine, still less that she is the equal of Anne. But I hardly know the definition of *prig* which would make her one. If it means a self-righteous person, a Pharisee, she is clearly no prig. If it means a "precisian," one who adopts or demands a moral standard more exacting than is current in his own time and place, then I can see no evidence that Fanny's standard differs at all from that by which Marianne condemns herself or Anne Elliot corrects Captain Benwick. Indeed, since Anne preaches while Fanny feels in silence, I am a little surprised that the charge is not leveled against Anne rather than Fanny. For Anne's *chastoiement*[3] of poor Benwick is pretty robust; "she ventured to recommend a larger allowance of prose in his daily study, and . . . mentioned such works of our best moralists, such collections of the finest letters, such memoirs of characters of worth and suffering, as occurred to her at the moment as calculated to rouse and fortify the mind by the highest precepts and the strongest examples of moral and religious endurances" (Chapter 11). Notice, too, the standards which Anne was using when she first began to suspect her cousin, Mr. Elliot: "she saw that there had been bad habits; that Sunday travelling had been a common thing; that there had been a period of his life (and probably not a short one) when he had been, at least careless on all serious matters." Whatever we may think of these standards ourselves, I have not the least doubt that they are those of all the heroines, when they are most rational, and of Jane Austen herself. This is the hard core of her mind, the Johnsonian element, the iron in the tonic.

How, then, does Fanny Price fail? I suggest, by insipidity. *Pauper videri*

Cinna vult et est pauper.[4] One of the most dangerous of literary ventures is the little, shy, unimportant heroine whom none of the other characters value. The danger is that your readers may agree with the other characters. Something must be put into the heroine to make us feel that the other characters are wrong, that she contains depths they never dreamed of. That is why Charlotte Brontë would have succeeded better with Fanny Price. To be sure, she would have ruined everything else in the book; Sir Thomas and Lady Bertram and Mrs. Norris would have been distorted from credible types of pompous dullness, lazy vapidity, and vulgar egoism into fiends complete with horns, tails, and rhetoric. But through Fanny there would have blown a storm of passion which made sure that we at least would never think her insignificant. In Anne, Jane Austen did succeed. Her passion (for it is not less), her insight, her maturity, her prolonged fortitude, all attract us. But into Fanny, Jane Austen, to counterbalance her apparent insignificance, has put really nothing except rectitude of mind; neither passion, nor physical courage, nor wit, nor resource. Her very love is only calf love—a schoolgirl's hero worship for a man who has been kind to her when they were both children, and who, incidentally, is the least attractive of all Jane Austen's heroes. Anne gains immensely by having for her lover almost the best. In real life, no doubt, we continue to respect interesting women despite the preposterous men they sometimes marry. But in fiction it is usually fatal. Who can forgive Dorothea for marrying such a sugarstick as Ladislaw, or Nelly Harding for becoming Mrs. Bold? Or, of course, David Copperfield for his first marriage.

Fanny also suffers from the general faults of *Mansfield Park,* which I take to be, if in places almost the best, yet as a whole the least satisfactory, of Jane Austen's works. I can accept Henry Crawford's elopement with Mrs. Rushworth: I cannot accept his intention of marrying Fanny. Such men never make such marriages.

But though Fanny is insipid (yet not a prig) she is always "right" in the sense that to her, and to her alone, the world of *Mansfield Park* always appears as, in Jane Austen's view, it really is. Undeceived, she is the spectator of deceptions. These are made very clear. In Chapter 2 we learn that the Bertram girls were "entirely deficient" in "self-knowledge." In Chapter 3 Sir Thomas departs for Antigua without much anxiety about his family because, though not perfectly confident of his daughters' discretion, he had ample trust "in Mrs. Norris's watchful attention and in Edmund's judgement." Both, of course, failed to justify it. In Chapter 12 when Crawford was absent for a fortnight it proved "a fortnight of such dullness to the Miss Bertrams as ought to have put them both on their guard." Of course it did not. In Chapter 16 when Edmund at last consents to act, Fanny is forced to raise the question, "was he not deceiving himself." In Chapter 34 when Crawford (whose manners are insufferable) by sheer persistence pesters Fanny into speech when she has made her desire for silence obvious, she says, "Perhaps, Sir, I thought it was a pity you did not always know yourself as you seemed to do at that moment." But deception is most fully studied in the person of Mary Crawford, "a mind led astray and bewildered, and without any suspicion of being so: darkened, yet fancying itself light." The New Testament echo in the language underlines the gravity of the theme. It may be that Jane Austen has not treated it successfully. Some think that she hated Mary and falsely darkened a character whom she had in places depicted as charming. It might be the other way round; that the author, designing to show deception at its height, was anxious to play fair, to show how the victim could be likable at times, and to render her final state the more impressive by raising in us false hopes that she might have been cured. Either way, the gap between Mary at her best and Mary in her last interview with Edmund is probably too wide; too wide for fiction, I mean, not for possibility. (We may have met greater inconsistency in real life; but real life does not need to be probable.) That last interview, taken by itself, is an alarming study of human blindness. We may—most of us do—disagree with the standards by which Edmund condemns Mary. The dateless and universal possibility in the scene is Mary's invincible ignorance of what those standards are. All through their conversations she is cutting her own throat. Every word she speaks outrages Edmund's feelings "in total ignorance, unsuspiciousness of there being such feelings" (Chapter 47). At last, when we feel that her ghastly innocence (so to call it) could go no further, comes the master stroke. She tries to call him back by "a saucy, playful smile." She still thought that possible. The misunderstanding is incurable. She will never know Edmund.

In *Persuasion* the theme of deception is much less important. Sir Walter is, no doubt, deceived both in his nephew and in Mrs. Clay, but that is little more than the mechanism of the plot. What we get more of is the pains of the heroine in her role of compelled observer. Something of this had appeared in Elinor Dashwood, and more in Fanny Price, constantly forced to witness the courtship of Edmund and Mary Crawford. But Fanny had also, at times, derived amusement from her function of spectator. At the rehearsals of *Lovers' Vows* she was "not unamused to observe the selfishness which, more or less disguised, seemed to govern them all" (Chapter 14). It is a kind of pleasure which we feel sure that Jane Austen herself had often enjoyed. But whether it were that something in her own life now began to show her less of the spectator's joys and more of his pains, forcing her on from "as if we were God's spies" to "break my heart for I must hold my tongue," or that she is simply exploring a new literary vein, it certainly seems that Anne's unshared knowledge of the significance of things she hears and sees is nearly always in some degree painful. At Kellynch she has "a knowledge which she often wished less, her father's character." At the Musgroves', "One of the least agreeable circumstances of her residence . . . was her being treated with too much confidence by all parties, and being too much in the secret of the complaints of each house" (Chapter 6). One passage perhaps gives the real answer to any charge of priggery that might lie against her or Fanny for the judgments they pass as spectators. Speaking of Henrietta's behavior to Charles Hayter, Jane Austen says that Anne "had delicacy which must be pained" by it (Chapter 9). This is not so much like the Pharisee's eagerness to condemn as the musician's involuntary shudder at a false note. Nor is it easily avoided by those who have standards of any sort. Do not our modern critics love to use the term "embarrassing" of literature which violently offends the standards of their own group? and does not this mean, pretty nearly, a "delicacy" on their part which "must be pained"? But of course all these spectator's pains sink into insignificance beside that very special, almost unendurable, pain which Anne derives from her understanding of Wentworth's every look and word. For *Persuasion,* from first to last, is, in a sense in which the other novels are not, a love story.

It remains to defend what I have been saying against a possible charge. Have I been treating the novels as though I had forgotten that they are, after all, comedies? I trust not. The hard core of morality and even of religion seems to me to be just what makes good comedy possible. "Principles" or "seriousness" are essential to Jane Austen's art. Where there is no norm, nothing can be ridiculous, except for a brief moment of unbalanced provincialism in which we may laugh at the merely unfamiliar. Unless there is something about which the author is never ironical, there can be no true irony in the work. "Total irony"—irony about everything—frustrates itself and becomes insipid.

But though the world of the novels has this serious, unyielding core, it is not a tragic world. This, no doubt, is due to the author's choice; but there are also two characteristics of her mind which are, I think, essentially untragic. The first is the nature of the core itself. It is in one way exacting, in another not. It is unexacting insofar as the duties commanded are not quixotic or heroic, and obedience to them will not be very difficult to properly brought up people in ordinary circumstances. It is exacting insofar as such obedience is rigidly demanded; neither excuses nor experiments are allowed. If charity is the poetry of conduct and honor the rhetoric of conduct, Jane Austen's "principles" might be described as the grammar of conduct. Now grammar is something that anyone can learn; it is also something that everyone must learn. Compulsion waits. I think Jane Austen does not envisage those standards which she so rigidly holds as often demanding human sacrifice. Elinor felt sure that if Marianne's new composure were based on "serious reflection" it "must eventually lead her to contentment and cheerfulness." That it might lead instead to a hair shirt or a hermitage or a pillar in the Thebaïd is not in Jane Austen's mind. Or not there. There is just a hint in *Persuasion* that total sacrifice may be demanded of sailors on active service; as there is also a hint of women who must love when life or when hope is gone. But we are then at the frontier of Jane Austen's world.

The other untragic element in her mind is its cheerful moderation. She could almost have said with Johnson, "Nothing is too little for so little a creature as man." If she envisages few great sacrifices, she also envisages no grandiose schemes of joy. She has, or at least all her favorite characters have, a hearty relish for what would now be regarded as very modest pleasures. A ball, a dinner party, books, conversation, a drive to see a great house ten miles away, a holiday as far as Derbyshire—these, with affection (that is essential) and good manners, are happiness. She is no Utopian.

She is described by someone in Kipling's worst story[5] as the mother of Henry James. I feel much more sure that she is the daughter of Dr. Johnson: she inherits his common sense, his morality, even much of his style. I am not a good enough Jamesian to decide the other claim. But if she bequeathed anything to him it must be wholly on the structural side. Her style, her system of values, her temper, seem to me the very opposite of his. I feel sure that Isabel Archer, if she had met Elizabeth Bennet, would have pronounced her "not very cultivated," and Elizabeth, I fear, would have found Isabel deficient both in "seriousness" and in mirth.

Louis Auchincloss

JANE AUSTEN AND THE GOOD LIFE

Jane Austen has always had to put up with a certain amount of condescension, even from her admirers. It used to be the fashion to illustrate
her books as if they were juveniles, with pictures of dainty ladies on tiny
feet and in huge hats tripping down cobbled streets to shop or make calls.
And who is not tired of having it pointed out that she wrote six novels
during the Napoleonic wars without ever mentioning Napoleon's
name? I was delighted recently to discover that she had spoken of this
herself, and as a fault, but not with a groveling twentieth-century guilt at
having scanted her duty to history. She simply regretted that she had not
used the emperor to provide her with an artistic contrast. She considered
that *Pride and Prejudice* was "too light and bright and sparkling" and
needed "the history of Buonaparte to increase the reader's delight at the
playfulness and epigrammaticism of the general style." She would have
shaped Buonaparte for her fictional purposes as Tolstoy was to do in *War
and Peace.*

The great events of the world do not much help the novelist of any
age in his task. As Mary McCarthy has pointed out, the world of the
novel is essentially a reasonable one, and the mighty things, at least of our
time—genocide, the bomb, the population explosion—are essentially
unreasonable. Jane Austen was just as aware of Napoleon as we are aware
of Moscow and Peking (more so, perhaps, with a favorite brother on active duty in the navy and a first cousin married to a Frenchman guil-
lotined in the Terror), but he was not usable. She rejected him, as she
rejected the Prince Regent's librarian's suggestion that she do a book on

the House of Coburg, in order to pursue the task that Charlotte Brontë and George Eliot were also to set for themselves: that of finding the good life.

Every time that I reread Jane Austen's peerless six, I discover that, although I always rate them closely together, I find that the order of my preference changes. In youth *Emma* and *Pride and Prejudice* were my favorites. In middle age they are *Sense and Sensibility* and *Mansfield Park,* and, after them, *Persuasion.* To me these three are bathed in a mood of what, for lack of a better term, I shall call moral beauty. The long, grave struggles of Marianne Dashwood, of Fanny Price, and of Anne Elliot for a life that is worth the living seem to me the finest parts of Jane Austen's work.

In *Emma* the heroine's path to happiness is essentially smooth. She has only to wake up to what is there before her. And Elizabeth Bennet and Darcy in *Pride and Prejudice* are kept apart by a series of simple misunderstandings on Elizabeth's part. Darcy's pride, once comprehended, is no hindrance. Indeed, it is an integral part of his sex appeal. But Marianne Dashwood in *Sense and Sensibility* is brought close to death by her reckless passion for Willoughby, and Fanny Price in *Mansfield Park* must endure a youth of mortification and semi-servitude before Edmund Bertram learns to value the love that he has inspired. For Marianne and for Fanny the search for the good life requires patience, courage, and discipline.

What, then, is this "good life" for a Jane Austen heroine? Well, to begin with, it is limited to a very small part of the social structure. The top of society has been made a desert by the arrogance and worldliness of such rich or titled folk as Mrs. Ferrars, Lady Catherine de Bourgh, and Sir Walter Elliot. Only Elizabeth Bennet, cleverest of the heroines, can find her oasis there. And if one descends the social ladder too far, to the Price family, for example, in *Mansfield Park,* one finds that Jane Austen was clearly of the opinion that the good life was not compatible with noisy, undisciplined children let loose in small rooms. No, there should be some degree of affluence to provide space, both for solitude and for genteel gatherings, in houses that should be always elegant, even when simple, and should, if the countryside permits, look out on pleasant landscapes. Jane Austen lived in an era of such universal good taste (almost inconceivable to us) that it was inevitable for her and her contemporaries to associate outward order with inward serenity.

Also in the good life there should be time for reading, music, drawing, and for edifying conversation. And in the good marriage there should be compatibility as well as love, and money as well as mutual respect, although, as Catherine Morland points out in *Northanger Abbey,* it does not matter which spouse supplies the money. But above all, both in life and marriage, there should be a guiding philosophy to restrain the individual from excess, the excess of hoping too much or of despairing too much, and a constant resignation to the whims of providence that may at any moment dash the cup from even devoutly worshipping lips. This last is most important of all.

Now if one is going to take the attitude, because today any young man should be able to support himself and because class distinctions have largely dwindled to eccentricities, that Jane Austen was a snob to premise marriage on a bank account and some degree of compatibility of social background, one may as well shut up her novels. She was of her time, and she accepted her time, not as an ideal one but as something to be made the best of. In her day (and indeed in all days but our own) it was a very dangerous thing to run out of money, and only a fool ignored this. But this did not mean that money was to be coveted unduly. When Elizabeth Bennet argues that, if it be imprudent for Wickham to court a portionless girl, it must be wise for him to court a rich one, Jane Austen makes it very plain that her heroine is joking. Such conduct on Wickham's part would be "mercenary," and to be mercenary is being bad indeed. Simply because a line is hard to draw, does not excuse a man from drawing it.

Some of Jane Austen's own contemporaries had a bit of trouble with this line. It bothered Sir Walter Scott, for example, that Elizabeth's heart should soften toward Darcy as she contemplates his handsome park at Pemberley. But I imagine that Jane Austen would have replied that so long as her heroine was not primarily motivated by the park, it was a perfectly proper item on the list of Darcy's attractions. Pemberley is part of Darcy's sex appeal, as Donwell Abbey is part of Knightley's, as social position is part of Emma Woodhouse's, and as poverty and loneliness are part of Fanny Price's. No doubt it is nobler in mating to be drawn only to the person of one's partner, and those who are able so neatly to compartmentalize their feelings are quite right to scold Jane Austen.

Money, then, must receive its rightful due, but not a jot more than its rightful due. This is also true of the separation of classes. Jane Austen finds it manifestly absurd for Lady Catherine de Bourgh to consider Elizabeth Bennet unworthy of her nephew, but she also finds it very wrong of Emma Woodhouse to persuade the illegitimate, nameless Harriet Smith that she is a fit match for Mr. Elton. Elizabeth will grace Pemberley; Harriet is not up to a rectory. That is the eighteenth century, and that is Jane Austen. But the good life could still be attained even by a poor girl, within the hierarchies of that harshly divided world. This is the theme of *Mansfield Park*.

Fanny Price is surely the least loved of Jane Austen's heroines, but she has grown on me steadily through the years. She is not gay like Elizabeth Bennet or pert like Emma; she lacks Catherine Morland's ingenuousness and Anne Elliot's charm, but then she is poorer and lower born than any of them. She comes alone as a child to the hostile luxury of Mansfield Park, a waif suddenly confronted with the splendor of a rich baronet's household, and she must put together her life out of the scraps that are flung to her. Only by rejecting the bad things that she sees—the snobbishness, the greediness, the sensuality, the flippancy, the hardness—and grasping to her heart the good—the love of graceful dimensions, the opportunity of libraries, the approaches to God and serenity in quiet and solitude—can she come out on top.

She has no help from anyone, except a few kind words from Edmund. Her other cousins make fun of her. Her uncle, Sir Thomas Bertram, is grave and terrifying, and he will not care for the inclinations of the heart when it comes to an advantageous match for a poor niece. Aunt Bertram is indolent, Aunt Norris tyrannical. The first regards Fanny as a paid companion, the second as a serving maid. A young neighbor, Henry Crawford, is out to break her heart, perhaps to seduce her. And to add to her woes, she is in love with Edmund, who doesn't even know it. But Fanny will never take second best: of that she is always sure. She will wait for Edmund, though she knows her love to be impossible, for even if by a miracle he should ever want to marry her, he could not do so without his family's consent. Yes, that is another of the tough conditions in Jane Austen's world. Even an unreasonable parent's consent must be obtained, even the horrible General Tilney's in *Northanger Abbey*.

Fanny must be the rebuttal to those who claim that Jane Austen is basically worldly. She stands out against everybody who urges compromise. She has no one to advise her or help her in her crisis. In the household of her rich uncle, Sir Thomas, she is a kind of upper servant. She is penniless and without prospects. Yet a rich and attractive young man, Henry Crawford, suddenly offers her his hand and fortune, and everyone, including her beloved cousin Edmund, congratulates her on her good luck. But she turns him down. Cinderella rejects Prince Charming! Why? Because she is in love with Edmund? But his heart is elsewhere engaged. No, the real reason is that she has seen Crawford heartlessly flirting with *both* her cousins, Maria and Julia, one of whom is engaged to another man. She knows he is rotten.

Crawford is nonetheless sincerely in love. His character is even improved by the experience, as Fanny recognizes. He goes up to London to obtain a commission for her brother, earning a valid claim to her gratitude. Furthermore, her rejection of him must be attended by disagreeable consequences to herself. Her uncle will accuse her of willfulness, self-conceit, and ingratitude and send her off to her parents' humble home in Portsmouth, that she may have a taste of the poverty from which he has rescued her and to which she can always be returned if she persists in rejecting eligible suitors. So what will poor Fanny have gained?

Simply her soul. Henry Crawford and his sister, Mary, for all their charm and popularity, are deeply corrupted individuals. And Fanny has divined this with much less information than the reader has. *She* has not heard them discussing Henry's cold-blooded plan to amuse himself for a few weeks by making Fanny fall in love with him—a plan which of course backfires. But Fanny has observed how Henry has behaved during the rehearsal of *Lovers' Vows,* the play that the young people of Mansfield are putting on for the neighboring gentry. She has watched him undermining Maria's engagement. His conduct has been clearly incompatible with the good life.

Much has been written about Jane Austen's prudishness about the amateur theatricals at Mansfield. Why should the Bertrams and Crawfords not put on a play? But *Lovers' Vows* to Sir Thomas Bertram must have seemed like *Hair* to a Westchester banker in 1968. Could ladies, unmarried ladies, appear in it? With its frank love scenes and its suggestiveness, it represents the intrusion of the worst of London into the sanctity of Mansfield Park. It is loud; it is vulgar; it is intimate. It is the bad life.

Fanny alone of all the household has nothing directly to do with it. She will not take a part. She is absolutely firm, as she will be later in her refusal to accept Crawford. Fanny may be a trifle fastidious about the noise and sloppy habits of her own family in Portsmouth, but there is never any danger that she will compromise her moral standards to get away from them. She is strong because her inner life accords with her outward decorum. Contrast her with Mary Crawford:

"I shall soon be rested," said Fanny; "to sit in the shade on a fine day and look upon verdure, is the most perfect refreshment."

After sitting a while, Miss Crawford was up again. "I must leave," said she; "resting fatigues me.—I have looked across the ha-ha till I am weary."

What we see in the Crawfords and in the Bertram sisters is outward decorum over a flawed interior. This will never do. Here is how Jane Austen sees Julia Bertram:

The politeness which she had been brought up to practise as a duty, made it impossible for her to escape; while the want of that higher species of self-command, that just consideration of others, that knowledge of her own heart, that principle of right which had not formed any essential part of her education, made her miserable under it.

It is all very well to call Fanny and Edmund prigs, but they are ranged against adversaries so dangerous that even priggishness may not be a weapon that they can afford to discard. Henry Crawford has made both the Bertram girls miserable; he will ultimately destroy Maria's marriage and reputation, and he has entertained a project that might have resulted in Fanny's seduction. Through all Jane Austen's veils we catch a glimpse of Lovelace. And his sister has plotted nothing less than the undermining of Edmund's chosen career; she yearns to turn a minister into a social idler. There is wickedness in *Mansfield Park*; under the good manners, the quiet routine, the gentle chat, there is a note of Miltonic struggle. In the end Jane Austen ceases to laugh at Mrs. Norris; we learn that Sir Thomas himself has come to feel her "as an hourly evil":

She was regretted by no one at Mansfield. She had never been able to attach even those she loved best, and since Mrs. Rushworth's elopement, her temper had been in a state of such irritation, as to make her everywhere tormenting. Not even Fanny had tears for Aunt Norris—not even when she was gone forever.

In the fullness of time the patient and intrepid Fanny comes into her own. Edmund is at last cured of his infatuation for Mary Crawford and comes to see that Fanny will be the perfect parson's wife, and Fanny herself is finally justified in making use of evidence in her possession to prove to him that Mary is "mercenary." Even a good girl, after all, must occasionally use her claws in the jungle. But never too much, never in excess. Fanny wins her Edmund in the end, together with the love and respect of all the Bertrams, but she is always aware that it could have worked out very differently and that she might just as easily have spent the rest of her life sitting on the sofa in the drawing room reading aloud to Aunt Bertram. Fanny has accepted the universe.

Fanny has had too hard a lot to develop much charm, but not so Anne Elliot in *Persuasion,* who is as attractive as she is good. She has been argued out of an engagement to a young naval officer seven years before the action of the novel commences, by her mentor, Lady Russell. Anne has not done wrong, according to her creator, in bowing to Lady Russell. Her fault, such as it is, lies simply in her failure to have tried harder to talk Lady Russell out of it. The sanctity of the older generation is strictly preserved in Jane Austen, but no more than it is in Trollope or Thackeray. Life, however, brings Anne a glorious second chance with her sailor, and, unlike most beneficiaries of such chances, she grabs it! But in the ecstasy of this long-awaited engagement she must not and does not lose her head. She will not risk all by violence as Marianne Dashwood did:

> An interval of meditation, serious and grateful, was the best corrective of everything dangerous in such high-wrought felicity, and she went to her room and grew steadfast and fearless in the thankfulness of her enjoyment.

To get money or social position or just a man—there is no great trick to that. Jane Austen tosses cheap successes to her cheap characters. A true sophisticate, she knew how easily the "great World" is duped. The mean and vulgar Lucy Steele can insinuate herself into the affections of Robert Ferrars and of his ultrasnobbish mother; the unscrupulous Willoughby can marry a fortune, and the cheat Wickham can be established by the man he tried to ruin; it is even prognosticated in the end of *Persuasion* that Mrs. Clay may end up as Lady Elliot. But what have such trashy folk to do with the good life? The finest taste is kept for the finest wine. Charlotte Lucas in *Pride and Prejudice* does not do absolutely wrong to marry the absurd Mr. Collins, but she would do better to become a governess. Fanny Price would never have so compromised.

A question may remain as to what extent Jane Austen's sense of the good life may have validity to our generation of readers. It seems to me that to intelligent novel lovers—at least those who are not put off by differences in mores—the moral beauty of the stories of Fanny Price and Anne Elliot should have the same effect today as they did when they were first published. We may not live in Jane Austen's world, but we can still admire her.

Kingsley Amis

WHAT BECAME OF JANE AUSTEN?

There is something to be said for the view, held by rational critics as well as by mere going-through-the-motions appreciators, that *Mansfield Park* is the best of Jane Austen's works. Although there is some loss of high spirits, that invigorating coldness prevails, so that we can believe at times that we are reading an eighteenth-century novel, and the dialogue reaches new heights of flexibility and awareness, so much so that there are some distinct anticipations of the modern novel. Further, we have in Mrs. Norris the most hauntingly horrible of the author's horrible characters, and in Sir Thomas Bertram the most fully and firmly drawn and—but for his final obduracy toward his elder daughter—most sympathetic of her patriarchs. And negatively, it might be added, there is less concern here with "the amorous effects of 'brass' " (in Mr. Auden's phrase), with the minutiae of social obligation, with distinctions between a Tweedledum labeled "well-bred" and a Tweedledee labeled "coarse"— with some of the things, in fact, which render parts of Jane Austen's other work distasteful.

Correspondingly, however, defects which are incidental elsewhere become radical in *Mansfield Park*. Not even *Pride and Prejudice,* which plainly foreshadows much of the Henry Crawford theme in the later book, exhibits as glaringly the author's inclination to take a long time over what is of minor importance and a short time over what is major. Nor does *Persuasion,* despite the sneering vulgarity with which the character of Mrs. Clay is treated, embody to any comparable degree the Austen habit of censoriousness where there ought to be indulgence and indulgence where there ought to be censure. These are patently moral "oughts," and it is by moral rather than aesthetic standards that *Mansfield Park,* especially, is defective. Although it never holds up the admirable as vicious, it continually and essentially holds up the vicious as admirable, an inversion rendered all the more insidious by being associated with such dash and skill, and all the more repugnant by the co-presence of a moralistic fervor which verges at times on the evangelical.

It must be said at once that the book succeeds brilliantly whenever it aims to hold up viciousness of character as vicious. Mrs. Norris is very fully visualized in domestic and social terms, but these are the lineaments of a moral repulsiveness, and it is a superb if unintentional stroke of moral irony whereby she alone shows charity toward the disgraced and excommunicated Maria. Sir Thomas, again, represents an essay, carried out with scrupulous justice, on the case of the humane and high-principled man whose defects of egotism and a kind of laziness (to be seen running riot in the character of his wife) betray him into inhumanity and are shown as instrumental in the disasters visited upon his daughters. More important still, the unworthiness of Henry and Mary Crawford is allowed to emerge with an effect of inevitability that is only heightened by the author's freedom, almost audacity, in stressing their sprightliness and even their considerable share of right feeling. This is an achievement which changes in ethical outlook have left undimmed and which testifies to a unique and enviable moral poise.

All these, however, are relative triumphs. The characters mentioned, especially the Crawfords, exist less in their own right than in order to show up by contrast the virtues of the central pair, not only in the status of persons but as embodiments of rival ideologies and ways of life. In both capacities the hero and heroine are deficient. The fact that as social beings they are inferior to the Crawfords, that Henry and Mary are good fun and the other two aren't, is a very large part of the author's theme and is perfectly acceptable, even though this particular disparity sometimes goes too far for comfort and further, one cannot help feeling, than can have been intended: to invite Mr. and Mrs. Edmund Bertram round for the evening would not be lightly undertaken. More basically than this, Edmund and Fanny are both morally detestable and the endorsement of their feelings and behavior by the author—an endorsement only withdrawn on certain easily recognizable occasions—makes *Mansfield Park* an immoral book. Let us consider first the less heinous of the two offenders.

Edmund's kindness to Fanny entitles him to initial respect, and the bantering form it occasionally takes recalls his far livelier forerunner, Henry Tilney of *Northanger Abbey*. But it is not long before Edmund is shocked by Mary Crawford's complaint—in company, too—that her uncle's rather ill-judged alterations to a cottage of his resulted in the garden being messed up for some time. Soon afterward he conducts, with the untiringly sycophantic Fanny, a postmortem on this affront to his "sense of propriety." This readiness to be shocked, in itself shocking, is not in evidence when, a few chapters later, the pair of them launch into a canting pietistic tirade against Mary's brother-in-law in her presence. Nor does the vaunted sense of propriety exclude boorishness—in reply, for instance, to a perfectly amiable suggestion from Henry Crawford about possible improvements to the parsonage. But it is his objections to the proposed private theatricals that finally establish Edmund as repulsive, and are thus worth setting out in some detail.

Any such amusement, he considers, is "open to some objections"—though without divulging these—and in this case "want of feeling" would be involved, because Sir Thomas is at sea and might get drowned round about now. (The reasonable argument, that Sir Thomas would object to his house being disordered—as in the event he does—is not stressed.) It further transpires that the play proposed, *Lovers' Vows,* is so vicious that merely to rehearse it "must do away all restraints." Such scruples, as Mrs. Q. D. Leavis notes in her introduction to the latest reprint of the novel, are "well grounded in conventional notions of decorum." But we are right to expect from Edmund something more intelligent, more liberal, more manly than that, and a cursory reading will show that *Lovers' Vows* is in fact innocuous rubbish. This being so, his eventual reluctant consent to participate, which we are invited to see as the tragic overthrow of a noble mind worked on by Mary Crawford, becomes a squalid and ridiculous belly flop, and his consequent humiliation is deserved in two senses, since it is earned—can we really be reading Jane Austen?—not by being too priggish, but by not being priggish enough.

If Edmund's notions and feelings are vitiated by a narrow and unreflecting pomposity, Fanny's are made odious by a self-regard utterly unredeemed by any humor—is this still Jane Austen?—or even lightness. She is mortified by being excluded—at her own obstinate insistence—from the theatricals. She pities herself and does others the kindness of hoping that they will never know how much she deserves their pity. She feels that Henry's addresses involve "treating her improperly and unworthily, and in such a way as she had not deserved." She indulges in righteous anger a good deal, especially when her own interests are threatened. She is disinclined to force herself to be civil to those—a numerous company—whose superior she thinks herself to be; such people she regards with unflinching censoriousness. She is ashamed of her own home in Portsmouth, where there is much "error" and she finds "every body underbred," and how relieved she is when the "horrible evil" of Henry lunching there is averted. Significantly, the climax of her objections to her mother is that Mrs. Price was too busy to take much notice of Miss Price from Mansfield Park. And, in the closing stages, her "horror" at the wretched Maria's elopement is such as to exclude pity in any word or thought.

This indictment could be greatly extended, notably in the direction of the "moral concern" Fanny feels at Mary's power over Edmund. The tendency of all this can perhaps be fixed by pointing out that the character of Fanny lacks self-knowledge, generosity, and humility, the three "less common acquirements" which her girl cousins are, near the outset, stated to lack and which, by implication, are to be demonstrated as existing in her. Instead it is a monster of complacency and pride who, under a cloak of cringing self-abasement, dominates and gives meaning to the novel. What became of that Jane Austen (if she ever existed) who set out bravely to correct conventional notions of the desirable and virtuous? From being their critic (if she ever was) she became their slave. That is another way of saying that her judgment and her moral sense were corrupted. *Mansfield Park* is the witness of that corruption.

A. S. Byatt and Ignês Sodré

FROM "JANE AUSTEN: *MANSFIELD PARK*"

BYATT: *Mansfield Park* has been described as one of the great works of Western European literature, and has also been described as a novel in which nobody can manage to like the heroine. Modern criticism has picked on it from all sorts of angles. It's been used to prove that Jane Austen was secretly concerned to make a point about slavery; it's been used to illustrate her involvement with Tory high politics. Feminist critics see it as a critique of patriarchy. What I want to talk about here is the novel I read as a child, and the novel I now read as an adult, as a writer.

SODRÉ: I think we read novels primarily for the pleasure of being told a story and being able to imagine new worlds, and the different ways in which we relate to these very "real" imaginary people, the characters in fiction. The first time we met, you joked about reinstating "the pleasure principle" in novel reading!

BYATT: I think it struck both of us that in this novel the family structure is at the center. We both felt, didn't we, that this is clear from that very first paragraph about Lady Bertram?

SODRÉ: Yes, I think it is interesting that Jane Austen starts with the three Ward sisters, because sibling relationships are going to be of central importance throughout the novel: definitely one of the things she wanted to explore, and we want to explore.

BYATT: "About thirty years ago Miss Maria Ward of Huntingdon, with only seven thousand pounds, had the good luck to captivate Sir Thomas Bertram, of Mansfield Park, in the county of Northampton, and to be thereby raised to the rank of a baronet's lady, with all the comforts and consequences of an handsome house and large income" (Chapter 1). The structure's like a fairy story, there are three sisters, and the word "captivate" suggests things we shall be talking about—enclosure and imprisonment—although at the superficial level it just means to charm and to attract.

SODRÉ: In the case of Miss Maria Ward we soon feel it must have been to captivate in the first way you imply, because there isn't anything tremendously charming about her personality at all! She had only external beauty and an extreme passivity which, it is implied, was pleasing to men, or to that man, Sir Thomas. But immediately after that Jane Austen brings in the world everybody's opinion on this marriage: "All Huntingdon exclaimed . . ."—she brings the satirical point of view.

> All Huntingdon exclaimed on the greatness of the match, and her uncle, the lawyer, himself, allowed her to be at least three thousand pounds short of any equitable claim to it. She had two sisters to be benefited by her elevation; and such of their acquaintance as thought Miss Ward and Miss Frances quite as handsome as Miss Maria, did not scruple to predict their marrying with almost equal advantage. But there certainly are not so many men of large fortune in the world, as there are pretty women to deserve them. Miss Ward, at the end of half a dozen years, found herself obliged to be attached to the Rev. Mr Norris, a friend of her brother-in-law, with scarcely any private fortune, and Miss Frances fared yet worse. [Chapter 1]

BYATT: How do you think the structure of the Ward family relates to the structure of the Bertram family and the Price family—and for that matter the Norris family—with which we then become concerned, which the three sisters build?

SODRÉ: Well, the three Ward sisters together create a new set of three sisters when Fanny, through being adopted at the suggestion of Mrs. Norris, becomes the third Bertram sister: the child of the poorest, least successful Ward sister eventually becomes the favorite, and by far the most successful of the three new sisters. But Jane Austen makes it clear that in this world most marriages are built on a false basis; this is going to be explored in much greater depth in the generation of the children, in terms of their choice of partners and their mistakes.

BYATT: Yes, it's as though the narrator of the first paragraph and the first chapter is a kind of gossiping social commentator speaking from a distance, and then she moves into the emotions of people after she's set out this satirical portrait of a society. It interests me very greatly, when we get into Lady Bertram's own family, just how much and how little we are told about what is quite an extensive group of people. Fanny is adopted from the Price family into the Bertram family as you say and becomes automatically in a sense the fairy princess. She's number three, and she's the stepsister; it's not that she's got ugly stepsisters, it's that she's the pretty or the good stepsister. And her first relationships that are described, her first intense relationships are with the brother she's left behind, and with Edmund, the second brother of the two sisters she's joined, with whom she falls in love. When Edmund finds her crying and says to her "You are sorry to leave Mamma," she doesn't correct him, but makes it clear that what she really wants is to write to her brother. And from that point he becomes her brother but also at that point becomes the hero of the novel, because of brotherly affection—because of noticing her feelings. The whole novel in a way is about people who don't notice other people's feelings, and the extraordinary rarity of people who do notice other people's feelings, or who can act on this noticing. And in that sense Edmund's first act of kindness is a central act that reverberates throughout the whole book.

SODRÉ: And this establishes what their love is based on, which is kindness and interest in the feelings of the other person. But of course, as you say, he thinks she's missing her mother when in fact she's missing her brother. This is important because it sets the scene for what I think is one of the central themes of the novel—the question of constancy. Fanny remains forever constant to what you might call an original love object—her brother. She declares her love for William, and at that moment, which is also when Edmund begins to appear to her as a kind brother, she starts transferring her love to him. In her choice of sexual partner, she moves only from William to Edmund—from a real brother to an adopted one. This is a very small step: she does not choose a partner from outside the family. On the other hand, the beginning of her own story is deeply concerned with a lack of constancy: she is given away to another family. Her parents were not constant to her. Indeed, Fanny herself is expected to be *in*constant, she is expected to cease to love her original family and to adopt a new one. This she has enormous trouble in doing because the Bertrams aren't very nice!

BYATT: And the motivation of the people who propose the transfer of this child from one family to another is suspect. It's an idle idea of Mrs.

Norris's, who is apparently offering to be a mother to one of her poor sister's children because she is childless, but in fact she proposes to do no such thing.

> When the subject was brought forward again, her views were more fully explained; and, in reply to Lady Bertram's calm enquiry of 'Where shall the child come to first, sister, to you or to us?' Sir Thomas heard, with some surprise, that it would be totally out of Mrs Norris's power to take any share in the personal charge of her. [Chapter 1]

She makes it perfectly clear that it's really Sir Thomas and Lady Bertram who will have the child. And Lady Bertram is a person almost incapable of deep feeling or deep affection, who simply lies on her sofa. So Sir Thomas, who is a man of principle, simply takes over providing for, if not loving, this child.

It's interesting that Jane Austen's second brother was given away in exactly this way. He attracted Mr. and Mrs. Knight, who asked if they might adopt him and left the whole of their fortune to him. As far as I can see from the biographies, nobody seems to have felt that this was an odd thing to do, and this seems, in fact, in the case of Jane Austen's family, not to have soured relations between the family of origin and the family of adoption. Which may cast some light on why in the end it seems to have been good for Fanny to move from a poorer household to a richer one, even if at first it seems rather frightening.

SODRÉ: Yes, I also get the feeling from the biographies that there weren't tremendous difficulties about this adoption, that relations between the families remained very friendly; Jane Austen's knowledge of a great house like Mansfield Park came at least partly from her intimate knowledge of her brother's rather grand home with the Knights. It is interesting that in the novel it is a girl that is adopted, not a boy. Mrs. Price herself doesn't understand why they should want a girl, when she has so many fine boys. But it is clear that a girl is needed for Mrs. Norris, who is a witch, to torment; she's adopted in a very different spirit. The Knights adopted because they needed a child . . .

BYATT: They needed an heir, yes.

SODRÉ: The Knights gave Edward Austen everything, whereas I think the spirit of Fanny's adoption is that she shouldn't be given almost anything; as far as Mrs. Norris, the *oldest* daughter in her family, is concerned, Fanny is brought into the family to take the role of the poor, inferior *youngest* one—in contrast to the wonderfulness of her other *older* nieces, Maria and Julia.

BYATT: Yes, very clever of Jane Austen to divide the adopting women into the very actively malevolent and the very passively neglecting without leaving anything in between, so that there is a gap where there should be an adult woman who cares. And there's a gap where there should be an adult man who cares, simply because Sir Thomas goes away or doesn't look. It raises the whole question of upbringing, which is one of the things people always say *Mansfield Park* is about. If Maria and Julia have been taught to think of themselves as very wonderful and have been taught to behave well without being taught principles, how does it come about that Edmund is so full of good principles? Who has taught them to him?

SODRÉ: One could just say that Jane Austen is being realistic: children make different use of what's happening in the family; although in fairy tales there is often only one "good" child, usually the youngest. But you are right, it does make one wonder, how could Edmund be all right, in this horrible family? William, who is the first person who loves Fanny, was his mother's favorite; it is therefore possible to imagine that he knows how to be a good "parent" to Fanny through identification with his own loving mother.

BYATT: You can in a way pick this out by observing *Mansfield Park* as though you were a real human being observing a real world. Toward the end of the book it becomes quite clear that Sir Thomas is in the habit of talking to Edmund, whereas he's completely incapable of talking to his son Tom, because Tom is perfectly incapable of listening to anything anybody says and just flies about being dissipated and has been a great disappointment. Sir Thomas's life consists of being disappointed by people who might expect to be first in his love and admiration, and finding substitutes and secondary people whom he loves much more. So that in the end he ends up with a family that consists of two substitute nieces—having lost (more or less) two daughters—and a satisfactory son and a less satisfactory son. And William of course, the good nephew. It's as though those people capable of affection are finally congregated into a rather narrow space which excludes all those who have been found incapable of responding with real warmth or kindness. Which includes the Crawfords, who are the intruders into this static world where Mrs. Norris hurts people and Lady Bertram ignores them.

SODRÉ: I think this separating out of "good" and "bad" qualities is important also in the way Mansfield itself is modified. Mansfield as a place is always idealized ("Mansfield will cure you," Mrs. Grant tells Mary Crawford)—but there is a sense in which it only remains that way if "good" people get in while the "bad" are let out. It improves with the presence of Fanny; in her passivity she is capable of transforming the home where she lives. Whereas in fact the innovators, supposedly the improvers, who are Henry and Mary, cause havoc.

BYATT: That's very interesting, because it's Fanny's love for William and Edmund's observing that she loves William and communicating this to Sir Thomas, who then invites William to Mansfield Park, that is instrumental in all sorts of changes. And his coming changes their perception of her. I'd never thought of it quite that way before, because you always think of the people who come into Mansfield as being the Crawfords. But of course William is very important, he too comes into Mansfield and is rather robust, and does things like announce that he likes dancing. So Sir Thomas responds by suggesting the ball. Here we have the fairy story again—this is the ball, at which the prince is to be met. Mrs. Norris feels violently that the ball ought to be for Maria or Julia, and she actually interrupts Sir Thomas to announce that of course he couldn't hold one because they're away, she tells him she knows what he's going to say—but he brushes her aside:

'My daughters,' replied Sir Thomas, gravely interposing, 'have their pleasures at Brighton, and I hope are very happy; but the dance which I think of giving at Mansfield, will be for their cousins.' [Chapter 26]

William's delight in dancing perhaps modifies some of the things that are usually said about the static nature of the people held up for admiration, and the extreme busybodiness and activity of the people whom we are meant not to like.

SODRÉ: I think there is something important about the transforming quality of Fanny's inner life—and this gets communicated almost without her making any external sign that it exists.

BYATT: I remember when I first read this book when I was really quite a little girl. Jane Austen was almost the first author in whom I met the convention that a woman couldn't speak if a man didn't ask her to marry him. They were the first women's novels I read in which the story was about waiting to see whether the man would speak, and silence was an essential part of being a woman no matter how violently you felt. Not only Fanny, but the much more active heroines such as Emma couldn't speak once they had realized what their feelings were. They simply had to be passive. I remember as a little girl thinking, is this my fate, is this the nature of being female? This kind of silence, this kind of waiting? It was a terrible shock to me. I think the convention certainly still existed when I was a young woman, you would never have asked a man to marry you, though you might by then have told him you loved him. Fanny, in a sense, is very purely bound by those conventions. You may see everything, but you must never speak. So your inner life becomes all your life and is lived with an intensity that is the greater because it can have no outside expression.

SODRÉ: This conventional behavior is also clearly built into Fanny's personality. Emma is completely different: she is quite forthright and only silent when bound by convention. Fanny, however, says almost nothing: she is bound not merely by convention, but by her psychological difficulties as well. Fanny's psychological makeup is the extreme opposite of Maria's and Julia's—she was brought up to think nothing of herself, even in her original family, so her self-esteem is extremely low; clearly Jane Austen feels that not enough attention is almost as bad as too much! Fanny is not only a virtuous heroine, thoughtful and unselfish, unlike her narcissistic, rather grandiose, cousins; she is also terrified of everybody and everything—a very neurotic heroine! She is very different from all the other Austen heroines; her excessive modesty can be irritating to readers, but Austen does see it as a sign of psychological weakness. Fanny is passive to an unhealthy degree, and it is clear in the end that she gets her "prince" only because there is no one else around.

BYATT: One moment of psychological truthfulness is when Fanny returns to Portsmouth and observes her sister Susan to be in a perpetual rage, fighting her mother and complaining about the servants. The awful battle between the siblings, about the little silver knife that was left by the little girl who died, made my hair stand on end with misery and grief when I first read it.

> Betsey, at a small distance, was holding out something to catch her eyes, meaning to screen it from Susan's.
>
> 'What have you got there, my love?' said Fanny, 'come and shew it to me.'
>
> It was a silver knife. Up jumped Susan, claiming it as her own, and trying to get it away; but the child ran to her mother's protection, and

Susan could only reproach, which she did very warmly, and evidently hoping to interest Fanny on her side. 'It was very hard that she was not to have her *own* knife; it was her own knife; little sister Mary had left it to her upon her death-bed, and she ought to have had it to keep herself long ago. But mamma kept it from her, and was always letting Betsey get hold of it; and the end of it would be that Betsey would spoil it, and get it for her own, though mamma had *promised* her that Betsey should not have it in her own hands.'

Fanny was quite shocked. Every feeling of duty, honour, and tenderness was wounded by her sister's speech and her mother's reply.

'Now, Susan,' cried Mrs Price in a complaining voice, 'now, how can you be so cross?' [Chapter 38]

Fanny does then reflect that her own nature had always been quieter and that she could never have thought as Susan did. And she broods away about how to teach Susan to behave better and to be more decorous. At that point Jane Austen has a little fun with Fanny, which Fanny herself is almost prepared to join in, about how difficult this is for her, how hard it is for her to think how to teach Susan how to behave better, since Susan is braver than she herself is. It is a moment of separation between Jane Austen and Fanny. I think they are very, very close in the sense that almost everything Jane Austen says that Fanny feels, she also implicitly or explicitly expresses approval of.

SODRÉ: Fanny the silent heroine is portrayed as extremely fearful and diffident: "she crept about in constant terror of something or other" (Chapter 2). Fanny feels and thinks very intensely, but finds it very difficult to communicate. If you have strong needs but you don't express them ever, either there is a kind of permanent desperation, or a more passive giving up—as, for instance, when Jane Austen says that Fanny could take pleasure in hearing about Maria's and Julia's going to balls because it never had occurred to her that she might have been invited too. Here Fanny seems to think that she will be a little girl forever; sometimes she seems masochistic. But for this silent, self-effacing heroine, any hope of having her needs satisfied depends on a relationship with a very particular, very special person: somebody who will listen to her when she hasn't said anything. Which is what Edmund does. She has this desire for Sir Thomas to respond to her, and he doesn't. She thinks, if only he said "My dear Fanny"—but he never says it—until the end, when he has finally learned from his experience, from all the terrible things that happened because of his neglect; then he becomes somebody who can be sensitive to needs that are not put into words.

BYATT: Yes, one of the most wonderful moments in the book every time you read it is when, although very angry with Fanny, Sir Thomas causes a fire to be put in her room:

> She was struck, quite struck, when on returning from her walk, and going into the east room again, the first thing which caught her eye was a fire lighted and burning. A fire! it seemed too much; just at that time to be giving her such an indulgence, was exciting even painful gratitude. She wondered that Sir Thomas could have leisure to think of such a trifle again; but she soon found, from the voluntary information of the housemaid, who came in to attend it, that so it was to be every day. Sir Thomas had given orders for it. [Chapter 32]

Sir Thomas produces warmth, that is, both really and figuratively. Warmth which Mrs. Norris has prevented her having throughout the book. Every time Mrs. Norris has anything to do with a fire, it's a disaster. There's a wonderful comic scene where she disarranges the fire that the butler has beautifully set up before the return of Sir Thomas. Just in order to have something to do she destroys the beautiful shape of it. Fanny is looking forward to the ball:

> . . . and was actually practising her steps about the drawing-room as long as she could be safe from the notice of her aunt Norris, who was entirely taken up at first in fresh arranging and injuring the noble fire which the butler had prepared. [Chapter 28]

We ought to talk about Maria and Julia here. We share so much in Fanny's feelings and her inner life, and her perception of the movement of the house, but very occasionally we're also told what *they* feel. We're told what they feel when they're battling to be with Henry Crawford on the seat of the barouche. We are told what Julia feels particularly, but also a little of what Maria feels, when they are both trying to get cast as Agatha in *Lovers' Vows*. But on the whole they are rather like silhouettes or counters. We're told very early on by a narrative voice that they were a kind of simulacrum, they had been taught good manners so they knew better than to behave badly, but they hadn't been taught good feelings so they never actually noticed what anybody felt. Mrs. Norris's favoritism has simply reinforced their sense of their own special superiority.

> . . . it is not very wonderful that with all their promising talents and early information, they should be entirely deficient in the less common acquirements of self-knowledge, generosity and humility. In every thing but disposition, they were admirably taught. [Chapter 2]

But they wouldn't make a vulgar scene at a party or anything because they were too well bred. And yet there is one sharply moving moment, which is when Maria, in the little wilderness at Sotherton, says "I cannot get out, as the starling said." Because one has had the feeling again and again all the way through *Mansfield Park* of "I cannot get out, I cannot get out"—the whole world is restrictive and encircling. And Maria is almost never offered as an object of our sympathy. And yet here she is, uttering one terrible phrase, and suddenly she is opened up. She has made the mistake of agreeing to marry Mr. Rushworth. For a moment you share her total panic at being confined. And also you know exactly—Jane Austen tells you exactly—by what degree of lack of self-knowledge she got into this mess.

SODRÉ: And also to what tremendous extent she has been abandoned by her parents—because even Sir Thomas, who ought to have known better, allowed her to marry Mr. Rushworth; he feels guilty about that in the end, because he knows that it was through his neglect that he allowed the marriage to take place. Fanny (who wants as desperately to get *in* as Maria wants to get *out*) is aware of his neglect; she says about Sir Thomas that "somebody who allowed a daughter to marry Mr Rushworth," has no delicacy of feeling.

BYATT: The novel is about intelligence, it's about persistent failures in intelligence. Sir Thomas was just not paying enough attention and was also not quite clever enough. And also is a bit reluctant to interfere, and so he lets Maria marry Mr. Rushworth. He did ask Maria the right questions, but accepted her answers too easily. He discovers the truth too late.

> In this quarter, indeed, disappointment was impending over Sir Thomas. Not all his good-will for Mr Rushworth, not all Mr Rushworth's deference for him, could prevent him from soon discerning some part of the truth—that Mr Rushworth was an inferior young man,

as ignorant in business as in books, with opinions in general unfixed, and without seeming much aware of it himself.

He had expected a different son-in-law; and beginning to feel grave on Maria's account, tried to understand *her* feelings. [Chapter 21]

SODRÉ: In the novel he goes through a process of emotional education. As you said, Sir Thomas can talk to Edmund but not to Tom. It is as if Sir Thomas needs a special child so that he can be a good father: he has to have his goodness brought out through contact with somebody who is more in touch; he couldn't be a good father to ordinary children, he needed some special contribution from the outside to be able to function—which is of course what Fanny provides. This reminds me of what you said about Fanny's cold room and his providing her with a fire (after years of not having noticed anything wrong in Mrs. Norris's treatment of Fanny!): presumably, at a symbolic level, that is the moment when he finally realizes he has always been cold to Fanny.

BYATT: He presumably (and it's interesting that we can talk about them in this speculative manner as though they were real people— I think it's one of Jane Austen's greatnesses that you don't feel you are doing anything wrong if you speculate about her people)—Sir Thomas was presumably not emotionally educated or he wouldn't have picked Lady Bertram to be his wife.

Alain de Botton

THE MODEST ART OF ALTERING LIFE

1.

Jane Austen began work on *Mansfield Park* in the spring of 1812 and published it the following year. The novel tells the story of Fanny Price, a shy, modest young girl from a penniless family in Portsmouth, who, in order to relieve her parents, is asked by her aunt and uncle, the plutocratic Sir Thomas and Lady Bertram, to come to Mansfield Park, their stately home, to live with them and their four children. Sir Thomas and Lady Bertram stand at the pinnacle of the English county hierarchy; they are spoken of with awe and reverence by their neighbors; their coquettish teenage daughters, Maria and Julia, enjoy a generous clothes allowance and have both been given their own horses; and their eldest son, Tom, bumptious and casually insensitive, spends his time in London clubs lubricating his friendships with champagne while focusing his hopes for the future on his father's death and the inheritance of an estate and title. Though adept at the self-deprecating manners of the English upper classes, Sir Thomas Bertram and his family never forget (and do not allow others to forget) their superior rank and all the distinction that must naturally accompany the ownership of a large landscaped garden upon which deer wander in the quiet hours between tea and dinner.

Fanny may have come to live under the same roof as the Bertram family, but she cannot be on an equal footing with them. Her privileges have been given to her at the discretion of Sir Thomas, her cousins patronize her, the neighbors view her with a mixture of suspicion and pity, and she is treated by most of the family like a lady-in-waiting whose company one enjoys but whose feelings one is fortunately never under any prolonged obligation to consider.

Before Fanny arrives in Mansfield Park, Jane Austen allows us to eavesdrop on the Bertram family's anxieties about their new charge. "I hope she will not tease my poor pug," remarks Lady Bertram. The children wonder what Fanny's clothes will be like, whether she will speak French and know the names of the kings and queens of England. Sir Thomas Bertram, in spite of having proffered the invitation to Fanny's parents, expects the worst: "We shall probably see much to wish altered in her and should prepare ourselves for gross ignorance, some meanness of opinions and a very distressing vulgarity of manner." His sister-in-law, Mrs. Norris, states that Fanny must early on be told that she is not, and never will be, *one of them.* Sir Thomas avers: "We must make her remember that she is not a *Miss Bertram.* I should wish to see Fanny and her cousins very good friends but they cannot be equals. Their rank, fortune, rights and expectations will always be different."

Fanny's arrival seems only to confirm the family's prejudices against those who have not grown up on estates with landscaped gardens. Julia and Maria discover that Fanny only has one nice dress, speaks no French, and doesn't know anything. "Only think, my cousin cannot put the map of Europe together," Julia runs to tell her aunt and mother, "nor can she tell the principal rivers in Russia and she has never heard of Asia Minor—How strange! Did you ever hear anything so stupid? Do you know, we asked her last night, which way she would go to get to Ireland; and she said, she should cross to the Isle of Wight." "Yes my dear," replies Mrs. Norris, "but you and your sister are blessed with wonderful memories, and your poor cousin has probably none at all. You must make allowances for her and pity her deficiency."

But Jane Austen takes a little longer to make up her mind about who is deficient and in what. She follows Fanny patiently around the corridors and reception rooms of Mansfield Park for a decade or more, she listens to her on her walks around the gardens and in her bedroom, she reads her letters, she eavesdrops on her observations of her family, she watches the movements of her eyes and mouth: she peers into her soul. And in the process, she picks up on a rare quiet virtue.

Unlike Julia or Maria, Fanny is not concerned with whether a young man has a large house and a title, she is offended by her cousin Tom's casual cruelty and arrogance, she flinches from her aunt's financial considerations of her neighbors. Meanwhile Fanny's relatives, ranked so highly in the standard county status hierarchy, are more troublingly placed in that other status system, the novelist's hierarchy of preference. Maria and her suitor Mr. Rushworth may have horses, houses, and inheritances, but Jane Austen has seen how they fell in love and she does not forget it:

> Mr Rushworth was from the first struck with the beauty of Miss Bertram, and being inclined to marry, soon fancied himself in love. Being now in her twenty-first year, Maria Bertram was beginning to think matrimony a duty; and as a marriage with Mr Rushworth would give her the enjoyment of a larger income than her father's, as well as ensure her a house in town, it became her evident duty to marry Mr Rushworth if she could.

Debrett's Baronetage of England, the *Who's Who* of its day, may hold Maria and Mr. Rushworth in high esteem. After such a paragraph, Austen cannot—nor will she let her readers. The novelist exchanges the normal lens through which people are viewed in society, a lens that magnifies wealth and power, for a moral lens, which magnifies qualities of character. Through this lens, the high and mighty may become small, the forgotten and retiring figures may grow large. Within the world of the novel, virtue is spread without regard to material wealth: the rich and well mannered are not (as in the dominant status schema) immediately good nor the poor and unschooled bad. Virtue may lie with the lame ugly child, the destitute porter, the hunchback in the attic, or the girl who doesn't know the first facts of geography. Certainly Fanny has no elegant dresses, has no money, and can't speak French—but by the end of *Mansfield Park,* she has been revealed as the noble one, while the other members of her family, despite their titles and accomplishments, have fallen into moral confusion. The daughters have married for money and paid an emotional price for their decision, Sir Thomas Bertram has allowed snobbery to ruin the education of his children, his wife has let her heart turn to stone. The hierarchical system of Mansfield Park has been turned on its head.

But Austen does not simply assert her concept of true hierarchy with the bluntness of a preacher, she enlists our sympathies for it and marshals our abhorrence for its opposite with the skill and humor of a great novelist. She does not *tell* us why her sense of priorities is important, she *shows* us why within the context of a story which also happens to make us laugh and grips us enough that we want to finish supper early to read on (as an early critic of Austen, Richard Whately, later the Archbishop of Dublin, put it in the *Quarterly Review* of 1822: "Miss Austen has the merit of being evidently a Christian writer: a merit which is much enhanced, both on the score of good taste, and of practical utility, by her religion being not at all obtrusive. She might defy the most fastidious critic to call any of her novels a 'dramatic sermon' "). Upon finishing *Mansfield Park,* we are invited to go back into the sphere from which Austen has drawn us aside and respond to others as she has taught us, to pick up on and recoil from greed, arrogance, and pride and to be drawn to goodness within ourselves and others.

Austen modestly and famously described her art as "the little bit (two inches wide) of ivory on which I work with so fine a brush, as produces little effect after much labour," but her novels are suffused with greater ambitions. Her art is an attempt, through what she called a study of "three or four families in a country village," to criticize and so alter life.

2.

For our part, Austen has an unusual capacity to describe our world even as she apparently concentrates only on being faithful to her own. When I first read *Mansfield Park* at twenty-one, I was at university and, of course, a version of Edmund. Maria was Claire (she lived down the corridor, studied macrobiology, and had shoulder-length chestnut hair in a center parting) and Mr. Rushworth was played by Robin, an economist whom she'd been seeing for three years—testimony, if one needs it, of the miraculous ability of novels to mold themselves around, and illuminate, our own lives. I would meet Fanny occasionally in lectures on the French Revolution.

There are books that speak to us of our own lives with a clarity we cannot match. They prevent the morose suspicion that we do not fully belong to the species, that we lie beyond comprehension. Our embarrassments, our sulks, our envy, our feelings of guilt, these phenomena are conveyed in Austen in a way that affords us bursts of almost magical self-recognition. The author has located words to depict a situation we thought ourselves alone in feeling, and for a few moments, we see ourselves more clearly and wish to become whom the author would have wanted us to be.

The value of a novel is not limited to its depiction of emotions and people akin to those in our own life—it stretches to an ability to describe these far better than we would have been able, to put a finger on perceptions that we recognize as our own, but could not have formulated on our own.

One effect of reading a book which traces the faint yet vital tremors of our psyche and social interactions is that, once we've put the volume down and resumed our own life, we may attend to precisely those things the author would have responded to had he or she been in our company. Our mind will be like a radar newly attuned to pick up certain objects floating through consciousness; the effect will be like bringing a radio into a room that we had thought silent, and realizing that the silence only existed at a particular frequency and that all along we in fact shared the room with waves of sound coming in from a Ukrainian station or the nighttime chatter of a minicab firm. Our attention will be drawn to the shades of the sky, to the changeability of a face, to the hypocrisy of a friend, or to a submerged sadness about a situation we had previously not even known we could feel sad about. The book will have sensitized us, stimulated our dormant antennae by evidence of its own developed sensitivity.

Fay Weldon

LET OTHERS DEAL WITH MISERY

London, May

My dear Alice,

In *Mansfield Park* there is a young lady, a Miss Crawford, who behaves very badly. She speaks slightingly of the clergy. She is quite without respect for the Admiral uncle in whose household she was brought up, and to whom therefore she should be grateful. She says she has a large acquaintance of various Admirals; she knows too much about their bickerings and jealousies, and of Rears and Vices she has seen all too many. "Now," she says, "do not be suspecting me of a pun, I entreat." But of course we do. Rears and Vices! Strong stuff! Miss Crawford mocks religious feeling. She remarks, on being shown round the Rushworth Elizabethan chapel, "Cannot you imagine with what unwilling feelings the former belles of the house of Rushworth did many a time repair to this chapel? The young Miss Eleanors and Miss Bridgets—starched up into seeming piety, but with their heads full of something very different—especially if the poor chaplain were not worth looking at—and, in those days, I fancy parsons were inferior even to what they are now."

That makes Fanny angry. So angry she can hardly speak. It is the only time in the whole book that she is swayed by unholy passion. She is angry, you see, on Edmund's behalf. Edmund is training to be a parson. Fanny is an unusual Austen heroine: she is good, almost unspeakably good. Edmund is more usual: he is of the Mr. Knightley mold. He is kind, noble, and instructive. He rather fancies Miss Crawford, in spite of her bad behavior, perhaps even because of it, and she is certainly the one character in the book with whom one would gladly spend a week on an offshore island: she is witty, lively, lovely, and funny at other people's expense. She is selfish—she unfeelingly makes use of Fanny's horse, to Fanny's detriment, since Fanny seems quite unable to take care of herself—and admits it. Miss Crawford, in fact, doesn't mind being *bad*. Fanny simply can't help being good.

Now, Jane Austen started to write *Mansfield Park* in 1812. She had been living in Chawton, with her mother and sister, since 1809. It is tempting to suggest that the struggle between Miss Crawford and Fanny was the struggle going on in the writer between the bad and the good. The bad bit, which could write in a letter to Cassandra, "Mrs Hall of Sherbourne was brought to bed yesterday of a dead child, some weeks before she expected, owing to a fright. I suppose she happened unawares to look at her husband." (Now, that's far, far worse than anything Miss Crawford ever said.) And the good bit, which struggles to live at peace in a modest home with her mother and sister, and to continue to believe that her father was "good and kind" (and not, as I tend to believe, the callous and egocentric model for Mr. Bennet), and takes in *Mansfield Park* the personification of Fanny. And even more tempting to go back to Jane Austen's early childhood, and see in that powerful description in *Mansfield Park* of the arrival of a small, timid girl into a strange family—on the whole kindly, but stupid—a portrait of herself, sent away to a school where she nearly died, among strangers, and to suggest that the split between good and bad never, in Jane Austen, quite reconciled and resulting in her early death, started there. The rebellious spirit, raging at being so cast out by mother and father, learning the defenses of wit and style— Miss Crawford. The dutiful side, accepting authority, enduring everything with a sweet smile, finding her defense in wisdom—Fanny. So tempting, in fact, that I shan't resist. I shall offer it to you as an explanation of Jane Austen's determination to make the unctuous Fanny a heroine.

And also add that she must have missed her father very much, but in a rather, to us, unexpected way. *Mansfield Park* was the first new novel she wrote after his death—though she worked over *Sense and Sensibility* and *Pride and Prejudice,* novels of which we know he approved. I think she was trying hard, especially hard, to be good: as if without his controlling spirit all morality and self-control might fly away, dissipate, unless everyone was very, very careful. When Sir Thomas, the patriarch, leaves his family to go to Antigua for a time, his fear is—and it seems to Jane

Austen a reasonable fear—that if they are without his direction, without his watchful attention, they will behave without restraint and rapidly go to pieces. And so indeed they do—Good heavens! Amateur theatricals!

Mansfield Park throbs with the notion that what women need is the moral care and protection of men. Fanny marries Edmund in the end (of course), "loving, guiding and protecting her, as he had been doing ever since her being ten years old, her mind in so great a degree formed by his care, and her comfort depending on his kindness, an object to him of such close and peculiar interest, dearer by all his own importance with her than anyone else at Mansfield, that he should learn to prefer soft light eyes [Fanny's] to sparkling dark ones [Miss Crawford's]."

Oh, Miss Austen, what wishful thinking do we not have here! It has come to my notice, Alice, that in the real world the worse women behave, the better they get on. (Discuss, with reference to your female friends, and their mothers.)

Well, perhaps we *should* look to fiction for moral instruction: we should not see it, as we have come to do, as a mirror to be held up to reality. Perhaps writing should not be seen as a profession, but as a sacred charge, and the writer of a bestseller not run gleefully to the bank, but bow his head beneath the weight of so much terrifying responsibility. To be able to influence, for good or bad, the minds of so many! In China they do not have "novels" in our sense: they have fiction, it is true, but fiction that points the way to good behavior, both at an individual and a social level. Such works are exhortations to hard work, honor, good cheer, and the power of positive thinking, and sell by the hundred millions. And in Russia any individual writer who flies, in the name of art, or truth, in the face of an accepted group morality, is seen as irresponsible, even to the point of insanity. It is a different way of looking at things. I have some sympathy with it. It is, oddly enough, readers and not writers who believe so passionately that writers should be free to write what they want. I do not think Jane Austen would have thought they should be: certainly not on the evidence of *Mansfield Park,* a book in which virtue is rewarded and bad behavior punished, and the abominable Maria, disgraced, is obliged to go and live with the awful Mrs. Norris. And serve both right.

Your loving Aunt,
Fay

James Collins

Jane Austen is very funny. In fact, she is very, very funny. Her characters are vivid. The poise of her sentences is perfect. Her plots are pretty good—at least, they keep you reading. She orchestrates her themes and the timbres of her characters in a way that is aesthetically complex and pleasing. It is these qualities that make Jane Austen's novels so brilliant. However, to write brilliant novels was not Jane Austen's foremost goal: What was most important to her was to provide moral instruction.

In their essence, Austen's books are moral works. They each have a hard moral core. Indeed, the real story in each of the novels is the story of how the characters deviate from or act in accordance with Austen's morality. *Northanger Abbey* is really "about" Catherine Morland's moral education: she learns that the world does not operate on the principles of a gothic novel. As the title indicates, the story of *Sense and Sensibility* is a moral one: it is the story of Elinor's self-command and Marianne's self-indulgence. The central event of both *Pride and Prejudice* and *Emma* is each heroine's discovery of her own moral weakness. *Mansfield Park* treats any number of moral issues, from the propriety of engaging in amateur theatricals to the consequences of leaving one's husband for another man. The premise of *Persuasion* is that Anne Elliot once sacrificed her happiness by doing her duty and obeying the admonishment of her moral guide, Lady Russell. Moral concerns are not only reflected in the large themes of the books, however: they are pervasive. Even the smallest act or the briefest dialogue or the mere description of a character's manner of dress may have moral content.

The modern reader is not very interested in moral instruction, and the modern author is not very interested in providing it. It is positively baffling nowadays to read Samuel Johnson as he complains about the moral lessons that Shakespeare fails to provide in some of his plays—given the multifarious genius of Shakespeare, how could anyone care about that, of all things? In modern times, it is often agreed, readers tend to appreciate Austen despite her didacticism rather than because of it. She can be positively priggish, and that is an embarrassment. Indeed, these days the reader who loves Jane Austen sort of blips over the moralizing sections and tells himself that they don't really count. It is possible simply to ignore this aspect of her work, just as it is possible to discuss a religious painting with hardly any reference to the artist's religious intent. But this seems absurd: ignoring a writer's central concern is a strange way to attempt to appreciate and understand her.

The question arises, then, of how to reconcile Austen's moralism with modern sensibility. To address this problem, it would be useful if we could find someone with this modern sensibility who actually reads Austen for her moral instruction (in addition to the literary pleasure she provides). How convenient that we have someone who fits that description available to us: me.

Yes, it is quite true. I find that reading Jane Austen helps me clarify ethical choices, helps me figure out a way to live with integrity in the corrupt world, even helps me adopt the proper tone and manner in dealing with others. By explaining how Austen helps me in these ways, I hope to show that her moralism and the modern mind are not, in fact, as inimical as is so often assumed.

I can immediately anticipate one objection: "How do we know," the skeptic asks, "that your 'sensibility' is really representatively 'modern'?" It's a fair question, for I am sure that Austen appeals to me, in part, precisely because she is not modern in her moral views. Some might call this attitude of mine "reactionary," but I prefer to think of it as representing the next turn of the wheel from our current relativism, and so as being supermodern.

To say that one values Austen's moral instruction may also produce skepticism because, after all, she was a spinster living in provincial England two hundred years ago. It hardly seems likely that such a person could offer anything that would be of use to those living in so different a world as our own. But of course our worlds aren't so very different. We see Austen's characters—vain, selfish, naïve, compassionate—in our own lives every day. Given that, I think her time and place are actually an advantage. In her circumscribed world, the problems of life may be examined with precision, and there is a kind of pressure on her characters that makes the experiments especially fruitful.

I believe, furthermore, that Austen was writing at a time that has particular relevance to our own. Austen lived on the cusp of the eighteenth-century Augustan and nineteenth-century Romantic ages. "Jane Austen," wrote Tony Tanner, "was brought up on eighteenth-century thought and was fundamentally loyal to the respect for limits, definition and clear ideas which it inculcated. Yet among writers who published in the same year as *Pride and Prejudice* were Byron, Coleridge, Scott and Shelley."[1] Romanticism still reigns, with as much power as ever. In our own time, every song, every advertisement, every movie, every person's conceptions of the possibilities of life, are based on Romantic principles. (Certainly modernism and postmodernism are simply two cats fighting in the Romantic bag.) No matter how much we may enjoy the "felicities of domestic life," as Austen put it in *Persuasion,* we still feel the enormous Romantic pull to do something more heroic and intense. Rather than digesting a good dinner while conversing with friends, we should be out forging the consciousness of our race in the smithy of our soul, or some damn thing. I don't really want to forge the consciousness of my race, but at the same time I don't want to miss out on all that Romanticism offers. This is where Austen comes to our rescue, for she is an Augustan familiar with Romanticism and so can criticize and make fun of it, which makes her more useful than either an Augustan Samuel Johnson or a modern writer in helping us face the Romantic challenge. Only she can so credibly show us that it is possible to have moderation *and* deep feeling, good dinners *and* good poetry.

I will add one final reason why Austen has credibility as a moral guide: her total lack of sentimentality. It sounds like posing, but Auden was absolutely right when he wrote that beside Austen, Joyce seems "innocent as grass." Her odious and horrible characters are truly odious and horrible. Someone like Aunt Norris—one of the worst—does not have a good side, or a complicating scene. Modern writers like to give their evil characters dimension and to raise them above being mere villains, to show their human and sympathetic side. I'm with Austen: let's keep the evil ones evil.

What then, are the values that Austen would teach us? Value-laden words and phrases appear again and again in her work, often in clusters:

self-knowledge, generosity, humility; self-command, just consideration of others, principle of right; elegance, propriety, regularity, harmony, peace and tranquillity, cheerful orderliness; good breeding, manners neither shy nor affectedly open; sensible, well-bred, well-informed, gentle address, amiable heart; tenderest compassion; good-humored, lively; good sense, warm attachment, liberality, propriety, delicacy of feeling; true gentility; upright integrity, strict adherence to truth and principle, disdain for trick and littleness; good understanding, correct opinion, knowledge of the world, a warm heart, steady, observant, moderate, candid, sensibility to what is amiable and lovely.

I appreciate Austen's moral instruction because it points one toward a more moral life—where "moral" refers not only to right principles but to conduct in general. I think of Austen's value system as a sphere with layers. The inmost core might be called "morals," the next layer we could call "sentiments," and finally the surface "manners." Morals are the fundamental principles: self-knowledge, generosity, humility, tenderest compassion, upright integrity. Who can say that Jane Austen is being moralistic or didactic in pressing these values on us? Is she being merely priggish? No: rather, she serves us well, just as she served her contemporaries. I am inspired and properly shamed when I see these words before me in black and white, calling me to right thought and behavior. Austen's emphasis on good order and propriety can seem dry and stiff. But anyone who reads *Mansfield Park* will feel the same relief that Fanny does at the change from the relative order of the Park to the rackety disorder of her family's house in Portsmouth. Similarly, Austen's regard for self-control, especially as expressed in *Sense and Sensibility,* can seem hard, but it must be remembered how the author clearly, along with Elinor, regards Marianne's emotionalism with the greatest compassion. Austen is not advocating a suppression of the feelings themselves— despite her faultlessly correct behavior, Elinor undergoes great suffering and feels every bit of it. What Austen is saying, as a modern psychologist might urge, is that one should try to prevent the disintegration of one's personality. Reading Austen I sometimes feel as if my morals are a wobbly figurine that her hand reaches out and steadies. Sentiments are built on the foundation of these morals: an amiable heart, sensibility to all that is lovely. Manners, in turn, arise from our sentiments. They have to do with behavior, with the way we work in the world: perfect good breeding, gentle address. I find myself reading words like these and wishing I could even aspire to having these qualities. It is surely as necessary in our day to have models of good sense and gentle manners held up for us.

How can morals, sentiments, and manners help me live in the world? What should my relations to the world be? Should I reject it entirely as corrupt and mercenary and spiteful and hypocritical and shallow? Or is there some other way, a way I can keep my integrity and sensitivity, but live in the world too? W. H. Auden stated the problem well when he wrote:

> Does Life only offer two alternatives: "You shall be happy, healthy, attractive, a good mixer, a good lover and parent, but on the condition that you are not overcurious about life. On the other hand you shall be sensitive, conscious of what is happening round you, but in that case you must not expect to be happy, or successful in love or at home in any company. There are two worlds and you cannot belong to them both. If you belong to the second of these worlds you will be unhappy because you will always be in love with the first, while at the same time you will despise it. The first world on the other hand will not return your love because it is in its nature to love only itself."[2]

In effect, Auden is asking if Life offers only the two alternatives of Sense and Sensibility, and one can sympathize with his cry of despair, for when the dilemma is put the way he puts it, the two seem hopelessly irreconcilable.

Austen comes to our rescue, though, for she does manage to modulate between Sense and Sensibility, rejecting the excesses of both. This complex of values appeals to me particularly because the combination of morals, sentiments, and manners provides a way of living that allows one both to be in the world and of the world and to enjoy the sweets of goodness and sensitivity as well. Austen does not write about bohemians and rebels; she doesn't want to change her world—"she would not alter a hair on anyone's head or move one brick," as Virginia Woolf wrote.[3] Austen's sympathetic characters participate fully in their society and accept its conventions, yet they have exquisitely well-tuned minds and hearts. Those are qualities Austen cherishes. It seems to me that her values enable us to live in the world with self-respect and without any of Auden's envy. Good sense does not have to be at war with sensibility. Moreover, the manners that Austen approves of provide a dignified, attractive, and pleasant means of interacting with the world.

As has often been said, irony is part of Austen's essence. It is not just her characteristic mode of expression: it is her characteristic mode of thought. Austen's irony represents a kind of resigned, knowing, and amused criticism of the world that also accepts the world. The double-ness of irony situates it both within the wretched, mercenary, hypocriti-cal, vicious world and also outside it. Austen's irony reflects a perfect understanding of all the ways the world is wretched and the belief that although you can't really fight it, you can at least separate yourself from it. In her ironic sentences there is movement with stability. She moves toward the object of criticism, then away from it, and then provides a gentle snap of closure at the end. Her ironies swirl and drop like the cast of a fly fisherman. This rhythmic motion seems to me ideal for both ac-cepting and rejecting the ways of the wretched world while maintaining balance.

The irony of Austen's characters also gives those of us who believe in decorum a way to handle hypocrites. Elinor Dashwood is rarely ironic, but she provides a good example: recall the conversation when the odi-ous John Dashwood, who has reneged on the deathbed promise to his father to help his half sisters, suggests to Elinor that Mrs. Jennings will leave them a bequest. Elinor replies, "Indeed, brother, your anxiety for our welfare and prosperity carries you too far." John Dashwood lacks generosity and integrity. Elinor insults him, but she does it in the politest possible way. Some might prefer that she frankly tell her half brother off, but that would simply provoke ill will. With irony, Elinor is able to re-spond to her brother's faulty morals without submitting to a lapse of manners herself.

If one is to argue that Austen's morality is useful for a person living today, one must deal with three hard cases. First, there is Fanny's objec-tion to the amateur theatricals in *Mansfield Park*. Then, there is Elinor Dashwood's refusal to pursue the man she loves, Edward Ferrars, when she learns that he is officially engaged to Lucy Steele, a woman who "joined insincerity with ignorance." Finally, there is Anne Elliot's avowal that she did the right thing by following the dictates of Lady Russell to refuse Captain Wentworth, even though this led to years of loveless mis-ery for them both. In all three cases, Austen endorses a morality that seems priggish and nearly absurd. What is the big deal with theatricals? Most readers find the entire fuss ridiculous. Elinor employs "every prin-ciple of honor and honesty directed to combat her own affection," and we must ask what kind of principles these are that deny her and Edward love for the sake of honoring the word of a naïve young man, as Edward was when he contracted his engagement with Lucy. Are such principles worth upholding when they result in mismatches and regret for Elinor and Edward? One has the same kind of reaction to Anne Elliot's attitude: what kind of value system puts obedience before love?

I confess that rather than being offended by Austen's strictness, I welcome it. Perhaps it is very old-fashioned—or perhaps it is supermodern—but I think one can find merit in the concepts of honor, duty, and obedience. Those strings have gone so slack that I don't see anything wrong in their being tightened by a sympathetic reading of this aspect of Austen; they will loosen again soon enough.

To dispense briefly with Elinor and Anne, I will say simply that their actions must be seen in the context of their own sincerely held beliefs. They have consciences. The lesson that it is sometimes right to sacrifice something we want for the sake of our conscience is not altogether misplaced.

With Fanny Price it almost seems as if Austen set out to create a character that has no manners and no personality, but is simply raw morality. There is a line in *Mansfield Park* that reads, "she had gained the most valuable knowledge we could acquire: knowledge of ourselves and our duty"—and poor Fanny seems all duty. She is famously disliked by readers, but I have to confess myself to be sympathetic. When I reread the novels in preparation for writing this essay, the only time I teared up was when Fanny tells Edmund that she would like to write her brother, whom she misses so much. I think her actions and attitudes can be defended. For all her poor health and fear, she is quite brave. She stands up to all the others when they want her to participate in the play, and she even withstands the terrible onslaught of Sir Thomas's disapproval when she refuses to marry Crawford. This shows a lot of strength. It is too rarely acknowledged that Fanny is right. Sir Thomas *does* disapprove of the theatricals, as Fanny said he would. There is something rackety and improper about the whole playacting project, and it would be churlish to say that by accurately advocating the wishes of a good, dignified, generous patriarch Fanny is simply being a silly prude. Still more important, the theatricals *do* lead to the very dreaded outcome: Henry Crawford and Maria Rushworth run off together, and their passion for each other would never have been inflamed had they not rehearsed love scenes together. So Fanny is not only brave, she is wise. (And she also grows to be very good-looking, a point that Austen emphasizes repeatedly and that casting directors often ignore.) Fanny is not simply adhering to an arbitrary and silly rule about whether amateur theatricals are proper: she is trying to forestall a circumstance that does end up causing real pain.

"The most valuable knowledge we could acquire: knowledge of ourselves and our duty." As Lionel Trilling wrote, the word "duty" grates on the modern ear, but it is crucial to Austen.[4] In his most emphatic speech about Frank Churchill, Mr. Knightley in *Emma* says that "there is one thing a man can always do: his duty, not by maneuvering and finessing but by vigour and resolution." But is Knightley referring to arbitrary social conventions or to some kind of rigid code of duty owed to an institution? No—he is referring to Frank's failure to visit his father, a failure to show generosity. To my ear, the word "duty" has a pleasingly stern ring, if it is remembered that the "duty" Austen means is the duty of self-knowledge, humility, and generosity, not the pointlessly self-denying duty required by "insipid propriety."

Another criticism of Austen is that she has difficulty making her characters both good and interesting. This is a serious charge. Kingsley Amis wrote something very wise when he said that "to invite Mr. and Mrs. Edmund Bertram round for the evening would not be lightly undertaken."[5] No, one would not want to have dinner with Edmund and Fanny (although I think Amis is a bit unfair to Edmund here, for he is capable of fairly interesting conversation—he certainly holds his own with Mary Crawford). It might be useful to use Amis's standard with Austen's other couples: would we want to have dinner with Mr. and Mrs. Henry Tilney? Probably not: his humor is too arch and she is too silly. Mr. and Mrs. Edward Ferrars? Definitely not. Edward Ferrars is quite dull and Elinor Dashwood, while an admirable person, is not a barrel of laughs either—let's be fair and say that on her own she wouldn't be so bad. Colonel and Mrs. Brandon? No, we probably wouldn't want to have dinner with them either: Colonel Brandon is no more charismatic than Edward Ferrars, and Marianne, we are told, has had most of the life wrung out of her. Things begin to look up with *Pride and Prejudice*— I think we would readily accept an invitation to dine at Pemberley (and also, I think with Charles and Jane Bingley). *Mansfield Park* we have discussed, which brings us to *Emma*. Yes, certainly, having dinner with Mr. and Mrs. George Knightley would be enjoyable. Finally, what about Captain and Mrs. Wentworth? Frankly, no. Anne Elliot is another meek, purely good character like Fanny, whom one can admire but not seek to know. This list is somewhat troubling, if we look to Jane Austen for a way to live: too many of her good people are bores. Yet, think of the heroines who are decidedly not bores: Lizzy and Emma! If the characters are properly weighted to reflect their prominence, Lizzy and Emma are far more important than all the others combined; they are witty, charming, lively—and they are good. The charge that Austen linked goodness with stodginess is thereby refuted.

I have been trying to argue that, rather than being offensive or a kind of embarrassment, Jane Austen's moral instruction is a merit of her work, even—or especially—for the modern reader. Her principles are of transcendent value, they are not "priggish," and her novels illustrate and advocate a way of being in the world that is ethical, sensitive, and practical. The best representative for the worthiness of Austen's approach to life, however, is Austen herself. The reflection of the first sentence of *Pride and Prejudice* shimmers beneath it: "It is a truth universally acknowledged that a single woman of small fortune must be in want of a husband." There is nothing ironic about that: in Austen's time it really was a universal truth. Austen's condition as a single woman without money and no longer young was, as she put it when describing Miss Bates in *Emma,* to stand "in the very worst predicament in the world for having much of the public favor." As that very phrase indicates, however, Austen was able to regard her predicament coldly, clearly, and without self-pity. If a novelist fails to live up to the precepts espoused in his or her own work—if the passionate democrat on the page is a snob and bigot in life—we aren't supposed to care. It's the work that matters, we are told. This has always seemed highly unconvincing to me. One doesn't even have to know about Jane Austen's life, however, to know that her work mirrored her own authentic soul. Simply reading the novels, it is obvious that the personality of the creator and the personality of the novels themselves are the same. The novels convey the poise, balance, forbearance, and humor of their creator. By reading them one is enfolded in her personality, a personality we might wish we could adopt ourselves, for it seems to resolve many of life's problems, moral and otherwise.

Janet Todd

WHY I LIKE JANE AUSTEN

When very young I did not pleasurably read Jane Austen. In my teens I wanted sensation in novels and art, the kind of thing Jane Austen mocked or might have mocked. I loved Dostoyevsky, Daphne du Maurier, Lawrence Durrell, and Laurence Olivier in *Richard III.* I thought the two Austen books I'd been forced to study in school—*Northanger Abbey* and *Pride and Prejudice*—very quiet stuff.

But now, after a longish, unquiet life, I find much excitement, admittedly refined excitement, in her pages and a great deal more besides: much—what word is there for it?—wisdom perhaps, or good pragmatic sense, something not especially available in the pages of Durrell or Dostoyevsky.

The good sense is curiously delivered. From all the novels emerges a kind of acceptance of things as they are. Limitations and difficulties are squarely faced, so that the message—if message there is—insinuates tolerance concerning what life sends: just try to make the best of it while seeing that things might be or might have been otherwise. The heroines do this or would do so if matters had turned out badly, as they nearly do. Elizabeth Bennet would not have broken her heart and pined for the rest of her days had Darcy failed to return and Elinor Dashwood, denied her first love, would have loved again and not distressed her mother with her grief. We readers have been delivered the joy of romance—and the understanding of something closer to anti-romance. The balance is common sense.

The genre provides the contentment of a satisfactory marriage. Yet, even without this good fortune the heroines must struggle to reach contentment. They have needed to exert themselves to take advantage of chance and so avoid that heavy what-might-have-been that shadows all Jane Austen's novels. In *Persuasion,* the most romantic of the works, Anne Elliot requires not only luck to get her handsome hero but also some definite, swift action: she has to put herself where she can be noticed by Captain Wentworth, watching him from doorways and windows and making herself speedily indispensable. She has learned romance with age, an unnatural development, as the novel says—but she has also learned more thoroughly to display some very salutary selfishness.

I find this strain of selfishness marks both of Austen's most virtuous heroines. When contemplating Louisa Musgrove, who is quite possibly near death after her stubborn jumping from the Cobb, "Anne wondered whether it ever occurred to [Captain Wentworth] now, to question the justness of his own previous opinion as to the universal felicity and advantage of firmness of character; and whether it might not strike him that, like all other qualities of the mind, it should have its proportions and limits. She thought it could scarcely escape him to feel that a persuadable temper might sometimes be as much in favour of happiness as a very resolute character." In other words, at this crucial time she thought that she herself might show to good advantage beside her injured competitor. In the midst of everyone else's misery over her cousin Maria's adultery, Fanny Price in *Mansfield Park* finds herself moving from utter desolation—in which state she imagines that "instant annihilation" might be best for all her Bertram relatives—to "being exquisitely happy" when she realizes that in the wake of this misery she can return to the family and play the important role of comforter. It's worth noting that no film or television adaptation catches these moments, for a look of triumph, unlike a rush of love, from either young woman would be unpalatable; the fleeting thought must stay on the page.

When invited to a dinner of the Shakespeare Club with Dickens in the chair in 1839, Leigh Hunt wondered what Shakespeare would think if he could walk into the room and ask whom the festivity was for. With typical Hunt arrogance he declared he knew the bard's mind: he would, said Hunt, be "surprised and pleased . . . to learn it was himself." Like all other enthusiastic readers, I too feel a personal intimacy with Jane Austen and often declare, perhaps a little tongue in cheek, what she would and would not have thought of her amazing contemporary fame.

Austen permits this intimacy to us all in an inimitable way, so that we believe we are peculiarly close to her as a person and would somehow be appreciated by her were we to know her. Her characters can seem to walk free of the books to live in quite other spheres and contexts. The narrator of the novels often gently mocks us for accepting the heroines as "real," but we go on doing it nonetheless. It would be hard to give up the belief, as numerous sequels and recreations testify. And, for all her mockery, Jane Austen once fostered this illusion herself when, in her letters and talks with her family, she playfully revealed the afterlives of her characters. Miss Steele of *Sense and Sensibility,* she reported, "never succeeded in catching the Doctor"; Mr. Woodhouse in *Emma* would prevent his daughter and Mr. Knightley from settling at Donwell for another two years, while delicate Jane Fairfax would outlive him a mere seven years. Visiting London in 1813 she claimed she was looking for pictures of her characters among the miniatures shown at the Society of Painters' display; she was pleased "particularly" with "a small portrait of Mrs Bingley," declaring "there never was a greater likeness." Mrs. Darcy was, however, not to be found at any of the exhibitions, perhaps because her husband "prizes any Picture of her too much" to wish it to be shown publicly.

With Linda Bree I have just finished editing the formerly unpublished and unfinished works for a volume entitled *Later Manuscripts,* the last of nine devoted to Jane Austen's oeuvre. I served as the general editor of this edition, which has been in preparation for the last eight years. I was, at the outset, reluctant to take on the task and yet drawn to it. I was even more reluctant to involve myself in the unfinished works. Yet, like the finished novels themselves, these grew on me, and I began to read them for pleasure, quite at odds with the critic and novelist E. M. Forster, who regarded *Sanditon* as weak and of small literary merit, and Austen's first serious editor, R. W. Chapman, who saw this last unfinished work as rough and harsh. I now find *The Watsons* and *Sanditon* inhabiting my mind as completely as *Emma* or *Pride and Prejudice.*

Perhaps this is in part because these unfinished works have not been, and cannot in their present state be, adapted for film and television. I can have my own mental pictures without the characters being embodied for me by Jennifer Ehle or Keira Knightley or Emma Thompson or Colin Firth. The wonderful, hypochondriac Parker family can be imagined as Jane Austen makes me imagine them, eyeing the potions on the mantelpiece or the buttered toast near the fire. The claustrophobic house where the Watson daughters have grown up squabbling and competing is very different from and more troubling than Longbourn in *Pride and Prejudice,* where the more indulged Bennet girls have been left to tumble up into womanhood. The village of Highbury in *Emma* (incidentally a much stronger presence in the book than in any adaptation) has its successor in the sparkling, windy village of Sanditon enfolded in its cliffs and sands. The characters in these unfinished novels have not had time to become "deep and intricate"—Elizabeth Bennet's phrase for Mr. Darcy—but there is something intricate about the beginning of both *The Watsons* and *Sanditon.*

It is this intricacy, of course, that is so abundantly present in the finished novels. The six finished novels converse with each other as if taking up different points of view, challenging previous assumptions and prejudices. *Mansfield Park* insists on sympathy for a heroine at odds with her counterpart in the book published immediately before, *Pride and Prejudice,* and takes to task the sprightly, too outspoken woman. Then in *Emma,* we have a rescue of this imperfect heroine, as if Mary Crawford from *Mansfield Park* had been allowed on this occasion a rather better background and a kinder set of circumstances. I love the way Jane Austen experiments with language, with deeply fraught conversation, with idle talk, and with essential social oiling. More than all other writers before her, she captures communal speech, the collective hum of a community whose members have lived together over many years and whose phrases and eccentricities of talk have been steadily circulating. In *Emma,* which, like a large number of other readers, I find Jane Austen's supreme achievement, Miss Bates's rambling speech takes in the whole village, and at moments the village seems to talk through her. And when in *Emma,* as in all the novels, the narrator speaks, her wry omniscience provides unity. "How nicely you talk," says simple sweet Harriet Smith to her new friend Emma, "I love to hear you. You understand every thing." As readers we come to feel much the same about Jane Austen's voice.

This voice can shock as well as delight and heal, for it does not always say exactly what we expect or want—often after we have been lulled into a sense of easy agreement. We can see this in much academic criticism, which tends to rebel against such moments. Contemporary critics often assume that Jane Austen would—or more often *should*—have clarified her insufficiently liberal views on agricultural enclosure, the laboring poor, and above all race and slavery. Sir Thomas Bertram in *Mansfield Park* goes to Antigua to be out of the way for the plot to develop: modern critics want to know what he was doing there—or they helpfully tell us, or, like Patricia Rozema in her film version of the novel, adapt the book in modern mode with correct and approved contemporary attitudes concerning slavery and the emphasis on a parent's duty to a child rather than the eighteenth-century's stress on a child's duty to a parent. In this film Sir Thomas, the patriarch, becomes a raping slave owner and the spendthrift son a sensitive child.

In *Persuasion,* the estranged hero and heroine are sitting on a sofa; between them is Mrs. Musgrove, a large lady who is struck by recalling that Captain Wentworth was once at sea with her dead son. She has begun to sob over his memory. The narrator's response is tart here: the boy was useless, nobody liked him, and he was better dead and out of the way. The expression of grief by a fat woman is distasteful, even silly; fat people don't look good crying. As Jane Austen expressed it, "Personal size and mental sorrow have certainly no necessary proportions. A large bulky figure has as good a right to be in deep affliction as the most graceful set of limbs in the world. But, fair or not fair, there are unbecoming conjunctions, which reason will patronize in vain—which taste cannot tolerate—which ridicule will seize." Political correctness makes sizism unacceptable. As with the moments of triumphant self-assertion in *Mansfield Park* and *Persuasion,* this episode is absent from the recent films.

On no evidence, critics assert that, if she had lived to revise this last novel, Jane Austen would have excised the passage on inelegant grief, for, as with other writers, we have a propensity to claim that what we don't like in an author was an error, an oversight, or an aberration. In this case the maneuver has a long history: in 1870, fifty-three years after Jane Austen's death, her nephew James Edward Austen-Leigh published his influential *Memoir of Jane Austen,* the work that began her long and lasting ascent into the very first rank of popular and canonical writers. Presenting his aunt as a decorous Victorian lady author, he explained the lapses in *Persuasion* by the fact that she had not entirely revised the work.

I am uneasy with but hardly distressed by the torrent of Austenmania that has flowed over us all in the last years. Few academics would have the foolhardiness now to say, as D. W. Harding did in a 1940 essay that helped begin the scholarly study of Austen, that her fate has been "to be read and enjoyed by precisely the sort of people whom she disliked." We wouldn't dare. The public wants to buy the books when they come in pink and silver covers—some of us buy mugs, tea towels, pens, and dolls from the National Portrait Gallery and Chawton Cottage. At the annual meetings of the Jane Austen Society of North America the participants dress up in Regency costume, perhaps imagining themselves frolicking in the gardens of the Duke of Devonshire's Chatsworth, embodiment of Pemberley in the latest filmic version of *Pride and Prejudice* (though Mr. Darcy, with a mere ten thousand pounds a year, could never have lived in such a place). Deidre Lynch cautioned "the career-conscious critic against letting the wrong people know of her desire to . . . wear Regency costume and dance at a Jane Austen Literary Ball," but I doubt there is in reality such shame.

While completing our work on the manuscripts, my coeditor and I have worried about the authenticity of prayers, plays, and poems attributed to Austen. Meanwhile the Internet and publishing houses bring new works celebrating Jane Austen to the public every month: *Mrs. Elton's Diary, Captain Wentworth's Diary, Mr. Darcy's Diary,* the sex scenes added to the novels, to name only a few. Then there is *Pride and Prejudice,* the play and the musical, the time-traveling Elizabeth Bennet; sequels galore; and all the spin-offs: *The Jane Austen Book Club, Miss Austen Regrets, A Walk with Jane Austen, Jane Austen, Detective,* and *The Jane Austen Cookbook.* A webpage addresses "all those brainy lovers out there who WANT their literature with a little funk, their books with a little BOOGIE . . . a literary/song mash-up where the button down babes of the 19th Century meet the bottoms up beauties of today."[1] *Lost in Austen* is not only a 2008 television serial of time travel but also an interactive fiction game that allows you to be Elizabeth Bennet as long as you want, while you can live permanently in a place called Austenland. If instead of languishing in the old-fashioned monarchy of the novels, you go to the Republic of Pemberley on the Web, you will find a free land where afflicted souls ask advice of Jane Austen and are told to embrace their inner Janeite, but where, if their Jane addiction is too great, they can be soothed by counselors. "To me, it's as if she's a modern-day psychotherapist who time-traveled back to the Regency period and writes a novel about everyone who spent time on her couch."[2]

Jane Austen seems the writer nearest to a composer of classical music, her novels well-wrought symphonies; turbulent depths coexist with ordered surfaces and the ratio of the expected to the unexpected feels just as it should. Each time I read her—and she is one of the few novelists who can be read and reread—I know I have not exhausted the books; something has again escaped me, as it does from a concert performance of a complex musical piece. It was beautiful, but did I listen as closely as I should? Like Lyme in *Persuasion,* Jane Austen's books "must be visited, and visited again."

John Wiltshire

WHY DO WE *READ* JANE AUSTEN?

Why do we read Jane Austen? The burgeoning of so many films based on her novels in the last decades means that the question has to be inflected today in a way unknown to previous generations. Why *do* we read Jane Austen? If you don't happen to like Joe Wright's sumptuous *Pride and Prejudice* (2005), you can go back to the famously successful *Pride and Prejudice* broadcast in seven episodes in 1995, and if that doesn't please you, well then, there's the earlier BBC video with a very different Mr. Darcy also still available. Or perhaps you feel that none of these can match the Hollywood version of 1940 starring Greer Garson and Laurence Olivier. Why, with so many entertainments to choose from, would you search out the novel, or revisit that old text you read at school or in college? To be frank, some people who think of themselves as fans of Jane Austen have not read her novels, or have read one or two of them so long ago it hardly counts. So I want to pose the question: why do we *read* Jane Austen? What do those of us who do read the novels find in them that none of the visual presentations—movies or teletexts (I shall call them both films)—quite give us? And why are we so confounded by the films, some of them sporting the message "by Jane Austen"? Are we puzzled by their simultaneous reminders of, and distance from, the texts they translate so gorgeously into visual terms? I shall be suggesting that the films, apparently inevitably, present us with a "Jane Austen" that a reader of the novels might hardly recognize, and that this has something quite special to do with the film as a medium, and with that tricky and amorphous quality, mood, or genre we call "romance."

On the face of it, Jane Austen's, of all classic novels, seem the most resistant to adaptation into a visual medium. Where does the famous conversation that opens *Pride and Prejudice* take place? " 'My dear Mr Bennet,' said his lady to him one day, 'have you heard that Netherfield Park is let at last?' " Does Mrs. Bennet open this topic on the way back from church, or in the drawing room, or perhaps in bed? The novel leaves it entirely to the reader to imagine, or rather not to imagine. We just enjoy the words, the conversation, appreciate the comic interplay of these just-introduced figures, and delight in the repartee that immediately displays their relationship. What does Mr. Collins look like? We're told that he is "a tall heavy looking young man." We certainly know that Elizabeth Bennet has "fine eyes," but really not much more, and we're never told specifically what she's wearing. Mr. Darcy is tall and handsome, but is he broad-shouldered and athletic as well? Who knows?

This restriction of the visual is so characteristic of Austen's work that it led one of her earliest admirers, George Henry Lewes, to speculate that she might have been shortsighted.[1] It isn't that the visual is absent (it is easy to think of instances to the contrary), merely that it is strictly rationed. Everyone's daily life is filled with objects, and so, necessarily, are films. But objects, like backgrounds, or settings, are rare in Austen's novels. When they are brought to our attention it's because they contribute to the dramatic interaction of characters. There's a moment, for example, in *Mansfield Park* when Edmund Bertram, with whom the heroine, Fanny, is in love, admires her dress. He has never mentioned her clothes before, and in fact neither has Jane Austen. "Your gown seems very pretty," he says. "I like these glossy spots. Has not Miss Crawford a gown something the same?" (Mary Crawford is the lively young lady with whom he's in love.) What at first is to Fanny a gratifying compliment immediately turns sour. We see, rather comically, that it's not she who is in Edmund's thoughts but her rival, Miss Crawford. Actually, it's both amusing and heartrending: Fanny has accepted being, as her Aunt Norris puts it, "the lowest and last," but it's a moot point whether the reiteration of such slights lessens their pain.

This conversation, which takes place on a February evening, begins with Edmund at first admitting he can't see Fanny's gown clearly. "As well as I can judge by this light," he says, "you look very nicely indeed." This is one of the rather rare moments when Jane Austen introduces a mention of something that is utterly intrinsic to the film as an artistic medium: lighting. A famous moment at Donwell Abbey in *Emma,* when the heroine's pleasure in the view is captured in the apostrophe "English verdure, English culture, English comfort, seen under a sun bright, without being oppressive," seems like another, but it is the weather, rather than the light, that turns out to be significant, for what is delightful to Emma certainly oppresses Frank Churchill when he turns up on the scene complaining fretfully of the heat. "They had a very fine day for Box Hill," opens the next chapter, and again it is nothing but a general evocation that sets the stage for the coming action. Like objects and settings, effects of light and lighting are absent, by and large, from Austen's minimalist art: but all are obligatory in the realist movie, and play crucial roles not only in film generally, but specifically in the genre to which Austen films belong—the costume drama, period film, or what is increasingly called "heritage cinema."[2]

So what is the pleasure of reading Jane Austen? Perhaps it is not so obvious to say that she is, first and foremost, a humorist. Not just a satirist (though she is that), not just a wit (that too), nor just heir to the rich tradition of situation comedy on the eighteenth-century stage, which afforded her a training in—to mention only techniques—the delights of the running gag, and the comic permutations of cross-purposes. By calling her a humorist I mean that she was gifted with an inveterate and irrepressible delight in the ridiculous. But her kind of humorousness could touch the serious, even the painful, and toward the end of her writing life, skirt the tragic. It could mean mockery, even parody, but more pervasively it is the gift of seizing on the pompous ("She is tolerable; but not handsome enough to tempt *me*"), the pretentious, the clichéd, or the transparently self-interested, and turning them to enjoyable effect, as Elizabeth Bennet herself does with Darcy's careless snub.

Jane Austen's enjoyment of the ridiculous was inseparable from her having an extraordinarily acute ear. If it was speech that was the focus of her amusement, it was accompanied by her own talent for precise and economical expression; so the pleasure she affords the reader is not only that of pinning down absurdity, but of a continuous expressive exactness that is always next door to satire. "It is a truth universally acknowledged, that a young man in possession of a good fortune, must be in want of a wife." Already tinged with parody, this famous opening sentence reveals itself, to a reader familiar with Austen, as devastatingly tongue-in-cheek. The irony lies in the mischievous little word "must." Think for a moment and you see how absurd that is, and then you realize that what is represented as "universal" to the unsuspecting reader is no more than the currency of the genteel, gossipy women's world that is at this moment being both addressed and subverted. There's a variation on *Pride and Prejudice*'s witticism hidden in the opening paragraph of *Mansfield Park* (1814), Austen's next, and very different, novel: "there certainly are not so many men of large fortune in the world, as there are pretty women to deserve them." "Deserve"! In the one phrase the transactions of the marriage market that are the paragraph's topic are recognized and exploded. Being inseparable from her native concision, Austen's wit is everywhere, even in the most subdued or innocent-sounding sentences. In *Emma* Mrs. Elton is described, in passing, as "elegant as lace and pearls could make her." At Box Hill, the same pretentious Mrs. Elton declares that she is "really tired of exploring so long on one spot." In *Sanditon,* Jane Austen's uncompleted last manuscript, a young lady goes into a gift shop and is tempted there by "all the useless things in the world that could not be done without." "He wished him to be a model of constancy; and fancied the best means of effecting it would be by not trying him too long" (Sir Thomas in *Mansfield Park*). But moments like these are only superficially Wildean (Gwendolen: "If you are not too long, I will wait here for you all my life," or Lady Bracknell, "I am not in favour of long engagements. They give people the opportunity of finding out each other's character before marriage"[3]) because Austen's wit is less spectacular than modest, in the service of a very un-Wildean temperate rationality, and because it belongs, more often than not, to her narrator.

In Jane Austen's era, one broad cultural phenomenon provided the most obvious opportunity for her wit, and that was the cult of sensibility. Increasingly, sympathetic feeling (or its expression) had become understood as the sign of virtue, and its possession the province of the genteel. This fashionable mode was greatly stimulated by the success in 1771 of Henry Mackenzie's novel *The Man of Feeling,* whose hero enjoys many situations in which he may drop an unavailing tear. Janet Todd has even suggested that the key to Jane Austen's novels is their critique of sensibility, in all its varieties.[4] *Northanger Abbey,* which was probably composed in the last years of the eighteenth century, certainly parodies and exposes the gothic novels that are one offshoot of the cult of feeling, as well as the empty sentimental protestations of Isabella Thorpe, the heroine's false friend. And just as certainly, Austen took sensibility as a target in her first published novel, *Sense and Sensibility* (1811), although she was so intelligent that her ridiculing of Marianne's affectations is inconveniently complicated by the recognition that "sensibility" might not just be a style, but could also be an aspect of a person's innate response to the world, and its expression the outcrop of youthful idealism.

But by the time of her mature writing, the cult of sensibility had passed its heyday, and morphed into something wider, one aspect of which was the prestige of benevolence. This was at least partly the result of the influence of the Evangelical movement, which itself shared the sentimentalist assumption that an "inner voice" rather than rational conviction was the best guide to virtue, or to piety. When Jane Austen writes of Fanny Price's adoption, discussed by the Bertrams in the first chapter of *Mansfield Park,* that "the pleasures of so benevolent a scheme were already enjoyed," she is nailing the inauthenticity inherent in benevolence and sensibility alike—that the satisfactions belonged to those with power, not to the objects of their apparent sympathy, or charity. In this Jane Austen is at one with the man she called "my dear Dr Johnson," the inveterate enemy of what they both called "cant."

Something more diffuse, still less easy to define and far more lastingly important, developed out of the belief that feeling in itself was evidence of moral virtue. "I am certain of nothing but of the holiness of the heart's affections and the truth of Imagination" a great Romantic poet was to write.[5] In the eighteenth century, "enthusiastic" meant half-mad, or at least intemperate; "rhapsody" meant incoherent, and "romantic" (or "romantick") meant wild, absurd, and morally suspect. By the early years of the nineteenth, people had come to feel that "enthusiasm" was a good thing, that a rhapsody could explore and express those aspects of human experience rationality could not reach, and that there was promise in the unknown, the intuitive, the strange and exotic. "Romantic" had started to sound like praise, and a romantic feeling or impulse could be understood as a recognition of the possibilities of human nature. There were, it was felt, mysteries in the soul, prompting toward the ideal, to which those phenomena of life that lie on the peripheries of consciousness, such as reveries and dreams, were our guides. In literature, these areas of human experience could be most aptly evoked and represented by dusk, nighttime, semidarkness, glimmerings, images read in flickering firelight: all tropes of the poetry and fiction of the age. They had come to signal an openness to experiences beyond the realm of reason's light.

One of the pleasures of reading Jane Austen is to see how, with a vocabulary more limited than that of almost any other great novelist, she captures the shifts and exposes the deceptions inherent in so much of the commonplace language of her age. And this is the case with the words that I have singled out, themselves only flags on the stream of change. The same word, in its context, and in the mouth of different characters, becomes a protean index of a culture being transformed. A "friend," for example, can be used in its eighteenth-century sense, as someone who helps you advance in the world, but also in its later, affective register, the one we are most familiar with. In her last completed novel, *Persuasion,* there is a famous description of the heroine Anne Elliot's feelings. "She had been forced into prudence in her youth, she learned romance as she grew older,—the natural sequel of an unnatural beginning." The word "romance" is poised precisely on the cusp of irony and allure. And "natural," being coupled with learning, is something rather different from that spontaneous nature espoused by others in her age. What is romantic about the saddened and wry wit in which this acceptance of the rights of feeling is phrased?

For if there is one thing that is as ingrained in Jane Austen's style as it is endemic in her thinking, it's her suspicion of the romantic in all its forms. This is what creates such a compelling tension between the form or genre in which her novels are composed, and their ideological or moral content. For they are, broadly speaking, committed to a "romantic" narrative in which affirmation of human possibility takes ultimate form in the marriage of love. If there is one belief that is at the heart of the romantic it is that human beings are, despite appearances, essentially good, and human possibility necessarily endless. Like Johnson, Austen would have no time for this. For them, human beings are inveterately self-interested and prone to evil, and this was, after all, a cornerstone of the mainstream Christianity to which they both subscribed. Hence they are skeptical when people parade their goodness—a sympathetic nature, a superior intelligence, a feeling heart. In practice this means that Jane Austen's delight in the ridiculous very often has a cutting edge, an implicit agenda, which consists in the undermining or exposure of romantic expression in all its protean manifestations, from Isabella Thorpe's fashionable jargon, to the Bertrams' sentimental adoption, to Mrs. Elton's desire to arrive at the Donwell Abbey picnic like a Gypsy and riding a donkey.

You can see this impulse at work in her earliest writings, even in the very first. Peter Sabor's edition of the *Juvenilia* has as its frontispiece an extract from the Parish Register of her father's church, St. Nicholas, Steventon, in which the young Jane Austen has experimented with various fantasy marriages. One of them reads "Edmund Arthur William Mortimer of Liverpool and Jane Austen of Steventon were married in this Church."[6] The romantic, olde English names of the groom ("Edmund," says Fanny Price in *Mansfield Park,* "is a name of heroism and renown—of kings, princes and knights") are sabotaged by his coming from "Liverpool," the ugly-sounding port, its contemporary wealth based on the slave trade. Jane Austen's juvenilia are devoted, by and large, to hilarious spoofs of the language and conventions of the sentimental and romantic novels of her time. It is as if as soon as Jane Austen detected a romantic impulse within herself she was moved to cancel and repel by ridicule what she understood as the siren calls of fallen human nature. And foremost among these is the allure of the fantasizing imagination, aided and abetted by literary models. "Dearest Miss Morland, what ideas have you been admitting?" cries the hero in shock when he perceives that Catherine has imagined that his father—an authoritarian patriarch to be sure—is a murderous gothic tyrant. "Why did such an idea occur to her . . . ? It ought not to have touched on the confines of her imagination," is Fanny Price's self-chastisement for even dreaming of cousin Edmund as her lover. These are some of the most earnest moments in the novels, but they are utterly congruent with the impulses behind Jane Austen's comedy.

One of the things that makes her novels exciting is that she is so acute a commentator on the intellectual and cultural currents of her time. Not that she pontificates about them; rather she detects their presence, notes with interest and amusement how they are reflected in the trivia of everyday life and speech. Her later novels, especially, focus on the immediately contemporary scene. They are precisely dated: *Mansfield Park* takes place after the abolition of the British slave trade in 1807, and *Persuasion* spans the months from April 1814 to March 1815, during which Napoleon was exiled to Elba in apparent final defeat. In *Sanditon,* uncompleted in early 1817, the subject is a fashionable resort town, and the postwar entrepreneur who is sponsoring its development regrets that a crescent has been called "Trafalgar" because "Waterloo is now more the thing." And it is certainly one function of the objects that do feature in her novels to register current trends, like the harp that the stylish Londoner Mary Crawford brings with her to Mansfield, at the height of fashion in 1808–9, but going down-market to country gentry like the Musgrove sisters by the time of *Persuasion*. In other novels, a host of social and even political implications hovers around the possession and playing of that newly developed instrument the pianoforte, which was to become a vehicle for the great Romantic composers.

Jane Austen, then, was a novelist exclusively and sharply focused on the contemporary. The heritage film in contrast, is by definition about the past. The social observation embedded in Austen's references to current trends cannot give a modern audience the same shock of recognition and delight. The objects, settings, and descriptions so cursorily indicated in Austen's writing must become fully visualized, presented; the films must be filled with faces, costuming, candles, crockery, and vistas of country houses shot across greensward, all signifying the past, not the present. The underlying purpose and market appeal of the heritage film cannot be, as with Austen, to note with amusement what the latest shift in language use or trendy possession denotes, but rather to honor, or commemorate, a milieu that has now acquired the patina of history. The films belong to our time, not to hers. And the language that gives the reader of Austen so continuous a pleasure is reduced to the minor presence that the visual has in her novels, subordinate to a whole repertoire of emotive effects, two of which, significantly, are Romantic music and period lighting. How do the films compare then with the novels?

The BBC production of *Northanger Abbey* in 1986 marked a turning point in the practice of adaptation. This film, with its visualization of gothic fantasies of abduction and rape, its spooky accompanying music, its inclusion of figures who do not appear in the book, its transformation of the novel's modern Northanger, equipped with the latest devices for domestic comfort, into an authentic medieval castle, surrounded by a moat and filled with narrow staircases and dark passages, in effect reversed the novel's intention and produced instead a re-gothicization of Jane Austen's anti-gothic satire. The vows of fidelity that had previously governed adaptations of classics were well and truly broken. From this time onward scriptwriters and producers were free to experiment with Austen's novels, to add scenes and characters, even to radically alter Austen's conception of her personages, under the rubric of creative reinvention, coupled with the duty or desire to communicate to a contemporary audience. And there is no doubt that this new license has had some positive results.

The multiplying film versions of Jane Austen's novels have a dual heritage: they are influenced quite as much by other films and by each other as by the books under whose names they are released. The 1986 *Northanger Abbey* is an example: its affiliations are with the then-fashionable directors Ken Russell and Federico Fellini, which meant turning Austen's novel upside down. This production in turn leads to Patricia Rozema's controversial 1999 version of *Mansfield Park,* known to some Austen readers as *Wuthering Park* because, like the earlier film, it replaces the fine modern house of the novel's title with a half-ruin, and similarly sets many episodes in darkness, including one in which the novel's timid, reticent heroine furiously rides her horse, bareback, to the soundtrack accompaniment of an orchestra, amid thunder and lightning.

Films are made of light. It is light that makes its audience, seated in the dark, spectators, not witnesses or participants. It is lighting that gives scenes their character and objects and persons their presence, a presence quite different from the quality they have in real life. And directors employ effects of light to generate or control the viewer's responses to the visual scene. In the heritage film this has special valence or narrative value, since the period quality of the *mise-en-scène* can be most immediately communicated by scenes lit by oil lamps or candles, or, more grandly, by candelabra and flaming sconces. All of the films based on Austen novels feature such sequences, whether in ballrooms, parlors, or bedrooms. But it is not so much the objects that bestow light, as that effects of old or preindustrial lighting themselves generate meanings which depend very often upon the encircling presence of darkness.[7] As in Romantic literature, darkness evokes the mysterious, the unknown. The shooting of many scenes set at night, or lit by uncertain and flickering light, is a means by which Austen's unromantic romances are romanticized anew.

This can be illustrated well by scenes in two of the best of recent Jane Austen adaptations, the *Sense and Sensibility* directed by Ang Lee (1995) and the more recent BBC three-part serial of 2008, with script by Andrew Davies. Many readers of the novel feel that Marianne's ultimate marriage to Colonel Brandon, a rather older man, is insufficiently prepared for, and results in what feels like a compromised, a disappointing, close. Brandon, seen through Marianne's eyes, is "silent and grave" throughout the novel's first chapters, and never seems like a romantic prospect. In both visual versions of the novel, this weakness (if it is that) is remedied with early scenes that dramatize Brandon's presence and suggest an early rapport or even attraction between the two figures.

In Jane Austen's novel, one of the skimpy indications of Brandon's feeling for Marianne is in this brief paragraph about her singing at the piano:

Marianne's performance was highly applauded. Sir John was loud in his admiration at the end of every song, and as loud in his conversation with the others while every song lasted . . . Colonel Brandon alone, of all the party, heard her without being in raptures. He paid her only the compliment of attention; and she felt a respect for him on the occasion, which the others had reasonably forfeited by their shameless want of taste. His pleasure in music, though it amounted not to that extatic delight which could alone sympathize with her own, was estimable when contrasted against the horrible insensibility of the others; and she was reasonable enough to allow that a man of five and thirty might well have outlived all acuteness of feeling and every exquisite power of enjoyment.

In Emma Thompson's script for the film, this is turned into a resonant moment:

INT. BARTON PARK. MUSIC ROOM. EVE.
    Everyone watches MARIANNE as she plays and sings. Behind them we see BRANDON entering. But he stays in the shadow of the door, and no one notices him. CLOSE on his face. He gazes at MARIANNE with an unfathomable look of grief and longing. He breathes in deeply. Suddenly, ELINOR feels his presence and looks around at him. After a few moments, she turns back, slightly puzzled. The song finishes. Everyone claps. The man ventures into the light . . .[8]

As directed by Lee, this becomes a carefully staged sequence which enhances Brandon's role. Marianne is seen at the pianoforte, performing at Barton Park for the Middletons and her family. To the soundtrack accompaniment of her singing, a gentleman is shown riding up to the front entrance of the house; then his silhouetted figure enters the house; gradually, as the camera tracks back with his progress through the hall, more light intermittently falls on his face, he throws his hat aside and moves forward, captured by the sound of music from the room he is approaching. Now clearly lit, he stands at the entrance, "silent and grave" indeed, but in intense stillness, the camera remaining focused on his face for several seconds without moving. The sound of Marianne's singing continues. The film employs music to forge an emotional connection between the future lovers, or rather to make the audience feel that emotion; the lighting of Brandon's entrance through the house, passing through an enfilade of shadows and illumination, generates a sense of momentous-ness, and picks up the "unfathomable" attraction that Thompson's script requires. It hardly needs to be said that the tart ironic treatment of Mar-ianne in Austen's brief recall of the scene (let alone the comedy of Sir John's talking over her playing) is completely overridden. What has been lost is the narrator's presence.

In the later three-episode television treatment, mindful of the earlier success of the film, Brandon is also shown mesmerized, or at least deeply moved, by Marianne's playing. Here the aura of the occasion is increased by the scene's filming in the dark parlor of what looks like an old manor house at night. A fire roars in the chimney, and candles on the piano and candelabra elsewhere provide dim, uncertain light. As Marianne plays, the film cuts to Brandon, his profile lit by a source of light outside the frame, intently listening. The camera swoops round him so that the lis-tening Brandon is now fronting the viewer, and then holds the shot, fo-cusing unmovingly on his face, intent, for several seconds, while the sound of Marianne's playing continues. The play of light in both films is utilized to suggest that a key moment in the narrative is being presented. The actors in both films convey mingled desire and anguish. In both it is the *mise-en-scène,* the collaborative effect of acting, camera movement, carefully controlled lighting, and music that seduces the audience's imagination.

One need not scorn the "Jane Austen" films, nor, as do many film critics, slight the whole genre of heritage film. They are made with de-votion and intelligence to succeed with a contemporary audience, and to that end use all of the technologies of persuasion available to the visual media. There are times—often because of superb acting—that they achieve what might be called, following Virginia Woolf, "moments of being"—sequences or interactions that lift the film out of the routine, the quotidian, or for readers who remember the novel from which they derive, cast the text in a new light, as do the examples I have mentioned. The weakest of them at least invite a reader to return to earlier films of the same novel, and hence, sometimes, to the book. But to do so, as I have argued, is to rediscover a much less "romantic" treatment of the story. Because cinema must do what Jane Austen never does, and fill the audience's mind with visual stimulation, with objects, backgrounds, fa-cial expressions, gestural implications, and with music, it is necessarily a quite different art from hers. It is an art of sensuous seduction, working on the audience's imagination and dreams, in which the play of light, as of sound, is instrumental. In the cinema, then, Jane Austen's subversions of romantic idealism are reinvented as romantic narratives, and the narrator disappears. Perhaps the very conditions of the cinema dispose it to effects quite distinct from the bracing, contemporary, ironic, comic, and intellectual writing that is the reason why we do read Jane Austen.

Amy Heckerling

THE GIRLS WHO DON'T SAY "WHOO!"

On any given evening, in the music/alcohol/flirting places where young people congregate, you will find them. Some are attractive, most merely dress as if they were, and at the slightest provocation (e.g., a touchdown on the TV, a Beyoncé song on the sound system) they will throw their arms up and shout. These are the girls who say "Whoo!" Sometimes "Whoo!" is replaced with "All right!" or "I love this song!" They may even entreat everyone to "Party!"

These females will dance, flick their hair back, or otherwise find ways to physicalize their *joie de vivre,* and hopefully get you to look at them. The whooping girls certainly have their antecedents. In the first half of the nineteenth century, they might have been giggling incessantly over the soldiers in town, as Lydia and Kitty do in *Pride and Prejudice.* They might feel the need to "take a turn around the room," as Mr. Bingley's sister does, in an obvious ploy to show off her figure. Possibly jumping off a high staircase into someone's arms seems to them like a hilarious idea, as Louisa from *Persuasion* thought.

But there are the girls who can't say "Whoo," who can't be so overwhelmed by the latest song that they must draw everyone's attention to their bodies, and who can't laugh hysterically at something they don't find funny. It is here, among the non-whooping females, that one finds a large portion of the Jane Austen fan base. She has made leading ladies of the sensible sisters. She created a world where dashing, if arrogant, men seem to fall madly in love with the women who have more brains than fancy ribbons (in the 1800s, they didn't have body glitter). This paradigm works so joyously well that one only wishes she had written dozens more in that vein.

And then there's *Emma*. "Handsome, clever, and rich, with a comfortable home and happy disposition . . ." Emma is the antithesis of the typical Jane Austen character. In fact, Austen is quoted as saying she had created, "a heroine that no one will like except myself." For once, Jane Austen was totally clueless.

And here's where I come in, a hundred and seventy-eight years later, walking around Central Park, talking with my friend Wallace Shawn while my daughter rollerbladed ahead of us. Everyone seemed to be drinking Snapple and listening to grunge music. While trying to write a teen comedy, I had given myself the task of figuring out what kind of characters I most enjoyed in films. A bizarre collection emerged, from James Cagney (especially in musicals) to Little Alex of *A Clockwork Orange*. It wasn't the crime or killings that interested me, it was seeing individuals who were confident, energetic, and most of all, happy. Happy really fascinated and confused me. How do people get that way? What are they thinking? What kind of stories are they in? Is it possible to have a character be happy throughout a story? Or must they arrive there only at the very end (i.e., "Happily ever after . . .")?

I remembered reading and loving the book *Emma* during a college course on nineteenth-century novels (*Bleak House,* bleech). After rereading it, one thing was apparent, the story was absolutely . . . OK, I don't want to say "modern." That implies that the present is somehow superior to other times, and authors of the past were quite clever if their works make sense now. Books that are more closely linked to their eras are then considered "corny" or "dated" by those standards. The novel *Emma* is better than "modern," it's timeless and universal. It had the perfect structure for the growth of an optimistic person.

1. Emma's attributes (confidence, imagination) and her faults (manipulativeness and self-deception) lead to successes. Hooking up the Westons makes her arrogant about her matchmaking skills, and she steps up her efforts on Harriet and Mr. Elton.
2. She is so self-deceived that she does not pick up on any of the clues the world presents to her. She can't see that Mr. Elton thinks all the female attention he's getting is because Emma is in love with him. She can't tell that Frank has no deep feelings for her and is just flirting to hide his relationship with Jane. She is confronted with the fact

that she has been wrong and her meddling has been destructive and hurtful to others. She realizes she is clueless.

3. She sadly resolves to change her ways. She will make amends to Miss Bates, whom she offended, she will try to help Jane, she won't butt in on other people's affections. When she is feeling her lowest, Knightley is the most smitten. And what do you know? Everyone winds up getting married.

Could anyone have laid out a better teen romance film? Even little details and bits were completely current. Harriet's souvenirs of her very slight connection to Mr. Elton are scarily identifiable to most lovelorn teenagers. The machinations of who rides with whom and in which carriage is easily updated to cars and what freeway you live near being the excuse for "alone time" with one's object of desire.

In writing the movie *Clueless,* I was presented with a very pleasurable puzzle—taking the people of the English countryside of 1815 and finding their equivalents in 1990s Beverly Hills.

Emma (Cher)—With all of her projects, her energy, her delusions, and her positive outlook, Emma was perfect for then, for now, for anytime.

Miss Taylor (Ms. Geist)—The governess would obviously become a teacher, as would her husband, Mr. Weston (Mr. Hall). This would allow Cher to do her matchmaking while at school.

George Knightley (Josh)—Emma's brother-in-law is the staple of romantic comedies—the person you are thrown together with, you're close to, but you don't realize you're in love with. As a brother- and sister-in-law, Emma and Knightley are at home with each other and can fight and be themselves. In California, the land of divorces and disjointed families, it seemed natural that a couple with children from previous marriages could come together. Attachments and annoyances develop, and even after the parents divorce, the children still have a relationship. Knightley (Josh) would still be close to his stepfather, and as in most families, Josh and Cher could fight, insult, and ultimately count on each other.

Harriet (Tai)—Harriet is the girl of low (illegitimate) birth whom Cher takes under her wing. Here's where things get tricky because this is America, land of equality and all. I didn't want Cher to consider herself better than someone with less wealth, but there had to be some sort of pecking order, some reason Harriet was on a lower rung socially so that Cher could feel like she was dispensing charity. So I changed illegitimacy to being from New York and having sex, drugs, and sloppy clothes.

Robert Martin (Travis)—Robert is a perfectly decent farmer who likes Harriet. High school isn't really divided up between landowners and farmers, but I needed the equivalent of a group, separate from Cher's crowd, that is looked down upon. Sadly, in high schools I observed that was often what they called the "FOBs" (Fresh Off the Boat, i.e., recent immigrants). Certainly nothing new there, but not how I wanted to present my fantasy world. Cher couldn't be racist, but she could have some attitude about the stoners. So Mr. Martin (Travis) became a pothead.

Mr. Elton (Elton)—In *Emma,* Mr. Elton is the rector, so he is in her crowd and has a high regard for himself. Instead of a rector, I made Elton's father a music executive so Elton could be needlessly stuck-up and consider himself too good for Harriet. After all, he could get backstage passes.

Frank Churchill (Christian)—When Emma meets Frank, she decides she'll be in love with him. She doesn't fall in love with him, but he's just too cute, too personable, and too right for her (on paper, at least). Her self-deception is so strong that it takes a long time for her to realize that: A) she doesn't love him, and B) he's unavailable. This presented another tricky problem: Frank is unavailable because he's secretly engaged to Jane Fairfax.

Jane Fairfax—Here is the one character that didn't work for me. Jane is a girl of "genteel poverty" and so Knightley thought her a better companion for Emma than Harriet (pesky low birth). This seemed snobby to me, and Jane Austen is usually the antithesis of snobbery. Of course, Knightley could be referring to Harriet's lack of intelligence (not her fault) or her flightiness, but Jane Fairfax is a bore. So out she went.

Then why would Frank (Christian) still be unavailable? I decided he should be gay. This way, we can easily see the extent of Cher's self-delusion. He seems so perfectly cast as her boyfriend, she can't see who he is.

I have one note on the style of the film, and here is one area where I have some beef with many of the Jane Austen films. The novels Jane

Austen wrote are classics, but that doesn't mean they should be interpreted in some sort of "classy" style. They don't require slow, swooping shots of idyllic landscapes. There is no mention in *Emma* of lush symphonic music heard as wind sweeps through the heather on the hill. The trees, clouds, and birds can do whatever they want. It's not about them, it's about the *people,* and the people in *Emma* are BUSY. The book has the pace of youth—sometimes headed the wrong way, but fast, restless, and exuberant.

And so the town of Highbury became Beverly Hills. A carriage became a car, a ball became a dance, and the village became the mall. Cher (Emma) realizes she can't control everyone's lives no matter how good her intentions are. Josh learns to lighten up as she learns to get a little more realistic. They have evolved into becoming right for each other, all by following what is laid out in the novel.

Jane Austen once called her writing, "the little bit (two inches wide) of ivory on which I work with so fine a brush, as produces little effect after much labour."

For myself, whenever I'm in a museum, I'll run past the oversize, epic pictures of gods and biblical figures or historical battles and make a beeline for the small, humanistic paintings of people in mundane places. There's a Vermeer of a young girl smiling too much at a soldier. His back is to us, but his pose is cocky. She's sitting at a table leaning slightly forward, the sunlight streaming through a window lights her face, but it also seems to glow from within because he's showing off for her. That is the same kind of genius we find in *Emma,* in the moments of everyday life—who likes whom, what they said, the sly hints, the looks, the phrases with hidden meaning . . . Sometimes the finest brushes paint the biggest truths.

David Lodge

READING AND REREADING *EMMA*

Jane Austen began work on *Emma* in January 1814 and completed the novel on March 29, 1815. In the meantime *Mansfield Park* had appeared and the edition was sold out in six months. Jane Austen's reputation was slowly growing, although her novels were published anonymously and she was known to the general public as "the author of *Pride and Prejudice.*" She received a message from the Prince Regent expressing his admiration and inviting the dedication of her next novel. Accordingly *Emma* appeared on December 29, 1815 (though the title page is dated 1816), dedicated to a man for whose personal character Jane Austen had scant respect. She was doubtless more gratified by a long and laudatory review of her novel in the influential *Quarterly Review,* written by no less a person than Sir Walter Scott. Since the review was unsigned, we do not know whether Jane Austen was aware that she had earned the praise of the most successful novelist of the day; but undoubtedly this review marked the peak of the modest fame she achieved in her own lifetime. She died a little more than a year later, with *Persuasion* written but not seen through the press. *Emma* was the last completely finished product of her maturity; and in the opinion of most modern judges it is, of all her novels, the one which most perfectly represents her genius.

If the reader is making his first acquaintance with *Emma,* let me urge him to read no further in this essay until he has finished Jane Austen's text. Of few novels can it be said with more justice that reading it and rereading it are quite different experiences. Probably the latter is more rewarding, but I should be sorry to deny anyone the pleasure of the former by "giving away" the story.

On first reading, *Emma* is a comedy of mysteries and puzzles (it is no coincidence that riddles, anagrams, and conundrums figure so prominently in the action) which challenge the reader's perspicacity quite as much as the heroine's. To be sure, put on our guard from the very first page against too close an identification with Emma's hopes and expectations, we may anticipate her realization of the true state of affairs—we may guess that Mr. Elton's attentions are directed not at Harriet but at herself long before his declaration; and we may suspect, before Emma is told, that there is some secret between Jane Fairfax and Frank Churchill. Indeed, one of the marks of Jane Austen's skill is that it does not matter, as regards the effectiveness of the narrative, at what point we anticipate Emma's discoveries, if at all: the book is protected against failure for any reader, however naïve, however sophisticated. But only an uncannily knowing reader could predict the fate of every character from the outset. On first reading we must to a large extent share the heroine's bafflement, curiosity, and suspense as to the course of events. When Frank Churchill facetiously announces to the company gathered on Box Hill, "I am ordered by Miss Woodhouse . . . to say, that she desires to know what you are all thinking of," he is in a sense stating what the novel, on first reading, is all about.

On second reading we do know what everybody is thinking of, and *Emma* becomes a comedy of ironies. From a position of privileged wisdom, we watch Emma entangle herself deeper and deeper in mistakes and misunderstandings, unwittingly preparing her own discomfiture and disappointment, while all the other characters are to some extent living in a similar world of illusion. Even Mr. Knightley does not escape unscathed, for we know that his legitimate disapproval of Emma's conduct derives some of its animus from unnecessary jealousy on Frank Churchill's account. The miracle is that the second reading does not cancel out the first, nor exhaust the interest of subsequent readings. As Reginald Farrer said:

> While twelve readings of *Pride and Prejudice* give you twelve periods of pleasure repeated, as many readings of *Emma* give you that pleasure, not repeated only, but squared and squared again with each perusal, till at every fresh reading you feel anew that you never understood anything like the widening sum of its delights.[1]

Thus while every sentence of description and dialogue reverberates with ironic significance on second reading, there is no passage which is not sufficiently interesting, amusing, and character-revealing to seem quite in place on first reading. Conversely, the ironic mode does not totally dominate the second reading because "our attention is so diversified by the thick web of linguistic nuance that we do not concentrate single-mindedly on the ironic results of the mystification."[2] We are unlikely to exhaust the subtleties of *Emma* even on a second reading, and we can never, therefore, assume a position of entirely detached superiority toward the heroine. Becoming aware at each rereading of what we "missed" before, we are compelled to acknowledge, like Emma herself, the fallibility of our human understanding. This is perhaps one reason why Jane Austen's prediction when she began *Emma*—"I am going to take a heroine whom no one but myself will much like"[3] has so often been falsified.

Of course, we must like Emma Woodhouse if the novel is to work; and of course Jane Austen's prediction was really a definition of the artistic problem she set herself: how to make us care for Emma in spite of her faults, but without glossing over those faults. Emma can be snobbish, cruel, selfish, and calculating in the field of personal relations—the way she exploits and manipulates poor Harriet in the matter of Robert Martin's suit is only one of many examples. Marvin Mudrick, indeed, argues that Emma never really loses these unpleasant qualities. He is skeptical about Emma's "reformation" and about the prospects of the marriage that rewards it.[4] But it is surely demonstrable that Emma really does change, for the better, and the title of the French translation of the novel, *La Nouvelle Emma,* was well chosen. One small but telling index of Emma's moral progress is her attitude to the Martin family, which shifts from crude snobbery ("The yeomanry are precisely the order of people with whom I feel I can have nothing to do") to an uneasy conflict between conscience and prejudice ("She would have given a good deal . . . to have had the Martins in a higher rank of life. They were so deserving, that a *little* higher should have been enough: but as it was, how could she have done otherwise?") to her final, sincere declaration: "It would be a great pleasure to know Robert Martin."

Emma does, then, learn from her mistakes; but this alone would not be enough to make her acceptable, from the outset, as a heroine. How does Jane Austen make us like her? First of all, by narrating the story very largely from her point of view. We see most of the action through

Emma's eyes and this naturally has the effect of making us identify with her interests and of mitigating the errors of her vision—since we *experience* those errors with her, and to some extent share them. Indeed, so powerful is the pull of sympathy exerted by this narrative method, that checks and balances have to be introduced in the form of discreet authorial comments and well-timed interventions from Mr. Knightley. Knightley is the nearest thing to a paragon of virtue in the novel, but Jane Austen has carefully prevented any *female* character from filling the same role and thus putting her heroine in the shade. Jane Fairfax is the only serious contender—indeed a more conventional lady novelist of the period would have made her the heroine; but the intrigue in which Jane is involved, as well as contributing to the mystery of the plot, conveniently makes her a passive and enigmatic, if not indeed a quite negative character. Mrs. Weston is a worthy woman, but since her story, in a sense, reaches its happy conclusion on the first page of the novel, she does not engage our interest very deeply. Beside the other women—the silly Harriet, the vulgar Mrs. Elton, the chattering Miss Bates, and all the other old women in the story (among whom Mr. Woodhouse should perhaps be counted)—Emma can only shine. And it must be acknowledged that Jane Austen has given her positive and attractive qualities. She is endlessly patient with her tiresome father. She has a cheerful and resilient temperament, and is not given to self-pity. And she is, quite simply, intelligent. She finishes her sentences (always a criterion of worth in Jane Austen); she has a fine sense of humor; her errors are the result not of stupidity, but of a quick mind that is not sufficiently extended by her limited and banal society, so that she is tempted to *invent* interest for herself. She is, to use her own word, "an imaginist." There is an interesting parallel to be drawn here between Emma and her creator, if we accept D. W. Harding's plausible suggestion that Jane Austen herself was as much provoked by her own milieu as attached to it, and that writing novels was a way of "finding some mode of existence for her critical attitudes."[5]

We misrepresent the novel if we suppose that the authorial voice is always judicially detached from Emma. There are many passages where the attitudes and verbal styles of the author and the character are so close that it is impossible to drive a wedge between them. Emma surely shares much of the credit for such witty lines as "Mr. Knightley seemed to be trying not to smile; and succeeded without difficulty, upon Mrs. Elton's beginning to talk to him." Or consider the scene where it is Emma's painful duty to explain to Harriet the misunderstanding about Mr. Elton's intentions. The artless pathos of the girl's response "really for the time convinced that Harriet was the superior creature of the two—and that to resemble Harriet would be more for her own welfare and happiness than all that genius or intelligence could do." The next paragraph continues:

> It was rather too late in the day to set about being simple-minded and ignorant; but she left her with every previous resolution confirmed of being humble and discreet, and repressing imagination all the rest of her life.

The dry candor of the first part of this sentence, checking the overemotional response, is deeply characteristic of Jane Austen; but again it is difficult to say whether this is an authorial observation or a wry reflection of Emma herself. The effect, anyway, is to confirm the solidarity of author and heroine in a commitment to *intelligent* virtue.

Some repression of Emma's imagination is necessary to this aim because there is a great moral difference between making literary fictions, as Jane Austen does, and imposing fictional patterns on real people, as Emma does. Furthermore, Emma's fictions are sentimental and self-indulgent, derived from inferior literary models: her fond belief that Harriet is of distinguished parentage, and that Jane Fairfax is amorously involved with Mr. Dixon, are good examples of this. When Emma finally achieves maturity and self-knowledge, and is rewarded by Knightley's declaration of love, the moment is marked by an emphatic rejection of sentimental romance:

> for as to any of that heroism of sentiment which might have prompted her to entreat him to transfer his affection from herself to Harriet, as infinitely the most worthy of the two—or even the more simple sublimity of resolving to refuse him at once and for ever, without vouchsafing any motive, because he could not marry them both, Emma had it not.

The ironic invocation of literary stereotypes is one of the ways by which Jane Austen reinforces the realism of her own fiction. "Realism" is a notoriously slippery word, but one that applies to *Emma* in almost any sense. Ian Watt, for instance, distinguishes between "realism of presentation" and "realism of assessment": qualities, exemplified by Richardson and Fielding respectively, which are in a sense mutually antagonistic, since the illusion of life discourages detached judgment and vice versa.[6] Yet *Emma* surely embraces and reconciles both these effects. It is rich in that faultless observation of motive and behavior and speech habits for which Jane Austen has always been justly admired, making her characters as interesting to us as are our own acquaintances, and in much the same way—simply as human beings. This illusion of life depends upon the events of the novel seeming to follow each other in a natural and casual sequence, yet we can see that they have also been carefully patterned to lead Emma through a series of errors and instructive recognitions. The small, close-knit society of Highbury makes it natural that there should be a good deal of mutual entertaining, but it also enables Jane Austen to bring her principal characters all together at various crucial moments—Mr. Weston's dinner party, the ball at the Crown, the expeditions to Donwell and Box Hill—where the illusions and deceptions of these human beings are subjected to intense social (and therefore highly dramatic) pressure. The rendering of so much of the action through Emma's eyes intensifies the realism of presentation, but the quiet authority of the author's voice guarantees realism of assessment. Perhaps we read *Emma* first mainly for the presentation, and subsequently mainly for the assessment, but, as I said earlier, one reading does not cancel out the other. Under analysis *Emma* reveals an amazing multiplicity of ends and means, all perfectly adjusted and harmonized.

Consider, for example, Jane Austen's handling of the most serious crisis in her heroine's history. At the nadir of Emma's fortunes, when she is stricken with guilt for having insulted Miss Bates and incurred Mr. Knightley's reproof, when she has discovered the truth about Jane Fairfax and Frank Churchill, with all its embarrassing reflections on her own conduct toward them, and when she has belatedly recognized her own love for Mr. Knightley but believes he is going to propose to Harriet, whose pretensions to such a match she has herself encouraged—at the point when all these circumstances converge to bring Emma's morale to its lowest ebb, we get this piece of description:

> The evening of this day was very long, and melancholy, at Hartfield. The weather added what it could of gloom. A cold stormy rain set in, and nothing of July appeared but in the trees and shrubs, which the wind was despoiling, and the length of the day, which only made such cruel sights the longer visible.

The passage was justly singled out for praise by R. W. Chapman,[7] but the "miracle of communication" is not, as he suggested, impossible to analyze. Jane Austen is, of course, exploiting the pathetic fallacy here—but so stealthily that we are not distracted from the reality of the moment by a conscious recognition of her artistry. This artistry does more than establish a general consonance between the heroine's mood and the weather. The words "the length of the day, which only made such cruel sights the longer visible" provide a delicately appropriate analogy for Emma's state of mind because the circumstances of her life, her very fixed social position in a small and inward-looking community (a fact frequently underlined in the course of the narrative), mean that she can expect no release from her disappointment and regret but is condemned to live with them indefinitely. Emma's situation, in short, can only make *such cruel sights* as Harriet's marriage to Mr. Knightley *the longer visible;* and this is stated explicitly a few lines later:

> The prospect before her now, was threatening to a degree that could not be entirely dispelled—that might not be even partially brightened. If all took place that might take place among the circle of her friends, Hartfield must be comparatively deserted; and she left to cheer her father with the spirits only of ruined happiness.

The words *prospect, threatening,* and *brightened* in this passage are drawn from the vocabulary of weather description and thus, together with the echo of the "despoiled" vegetation in "ruined happiness," link it to the earlier one. And the whole scene recalls to Emma the very first scene of the novel when, "the wedding over and the bride-people gone, her father and herself were left alone to dine together with no prospect of a third to cheer a long evening." On that occasion Mr. Knightley had provided an unexpected and welcome third; but there are several reasons why he cannot be looked for now.

To her credit, however, Emma does not collapse under the pressure of these distressing thoughts. The chapter ends:

> . . . the only source whence any thing like composure could be drawn, was in the resolution of her own better conduct, and the hope that, however inferior in spirit and gaiety might be the following and every winter of her life to the past, it would yet find her more rational, more acquainted with herself, and leave her less to regret when it were gone.

The pessimistic strain of seasonal imagery is sustained in "every winter of her life," which has the effect of making Emma's future appear as one long winter. But the importance of this passage is that it describes Emma's first really disinterested effort at moral reform, inasmuch as she hopes to gain nothing except self-respect from her good resolution. In fact, she is rewarded the very next day, of which we get this description at the beginning of the next chapter:

> The weather continued much the same all the following morning; and the same loneliness, and the same melancholy, seemed to reign at Hartfield—but in the afternoon it cleared; the wind changed into a softer quarter; and the clouds were carried off; the sun appeared; it was summer again. With all the eagerness which such a transition gives, Emma resolved to be out of doors as soon as possible.

Walking in the garden, Emma is joined by Mr. Knightley, who in due course makes his most welcome proposal. The change in the weather is thus a natural circumstance which brings the couple together, giving them the time and the privacy to disentangle their misconceptions and reach an understanding; but it is also effectively symbolic. "It was summer again." The restoration of weather appropriate to the season intimates the restoration of happiness to Emma, and of comedy to the novel.

Lionel Trilling

FROM "*EMMA* AND THE LEGEND OF JANE AUSTEN"

1

It is possible to say of Jane Austen, as perhaps we can say of no other writer, that the opinions which are held of her work are almost as interesting, and almost as important to think about, as the work itself. This statement, even with the qualifying "almost," ought to be, on its face, an illegitimate one. We all know that the reader should come to the writer with no preconceptions, taking no account of any previous opinion. But this, of course, he cannot do. Every established writer exists in the aura of his legend—the accumulated opinion that we cannot help being aware of, the image of his personality that has been derived, correctly or incorrectly, from what he has written. In the case of Jane Austen, the legend is of an unusually compelling kind. Her very name is a charged one. The homely quaintness of the Christian name, the cool elegance of the surname, seem inevitably to force upon us the awareness of her sex, her celibacy, and her social class. "Charlotte Brontë" rumbles like thunder and drowns out any such special considerations. But "Jane Austen" can by now scarcely fail to imply femininity, and, at that, femininity of a particular kind and in a particular social setting. It dismays many new readers that certain of her admirers call her Jane, others Miss Austen. Either appellation suggests an unusual, and questionable, relation with this writer, a relation that does not consort with the literary emotions we respect. The new reader perceives from the first that he is not to be permitted to proceed in simple literary innocence. Jane Austen is to be for him not only a writer but an issue. There are those who love her; there are those—no doubt they are fewer but they are no less passionate—who detest her; and the new reader understands that he is being solicited to a fierce partisanship, that he is required to make no mere literary judgment but a decision about his own character and personality, and about his relation to society and all of life.

And indeed the nature of the partisanship is most intensely personal and social. The matter at issue is: What kind of people like Jane Austen? What kind of people dislike her? Sooner or later the characterization is made or implied by one side or the other, and with extreme invidiousness. It was inevitable that there should arise a third body of opinion, which holds that it is not Jane Austen herself who is to be held responsible for the faults that are attributed to her by her detractors, but rather the people who admire her for the wrong reasons and in the wrong language and thus create a false image of her. As far back as 1905 Henry James was repelled by what a more recent critic, Professor Marvin Mudrick, calls "gentle-Janeism" and he spoke of it with great acerbity. James admired Jane Austen; his artistic affinity with her is clear, and he may be thought to have shared her social preferences and preoccupations. Yet James could say of her reputation that it had risen higher than her intrinsic interest warranted: the responsibility for this, he said, lay with "the body of publishers, editors, illustrators, producers of magazines, which have found their 'dear,' our dear, everybody's dear Jane so infinitely to their material purpose."[1] In our own day, Dr. Leavis's admiration for Jane Austen is matched in intensity by his impatience with her admirers. Mr. D. W. Harding in a well-known essay[2] has told us how the accepted form of admiration of Jane Austen kept him for a long time from reading her novels, and how he was able to be at ease with them only when he discovered that they were charged with scorn of the very people who set the common tone of admiration. And Professor Mudrick, in the preface to his book on Jane Austen,[3] speaks of the bulk of the criticism of her work as being "a mere mass of cozy family adulation, self-glorif[ication] . . . and nostalgic latterday enshrinements of the gentle-hearted chronicler of Regency order." It is the intention of Professor Mudrick's book to rescue Jane Austen from coziness and nostalgia by representing her as a writer who may be admired for her literary achievement, but who is not to be loved, and of whom it is to be said that certain deficiencies of temperament account for certain deficiencies of her literary practice.

The impatience with the common admiring view of Jane Austen is not hard to understand and sympathize with, the less so because (as Mr.

Harding and Professor Mudrick say) admiration seems to stimulate self-congratulation in those who give it, and to carry a reproof of the deficient sensitivity, reasonableness, and even courtesy, of those who withhold their praise. One may refuse to like almost any author and incur no other blame from his admirers than that of being wanting in taste in that one respect. But not to like Jane Austen is to put oneself under suspicion of a general personal inadequacy and even—let us face it—of a want of breeding.

This is absurd and distasteful. And yet we cannot deal with this unusual—this extravagantly personal—response to a writer simply in the way of condemnation. No doubt every myth of a literary person obscures something of the truth. But it may also express some part of the truth as well. If Jane Austen is carried outside the proper confines of literature, if she has been loved in a fashion that some temperaments must find objectionable and that a strict criticism must call illicit, the reason is perhaps to be found not only in the human weakness of her admirers, in their impulse to self-flattery, or in whatever other fault produces their deplorable tone. Perhaps a reason is also to be found in the work itself, in some unusual promise that it seems to make, in some hope that it holds out.

2

Of Jane Austen's six great novels *Emma* is surely the one that is most fully representative of its author. *Pride and Prejudice* is of course more popular. It is the one novel in the canon that "everybody" reads, the one that is most often reprinted. *Pride and Prejudice* deserves its popularity, but it is not a mere snobbery, an affected aversion from the general suffrage, that makes thoughtful readers of Jane Austen judge *Emma* to be the greater book—not the more delightful but the greater. It cannot boast the brilliant, unimpeded energy of *Pride and Prejudice,* but that is because the energy which it does indeed have is committed to dealing with a more resistant matter. In this it is characteristic of all three novels of Jane Austen's mature period, of which it is the second. *Persuasion,* the third and last, has a charm that is traditionally, and accurately, called "autumnal," and it is beyond question a beautiful book. But *Persuasion,* which was published posthumously and which may not have been revised to meet the author's full intention, does not have the richness and substantiality of *Emma.* As for *Mansfield Park,* the first work of the mature period, it quite matches *Emma* in point of substantiality, but it makes a special and disturbing case. Greatly admired in its own day—far more than *Emma*—*Mansfield Park* is now disliked by many readers who like everything else that Jane Austen wrote. They are repelled by its heroine and by all that she seems to imply of the author's moral and religious preferences at this moment of her life, for Fanny Price consciously devotes herself to virtue and piety, which she achieves by a willing submissiveness that goes against the modern grain. What is more, the author seems to be speaking out against wit and spiritedness (while not abating her ability to represent these qualities), and virtually in praise of dullness and acquiescence, and thus to be condemning her own peculiar talents. *Mansfield Park* is an extraordinary novel, and only Jane Austen could have achieved its profound and curious interest, but its moral tone is antipathetic to contemporary taste, and no essay I have ever written has met with so much resistance as the one in which I tried to say that it was not really a perverse and wicked book. But *Emma,* as richly complex as *Mansfield Park,* arouses no such antagonism, and the opinion that holds it to be the greatest of all Jane Austen's novels is, I believe, correct.

Professor Mudrick says that everyone has misunderstood *Emma,* and he may well be right, for *Emma* is a very difficult novel. We in our time are used to difficult books and like them. But *Emma* is more difficult than any of the hard books we admire. The difficulty of Proust arises from the sheer amount and complexity of his thought, the difficulty of Joyce from the brilliantly contrived devices of representation, the difficulty of Kafka from a combination of doctrine and mode of communication. With all, the difficulty is largely literal; it lessens in the degree that we attend closely to what the books say; after each sympathetic reading we are the less puzzled. But the difficulty of *Emma* is never overcome. We never know where to have it. If we finish it at night and think we know what it is up to, we wake the next morning to believe it is up to something quite else; it has become a different book. Reginald Farrer speaks at length of the difficulty of *Emma* and then goes on to compare its effect with that of *Pride and Prejudice.* "While twelve readings of *Pride and Prejudice* give you twelve periods of pleasure repeated, as many readings of *Emma* give you that pleasure, not repeated only, but squared and squared again with each perusal, till at every fresh reading you feel anew that you never understood anything like the widening sum of its delights."[4] This is so, and for the reason that none of the twelve readings permits us to flatter ourselves that we have fully understood what the novel is doing. The effect is extraordinary, perhaps unique. The book is like a person—not to be comprehended fully and finally by any other person. It is perhaps to the point that it is the only one of Jane Austen's novels that has for its title a person's name.

For most people who recognize the difficulty of the book, the trouble begins with Emma herself. Jane Austen was surely aware of what a complexity she was creating in Emma, and no doubt that is why she spoke of her as "a heroine whom no one will like except myself." Yet this puts it in a minimal way—the question of whether we will like or not like Emma does not encompass the actuality of the challenge her character offers. John Henry Newman stated the matter more accurately, and very charmingly, in a letter of 1837. He says that Emma is the most interesting of Jane Austen's heroines, and that he likes her. But what is striking in his remark is this sentence: "I feel kind to her whenever I think of her." This does indeed suggest the real question about Emma, whether or not we will find it in our hearts to be kind to her.

Inevitably we are attracted to her, we are drawn by her energy and style, and by the intelligence they generate. Here are some samples of her characteristic tone:

"Never mind, Harriet, I shall not be a poor old maid; it is poverty only which makes celibacy contemptible to a generous public!"

Emma was sorry; to have to pay civilities to a person she did not like through three long months!—to be always doing more than she wished and less than she ought!

"I do not know whether it ought to be so, but certainly silly things do cease to be silly if they are done by sensible people in an impudent way. Wickedness is always wickedness, but folly is not always folly."

"Oh! I always deserve the best treatment, because I never put up with any other . . ."

[On an occasion when Mr. Knightley comes to a dinner party in his carriage, as Emma thinks he should, and not on foot:] ". . . There is always a look of consciousness or bustle when people come in a way which they know to be beneath them. You think you carry it off very well, I dare say, but with you it is a sort of bravado, an air of affected unconcern; I always observe it whenever I meet you under these circumstances. *Now* you have nothing to try for. You are not afraid of being supposed ashamed. You are not striving to look taller than any body else. *Now* I shall really be happy to walk into the same room with you."

We cannot be slow to see what is the basis of this energy and style and intelligence. It is self-love. There is a great power of charm in self-love, although, to be sure, the charm is an ambiguous one. We resent it and resist it, yet we are drawn by it, if only it goes with a little grace or creative power. Nothing is easier to pardon than the mistakes and excesses of self-love: if we are quick to condemn them, we take pleasure in forgiving them. And with good reason, for they are the extravagance of the first of virtues, the most basic and biological of the virtues, that of self-preservation.

But we distinguish between our response to the self-love of men and the self-love of women. No woman could have won the forgiveness that has been so willingly given (after due condemnation) to the self-regard of, say, Yeats and Shaw. We understand self-love to be part of the moral life of all men; in men of genius we expect it to appear in unusual intensity and we take it to be an essential element of their power. The extraordinary thing about Emma is that she has a moral life as a man has a moral life. And she doesn't have it as a special instance, as an example of a new kind of woman, which is the way George Eliot's Dorothea Brooke has her moral life, but quite as a matter of course, as a given quality of her nature.

And perhaps that is what Jane Austen meant when she said that no one would like her heroine—and what Newman meant when he said that he felt kind to Emma whenever he thought of her. She needs kindness if she is to be accepted in all her exceptional actuality. Women in fiction only rarely have the peculiar reality of the moral life that self-love bestows. Most commonly they exist in a moonlike way, shining by the reflected moral light of men. They are "convincing" or "real" and sometimes "delightful," but they seldom exist as men exist—as genuine moral destinies. We do not take note of this; we are so used to the reflected quality that we do not observe it. It is only on the rare occasions when a female character like Emma confronts us that the difference makes us aware of the usual practice. Nor can we say that novels are deficient in realism when they present women as they do: it is the presumption of our society that women's moral life is not as men's. No change in the modern theory of the sexes, no advance in status that women have made, has yet contradicted this. The self-love that we do countenance in women is of a limited and passive kind, and we are troubled if it is as assertive as the self-love of men is permitted, and expected, to be. Not men alone, but women as well, insist on this limitation, imposing the requirement the more effectually because they are not conscious of it.

But there is Emma, given over to self-love, wholly aware of it and quite cherishing it. Mr. Knightley rebukes her for heedless conduct and says, "I leave you to your own reflections." And Emma wonderfully replies: "Can you trust me with such flatterers? Does my vain spirit ever tell me I am wrong?" She is "Emma, never loth to be first," loving preeminence and praise, loving power and frank to say so.

Inevitably we are drawn to Emma. But inevitably we hold her to be deeply at fault. Her self-love leads her to be a self-deceiver. She can be unkind. She is a dreadful snob.

Her snobbery is of the first importance in her character, and it is of a special sort. The worst instance of it is very carefully chosen to put her thoroughly in the wrong. We are on her side when she mocks Mrs. Elton's vulgarity, even though we feel that so young a woman (Emma is twenty) ought not set so much store by manners and tone—Mrs. Elton, with her everlasting barouche-landau and her "*caro sposo*" and her talk of her spiritual "resources," is herself a snob in the old sense of the word, which meant a vulgar person aspiring to an inappropriate social standing. But when Emma presumes to look down on the young farmer, Robert Martin, and undertakes to keep little Harriet Smith from marrying him, she makes a truly serious mistake, a mistake of nothing less than national import.

Here it is to be observed that *Emma* is a novel that is touched—lightly but indubitably—by national feeling. Perhaps this is the result of the Prince Regent's having expressed his admiration for *Mansfield Park* and his willingness to have the author dedicate her next book to him: it is a circumstance which allows us to suppose that Jane Austen thought of herself, at this point in her career, as having, by reason of the success of her art, a relation to the national ethic. At any rate, there appears in *Emma* a tendency to conceive of a specifically English ideal of life. Knightley speaks of Frank Churchill as falling short of the demands of this ideal: "No, Emma, your amiable young man can be amiable only in French, not in English. He may be very 'aimable,' have very good manners, and be very agreeable; but he can have no English delicacy towards the feelings of other people: nothing really amiable about him." Again, in a curiously impressive moment in the book, we are given a detailed description of the countryside as seen by the party at Donwell Abbey, and this comment follows: "It was a sweet view—sweet to the eye and the mind. English verdure, English culture [agriculture, of course, is meant], English comfort, seen under a sun bright without being oppressive." This is a larger consideration than the occasion would appear to require; there seems no reason to expect this vision of "England's green and pleasant land." Or none until we note that the description of the view closes thus: ". . . and at the bottom of this bank, favourably placed and sheltered, rose the Abbey-Mill Farm, with meadows in front, and the river making a close and handsome curve around it." Abbey-Mill Farm is the property of young Robert Martin, for whom Emma has expressed a principled social contempt, and the little burst of strong feeling has the effect, among others, of pointing up the extremity of Emma's mistake.

It is often said, sometimes by way of reproach, that Jane Austen took no account in her novels of the great political events of her lifetime, nor of the great social changes that were going on in England. "In Jane Austen's novels," says Arnold Hauser in his *Social History of Art,* "social reality was the soil in which characters were rooted but in no sense a problem which the novelist made any attempt to solve or interpret." The statement, true in some degree, goes too far. There is in *some* sense an interpretation of social problems in Jane Austen's contrivance of the situation of Emma and Robert Martin. The yeoman class had always held a strong position in English class feeling, and, at this time especially, only stupid or ignorant people felt privileged to look down upon it. Mr. Knightley, whose social position is one of the certainties of the book, as is his freedom from any trace of snobbery, speaks of young Martin, who is his friend, as a "gentleman farmer," and it is clear that he is on his way to being a gentleman pure and simple. And nothing was of greater importance to the English system at the time of the French Revolution than the relatively easy recruitment to the class of gentlemen. It made England unique among European nations. Here is Tocqueville's view of the matter as set forth in the course of his explanation of why England was not susceptible to revolution as France was:

It was not merely parliamentary government, freedom of speech, and the jury system that made England so different from the rest of contemporary Europe. There was something still more distinctive and more far-reaching in its effects. England was the only country in which the caste system had been totally abolished, not merely modified. Nobility and commoners joined forces in business enterprises, entered the same professions, and—what is still more significant—intermarried. The daughter of the greatest lord in the land could marry a "new" man without the least compunction . . .

Though this curious revolution (for such in fact it was) is hidden in the mists of time, we can detect traces of it in the English language. For several centuries the word "gentleman" has had in England a quite different application from what it had when it originated . . . A study of the connection between the history of language and history proper would certainly be revealing. Thus if we follow the mutation in time and place of the English word "gentleman" (a derivative of our *gentilhomme*), we find its connotation being steadily widened in England as the classes draw nearer to each other and intermingle. In each successive century we find it being applied to men a little lower in the social scale. Next, with the English, it crosses to America. And now in America, it is applicable to all male citizens, indiscriminately. Thus its history is the history of democracy itself.[5]

Emma's snobbery, then, is nothing less than a contravention of the best—and safest—tendency of English social life. And to make matters worse, it is a principled snobbery. "A young farmer . . . is the very last sort of person to raise my curiosity. The yeomanry are precisely the order of people with whom I feel that I can have nothing to do. A degree or two lower, and a creditable appearance might interest me; I might hope to be useful to their families in some way or other. But a farmer can need none of my help, and is therefore in one sense as much above my notice as in every other he is below it." This is carefully contrived by the author to seem as dreadful as possible; it quite staggers us, and some readers will even feel that the author goes too far in permitting Emma to make this speech.

Snobbery is the grossest fault that arises from Emma's self-love, but it is not the only fault. We must also take account of her capacity for unkindness. This can be impulsive and brutal, as in the witticism directed to Miss Bates at the picnic, which makes one of the most memorable scenes in the whole range of English fiction; or extended and systematic, as in her conspiracy with Frank Churchill to quiz Jane Fairfax. Then we know her to be a gossip, at least when she is tempted by Frank Churchill.

She finds pleasure in dominating and has no compunctions about taking over the rule of Harriet Smith's life. She has been accused, on the ground of her own estimate of herself, of a want of tenderness, and she has even been said to be without sexual responsiveness.

Why, then, should anyone be kind to Emma? There are several reasons, of which one is that we come into an unusual intimacy with her. We see her in all the elaborateness of her mistakes, in all the details of her wrong conduct. The narrative technique of the novel brings us very close to her and makes us aware of each misstep she will make. The relation that develops between ourselves and her becomes a strange one— it is the relation that exists between our ideal self and our ordinary fallible self. We become Emma's helpless conscience, her unavailing guide. Her fault is the classic one of hubris, excessive pride, and it yields the classic result of blindness, of an inability to interpret experience to the end of perceiving reality, and we are aware of each false step, each wrong conclusion, that she will make. Our hand goes out to hold her back and set her straight, and we are distressed that it cannot reach her.

There is an intimacy anterior to this. We come close to Emma because, in a strange way, she permits us to—even invites us to—by being close to herself. When we have said that her fault is hubris or self-love, we must make an immediate modification, for her self-love, though it involves her in self-deception, does not lead her to the ultimate self-deception—she believes she is clever, she insists she is right, but she never says she is good. A consciousness is always at work in her, a sense of what she ought to be and do. It is not an infallible sense, anything but that, yet she does not need us, or the author, or Mr. Knightley, to tell her, for example, that she is jealous of Jane Fairfax and acts badly to her; indeed, "she never saw [Jane Fairfax] without feeling that she had injured her." She is never offended—she never takes the high self-defensive line—when once her bad conduct is made apparent to her. Her sense of her superiority leads her to the "insufferable vanity" of believing "herself in the secret of everybody's feelings" and to the "unpardonable arrogance" of "proposing to arrange everybody's destiny," yet it is an innocent vanity and an innocent arrogance which, when frustrated and exposed, do not make her bitter but only ashamed. That is why, bad as her behavior may be, we are willing to be implicated in it. It has been thought that in the portrait of Emma there is "an air of confession," that Jane Austen was taking account of "something offensive" that she and others had observed in her own earlier manner and conduct, and whether or not this is so, it suggests the quality of intimacy which the author contrives that we shall feel with the heroine.

Then, when we try to explain our feeling of kindness to Emma, we ought to remember that many of her wrong judgments and actions are directed to a very engaging end, a very right purpose. She believes in her own distinction and vividness and she wants all around her to be distinguished and vivid. It is indeed unpardonable arrogance, as she comes to see, that she should undertake to arrange Harriet Smith's destiny, that she plans to "form" Harriet, making her, as it were, the mere material or stuff of a creative act. Yet the destiny is not meanly conceived, the act is meant to be truly creative—she wants Harriet to be a distinguished and not a commonplace person, she wants nothing to be commonplace, she requires of life that it be well shaped and impressive, and alive. It is out of her insistence that the members of the picnic shall cease being dull and begin to be witty that there comes her famous insult to Miss Bates. Her requirement that life be vivid is too often expressed in terms of social deportment—she sometimes talks like a governess or a dowager—but it is, in its essence, a poet's demand.

She herself says that she lacks tenderness, although she makes the self-accusation in her odd belief that Harriet possesses this quality; Harriet is soft and "feminine," but she is not tender. Professor Mudrick associates the deficiency with Emma's being not susceptible to men. This is perhaps so; but if it is, there may be found in her apparent sexual coolness something that is impressive and right. She makes great play about the feelings and about the fineness of the feelings that one ought to have; she sets great store by literature (although she does not read the books she prescribes for herself) and makes it a condemnation of Robert Martin that he does not read novels. Yet although, like Don Quixote and Emma Bovary, her mind is shaped and deceived by fiction, she is remarkable for the actuality and truth of her sexual feelings. Inevitably she expects that Frank Churchill will fall in love with her and she with him, but others are more deceived in the outcome of this expectation than she is—it takes but little time for her to see that she does not really respond to Churchill, that her feeling for him is no more than the lively notice that an attractive and vivacious girl takes of an attractive and vivacious young man. Sentimental sexuality is not part of her nature, however much she feels it ought to be part of Harriet Smith's nature. When the right time comes, she chooses her husband wisely and seriously and eagerly.

There is, then, sufficient reason to be kind to Emma, and perhaps for nothing so much as the hope she expresses when she begins to understand her mistakes, that she will become "more acquainted with herself." And, indeed, all through the novel she has sought better acquaintance with herself, not wisely, not adequately, but assiduously. How modern a quest it is, and how thoroughly it confirms Dr. Leavis's judgment that Jane Austen is the first truly modern novelist of England. "In art," a critic has said, "the decision to be revolutionary usually counts for very little. The most radical changes have come from personalities who were conservative and even conventional . . ."[6] Jane Austen, conservative and even conventional as she was, perceived the nature of the deep psychological change which accompanied the establishment of democratic society—she was aware of the increase of the psychological burden of the individual, she understood the new necessity of conscious self-definition and self-criticism, the need to make private judgments of reality.[7] And there is no reality about which the modern person is more uncertain and more anxious than the reality of himself.

Eva Brann

THE PERFECTIONS OF JANE AUSTEN

1.

Jane Austen wrote a perfect number of perfect novels. In the probable order of her last attention to them these six are: *Northanger Abbey, Sense and Sensibility, Pride and Prejudice, Mansfield Park, Emma,* and *Persuasion.* Their perfection, which I shall treat as a given, presents at once an invitation and a difficulty. Devoted novel readers know that their attention is ever divided between the tale and their delight in its telling. And so, while reading, I find myself continually forming the question: Just what is so wonderful here? What *is* the essence of this perfection? But here arises the difficulty: it appears to be the nature of perfect works that they have no crevices by which to force an entry. Ordinarily in dealing with an ostensibly truth-telling text we bustle into it, we expound, expose, penetrate to something carefully secreted, decently hidden, unintended, or false. I wonder whether such burrowing is ever quite in harmony with the author's hopes, except perhaps in the case of the Platonic dialogues. At any rate, confronted with these novels and ashamed to force unseemly entries, I am driven to the thought that their kind of perfection is impenetrable and has no obscure depth; that it presents a smooth, continuous plane, which is not a surface because it has no hidden center. These works repel interpretative assault, whether it is attempted through a long siege of cyclical reading or in a straight dash through the six. And yet there is no escaping the insistent desire to lay hold of the essence of those novels, a desire that is really the wish to capture and fix their pleasure by an adequate reflection on its cause. But since a penetration of the novels seems to be a doomed undertaking—their essence apparently being that they have none—I thought I might satisfy myself by attempting merely to articulate and itemize the various perfections and felicities that make the novels what they are.

2.

Let me, then, go on to the enumeration of Jane Austen's perfections. It will include some items concerned with her matter and others with her form, and cutting across this distinction, some items dealing with what she is given and others with what she herself makes.

It is, of course, this very harmonious fitting of setting and talent, matter and form, that distinguishes her novels. The felicity of the fit is displayed in the fact that her romances are neither purely "conventional" nor purely "unconventional." The distinction is irrelevant, for it fails to take into account her characteristic attitude of detached tolerance.

3.

The first of my articulable felicities is the circumstance that there is one and only one outcome for all the novels—marriage. Not that courtship and marriage are the theme of the novels; properly speaking, they do not have "themes," since they are not about notions but about people, albeit people with dominant and distinctive character traits. Of the three novels whose titles might appear to show otherwise, one, *Pride and Prejudice,* was an irresistible phrase borrowed from Jane Austen's predecessor, Fanny Burney; the second, *Sense and Sensibility,* was originally named after the heroines, "Elinor and Marianne," and *Persuasion* was named posthumously by her brother.

What I mean is rather that each novel in fact ends in one, two, or three marriages, not to speak of the under-heroines' alliances which occur on the way, or those catastrophic counterparts of legitimate unions, forced marriages after elopement.

The singleness of story is a source of perfection first because it excludes all exotic scenes or violent action. Instead it fixes our interest on the course, in all its subtle possibilities, of a small but essential part of human affairs—on the settling of a woman for life. It stands to reason that the perfection of subtlety requires a standard plot concerning an unspectacular but crucial human event.

A second happy aspect of this choice of matter is that under Jane

Austen's management it causes every novel to end happily. For example, here is the ending of *Emma;* Mrs. Elton, an ill-disposed commentator, begins:

> 'Very little white satin, very few lace veils; a most pitiful busi-
> ness! . . . '—But in spite of these deficiencies, the wishes, the hopes, the
> confidences, the predictions of the small band of true friends who wit-
> nessed the ceremony, were fully answered in the perfect happiness of
> the union.

Jane Austen never, except in fun, entertained the romantic notion that the pleasure of the reader or the gravity of the novel could be increased by providing a spuriously disastrous conclusion, such as Charlotte Brontë gave her novel *Villette.* That otherwise wonderful work ends with a doom-laden paragraph strongly suggesting that Lucy Snowe's husband-to-be is lost at sea, leaving her with the chilly consolation of a prospering girls' school. Jane Austen, on the other hand, knows what the angels know—that happiness is more worthy of note than unhappiness. And since she has it in her novelist's power to make a second world, she chooses, with golden rationality, to make it a happy world, and, with sparkling invention, an absorbing one. Of course, she presupposes a sensible reader—I mean one who knows enough of happiness to prefer it to other states.

4.

But there is also a more strictly novelistic, I hesitate to say, compositional, reason for her choice of this one universal ending.

All the novels are essentially about young women. The youngest heroine, Fanny Price of *Mansfield Park,* comes on the scene when she is ten, though she does not stay ten for long, since, as Jane Austen observed in a letter, "One does not care for girls till they are grown up." The oldest is Anne Elliot of *Persuasion,* who passes from a faded twenty-seven to a blooming, engaged twenty-eight in the course of the novel. Except for Emma, whose whole behavior marks her as having no sibling, all the women bear themselves very much as sisters—their characters are formed by and displayed in sisterly affection. These young women develop an attachment to a man; it is reciprocated. Internal and external difficulties intervene; there is demonstrative or silent suffering fully reported, the former with somewhat checked sympathy, the latter with warm admiration. (It should be noted here that this authoress never pretends to describe the inner life of the men as she does that of her women.) Then, shortly before the close of the story, the young woman briefly vanishes, usually into the spacious seclusion of a shrubbery or a promenade. For crucial declarations are made and received in privacy, and though the woman's response is shaped by her breeding, it is not a part of social intercourse. Her answer is therefore at most reported indirectly, as in *Emma:*

> What did she say? Just what she ought, of course. A lady always does. She said enough to show there need not be despair—and to invite him to say more himself.

Consequently, in an opus entirely about the coming together of women with men, no one ever quite enunciates the words "I love you."

The engagement is announced, loose ends are tied up, the union is brought about, and with a prognostication of their future happiness, explicitly including the continuation of the sisterly bond, the heroines are finally dismissed from view.

This pattern follows from the facts of life, as well as from the demands of fiction. The getting or forgoing of a husband is the great hazard in a woman's life, the greatest occasion for an exercise of sensibility and an exertion of sense. The early twenties, the very period in life, according to Jane Austen, "for the strongest attachments to be formed," therefore contain the moment when she is most alive—when she most has the principle of motion within herself.

That is by no means to say that life is over when the era of courtship ends—a very unlikely view for an unmarried woman who regarded the single woman's "dreadful propensity for being poor" as among the strongest arguments for matrimony, and who allows her Emma this rejoinder to a young friend who exclaims,

> '. . . you will be an old maid, and that's so dreadful!'
> 'Never mind, Harriet, I shall not be a poor old maid, and it is poverty only which makes celibacy contemptible to a generous public!'

On the contrary, the busy tranquillity and solid comfort that constitute continuous happiness begin exactly when a woman is settled, one way or another, for life. There are in the novels numerous satisfying descriptions of sedate marital existences and comfortably confirmed spinsterhoods. Later life has lost just one property, which is cleanly described in a letter Jane Austen wrote to Fanny Knight:

> Ah! What a loss it will be when you are married. You are too agreeable in your single state, too agreeable as a Neice. I shall hate you when your delicious play of mind is all settled down into conjugal and maternal affections.

What is lost is the *liveliness,* the inner motion of the girl. "Marriage is a great improver," Jane Austen drily observes in a letter, because it fixes the feelings and makes fast the character.

Now a person whose inner motion has been damped, who displays a settled mind and steady sentiments, is a comic character, in the six novels, and in life. The young heroines are sometimes themselves witty, and often provoke an affectionate smile, but they are not comic, while all the old married couples and spinsters are, for all their virtues, or even because of them, comic—I mean, comical. What makes them so is that they are quite literally, "creatures of habit." For their nature is not so much a spring of fresh life as a source of self-reproduction. (A view of the comic as a "mechanical inelasticity" and "fundamental absentmindedness" of the living soul, which almost fits the case, is to be found in Henri Bergson's essay "Laughter.") They (I could say "we") seem to mimic their own settled selves; all their activity has turned into "behavior," a kind of deliciously petrified self-expression. They have practiced being themselves so long that it comes by habit. They live through a recognizable ritual which feeds the human delight in identifying images. By so escaping their own notice such beings particularly invite fascinated observation; their well-bred absurdities embellish the world like elegant arabesques.

A prime example of this mode of being is found in the most happily married of all the married couples, Admiral and Mrs. Croft in *Persuasion.* They are out driving their gig, comfortably conversing the while, and such is the old sailor's handling of the craft that Mrs. Croft has to intervene:

> "My dear admiral, that post!—we shall certainly take that post!"
> But by coolly giving the reins a better direction herself, they happily

passed the danger; and by once afterwards judiciously putting out her hand, they neither fell into a rut, nor ran foul of a dung-cart; and Anne, with some amusement at their style of driving, which she imagined no bad representation of the general guidance of their affairs, found herself safely deposited by them at the cottage.

The happy consequence, then, of the arrangement by which the heroines pass out of view with marriage, is that each novel has a foreground of liveliness against a background of life; each novel contains two perfectly perspicuous kinds of imitation, one of living character and the other of completed "characters." However, it should be noted that these "characters" too have a dignity, which derives from the intimations we are given that their lives have roots and ramifications not properly included in a novel.

5.

Nothing can be clearer than this—the novels are themselves imitations of life and contain imitations of human beings, especially of human beings in society, conversing. No symbols, metaphors, mere patterns, or levels of abstraction are to be found in them. Certainly there are revelations, correspondences, significances. But nothing is ever there for mere form's sake or to suggest or stand for something else—which is why the novels so repel literary criticism.

6.

Jane Austen imitates a moral world—a world to whose conduct and virtue, manners and morals, she and her sister and her family and her neighborhood were bred. We must be grateful to it for being a dignified and shapely world, whose favorite epithets convey a sense of clarity concerning what is worthy and unworthy—a world in which the words "comfort" and "consequence" and "connections," in all their sedate rationality, have a clear reference; where a well-considered outing is termed an "eligible scheme"; where considerate people act "upon a system"; a quiet evening spent in talk is "conversible"; and "the rational pleasures of an elegant society" are highly valued. Although the novels are devoid of even the slightest didactic taint, they do teach—if nothing else, the shape and ways of one integral world.

To keep this world plausible she exercises her most admirable restraints. She admits nothing very vicious and nothing very violent, for most novel reader's lives are not directly determined by such things, whatever hyperbolic spirits may claim. Her unpublished and unfinished works are, to be sure, significantly more pungent than those she released. Her very early sketches contain burlesque murders, the heroine of a short later novel which she withheld from publication, Lady Susan, is unprincipled, hypocritical, scheming, crude, and cruel, and the fragmentary novel *The Watsons* may have remained so precisely because it promised to become too sordid. But the published works deal only with domesticated vices and with venial sins whose punishment is simply exile from her world—witness the beginning of the last chapter in *Mansfield Park*:

> Let other pens dwell on guilt and misery. I quit such odious subjects as soon as I can, impatient to restore everybody, not greatly at fault themselves, to tolerable comfort, and to have done with the rest.

Nonetheless, within her scope, there is clear wrong as well as right, and a diction to match—lucidly determined in condemning and sweetly reasonable in condoning. And since it is the most universal and necessary of social activities to pass judgment on others, they are all disapproved or approved. Indeed, she thinks too much of her characters not to judge their actions as she would her own. She never withholds judgment since she knows firmly what romantic ironists later obscured: that in fiction vices not condemned are celebrated. But it should be said that she always assigns to her people some saving graces, and, more important, some saving flaws—for she writes to her niece: ". . . pictures of perfection, as you know, make me sick and wicked."

7.

Now the chief flaws of manner, disposition, and principle that she admits are reserve (that is, a mean lack of openness), ill-breeding, love of change and restlessness (said to be the consequence of vanity and extravagance) and its attendant irregularity of life, coldheartedness, inconsiderateness, indelicacy, and finally, irrationality.

The virtues are of course everything opposite. For them there is a vocabulary of excellence which for my part I find wins my deepest accord. It contains terms like "integrity" and "candor" (meaning a well-disposed receptivity) and clusters like "goodnatured, useful, considerate, or benevolent." It expects that a woman know how to govern her feelings and be "acquainted with herself" (that is, that she have self-control and self-knowledge), and first and last, that she be "rational," that is, willing to act in accord with her principles. In sum, it requires her to be at once "amiable" and "well-principled," terms that in conjunction curiously well describe the womanly English equivalent of the Greek *kalos kagathos,* the generous and upright man.

"Amiable," which is in *Emma* contrasted with French "*aimable,*" agreeable, is defined there as an "English delicacy towards the feelings of other people," uncondescending graciousness. As for principles, "active principles"—these are the common maxims of moral action, and not in need of articulation, certainly not in a novel, which is no place for an inquiry into virtue. There are moments, as in the following passage from *Mansfield Park,* when Jane Austen comes close to enunciating them, only to glide away after all:

> Henry Crawford had too much sense not to feel the worth of good principles in a wife, though he was too little accustomed to serious reflection to know them by their proper name, but when he talked of her as having such a steadiness and regularity of conduct, such a high notion of honor, and such an observance of decorum as might warrant any man in the fullest dependence on her faith and integrity, he expressed what was inspired by the knowledge of her being well-principled and religious.

The ladies and gentlemen of her novels do not *reflect* on principles within them, and neither does she. Nonetheless, although unarticulated, they are the basis of all active excellence.

8.

Jane Austen's world is as merry as it is good. All the novels are perfect comedies—mirthful throughout and happy in outcome. Despite their brightness and lightness these novels are in no way trivial—they are simply not concerned with those terrific follies presented to the scourge of public laughter in classical comic drama.

Her humor has none of the hell-bent strenuousness of Sterne's (whose books she knew). He, it seems to me, tries to tickle his reader with a club, so that after a while it becomes hard even to manage a grin, but she usually elicits what she calls for, be it smile, chuckle, or loud laughter—on the seventh reading as on the first.

A pleasant way, and the least foolish, to approach this perfection of hers is simply to give examples of some of the fun she can think up.

Sometimes it is dignified nonsense, like the axiomatic beginning of *Pride and Prejudice:*

> It is a truth universally acknowledged, that a single man in possession of a good fortune, must be in want of a wife.

Sometimes it is an evanescently devastating stroke, like the observation made of that insufferable philistine Mr. Elton in *Emma:*

> He had caught both substance and shadow—both fortune and affection, and was just the happy man he ought to be . . .

Each novel also has its own pervasive humorous mode. The juvenile works of her middle teens are spirited and distinctly ungenteel burlesques, whose heroines introduce themselves by reporting that their "Mother was the natural Daughter of a Scotch peer by an Italian opera-girl," and who perish from having performed too many fainting spells on the wet grass, or coolly begin letters as follows:

> I murdered my father at a very early period of my life, I have since murdered my mother and I am now going to murder my sister.

The prevailing mode of her first published novel, on the other hand, is epigrammatic, chiefly because two of its people, Elizabeth Bennet and her father, are themselves witty. For instance, Elizabeth drily observes concerning the great commotion in the Collins household caused by a visit of their noble patroness:

> And is that all? . . . I expected at least that the pigs were got into the garden, and here it is nothing but Lady Catherine and her daughter.

Or she formulates this diagnostic test: "Is not general incivility the very essence of love?"

I have often wondered why *Mansfield Park* makes me continually smile, although its two young people are so very good and are allowed to prose on and on about it. Edmund only too truly observes of himself that:

> "You need not hurry when the object is only to prevent my saying a bon-mot, for there is not the least wit in my nature. I am a very matter-of-fact, plain spoken being, and may blunder on the borders of a repartee for half an hour together without striking it out."
>
> A general silence succeeded.

While Fanny, by way of spirit, at most manages a gentle line of poetry or an exclamation like: " 'The evergreen! How beautiful, how welcome, how wonderful the evergreen!' " Fanny is, as Edmund says, "of all human creatures the one over whom habit had most power . . ." But that is just it, the clue to the humor: the future Reverend and Mrs. Bertram are incipient comic figures; they are the elderly comic background of another novel in the making.

Emma, finally, is a comedy of errors: Emma is mistaken about Mr. Elton, Mr. Knightley, Harriet Smith, Jane Fairfax, and Frank Churchill, while Frank Churchill, Elton, Knightley, and Harriet Smith are mistaken about Emma. Mr. and Mrs. Weston are mistaken about Frank Churchill and Emma, and Harriet Smith is mistaken about Mr. Knightley and Jane Fairfax, while Miss Bates and Mr. Woodhouse live in a gentle fog of general misapprehension.

The light and unstrained effect of all her humor has everything to do with its being not a laborious construction but an immediate way of seeing the world: she simply lets her people be. Her moving principle is not a detached ironical motor, but a spring of disinterested love, or better, acute fondness, for her world. I would say that it is to the theatre of appearance what theory is to the world of being.

9.

Most felicitous of her perfections is her knowledge of the human heart.

The novel most fragrant with feeling is her last, *Persuasion.* The heroine, Anne Elliot, is, to begin with, walking proof of Jane Austen's dictum concerning losses in love:

> . . . it is no creed of mine, you must be well aware, that such sort of Disappointments kill anybody.

Persuasion is the novel in which the greatest things are most frankly at stake. When Anne finally holds in her hands a letter from Captain Wentworth, the man whom she had eight years before dutifully refused, yielding to the well-meant but narrow-minded persuasions of Lady Russell, she feels that "On the contents of that letter depended all which this world could do for her." The impression that this story is in earnest as no other is aided by a peculiar device, the presence of real dates, which occur in this work alone. Anne was born on August 9, 1787, and is a faded twenty-seven at the time the novel takes place, about 1814. The wars of those years are the tense, invisible, remote backdrop beyond the story. But the immediate setting within which Anne subdues and nurses her long-carried feeling is a delicious swirl of crosscurrents: shamefaced desire for establishment, natural preference derailed by envy, interfering ambition thwarted with counter-designs. Quietly, amid these comic machinations, Anne passes through the stations of her love: a walk in the company of the irreconciled Wentworth, when "Her pleasure . . . must arise from the exercise and the day"; a shy but articulate disquisition on the intensification of feeling resulting from the confinement of a woman's life; the agitations of the day of mutual understanding; and finally—the most quietly rhapsodic description of "high-wrought felicity" I know of—that evening party and its undercurrent of secret bliss, where Anne moves about in "delicious consciousness" making conversation with her friends,

> and with Captain Wentworth, come moments of communication continually occurring, and always the hope of more, and always the knowledge of his being there.

10.

Having articulated as well as I am able the perfections that belong to Jane Austen's novels I need probably add nothing concerning the mere delight that comes from reading them—especially aloud among friends, as was the habit of the Austen household. But there is something more to be said about their peculiar efficacy.

Novels are started for many reasons: to fulfill a promise to an enthusiastic friend, to get on with the project of having read everything, to abide a while in pleasurable passivity. But they are generally finished because they become absorbing. The question is whether this absorption is good for the soul. Jane Austen herself mounts a comic defense of any novel written with "genius, wit and taste" in *Northanger Abbey:*

> . . . I will not adopt that ungenerous and impolitic custom so common with novel writers of degrading by their contemptuous censure the very performances to the number of which they are themselves adding— joining with their greatest enemies in bestowing the harshest epithets on such works, and scarcely ever permitting them to be read by their own heroine, who if she accidentally take up a novel, is sure to turn over its insipid pages with disgust . . .

Yet I think there is also a serious apology to be proposed for these six novels, and for these alone. I am anxious to make it because I have myself experienced an efficacy of theirs often attested to in literature: their ability to re-collect the soul whenever it finds itself in places diffuse, dreary, enormous, or savage.

In the *Republic,* Socrates speaks of "a certain ancient quarrel between philosophy and poetry," in which philosophy can be said to charge fiction makers with a double crime: first the shameless fabrication of images which insidiously obstruct the search for being, and then the reckless vivification of these shades by means of a lurid singularity—so that the more brilliant the fiction, the greater the blame. Jane Austen sidesteps the first charge by being so candidly imitative and yet so careful to refrain from touching the last things as to offer not the least impediment to philosophy, while she meets the second by conforming all her fictions to a serenely normal pattern—she never even invents an authoress. The wonder is that figures so carefully middling in stature are nonetheless so absorbing: Sir Walter Scott caught the essence of her excellence when he observed that she "renders ordinary, commonplace things and characters interesting from the truth of the description and the sentiment."

But if Jane Austen's prosaic poetry is neither false nor egregious and her six novels give delight and hurt not, then that "ancient quarrel" is here for once composed, and these fictions, at least, can be loved rationally.

11.

In conclusion, let me once more reckon up the perfections and felicities that invite this rational love.

Jane Austen's novels celebrate that middling class of mankind to which it is, after all, most feasible and most fitting to belong. They reform the dispersed soul and inculcate respect for the concealed heart. They afford the example of a correct and uncorrupted tongue, and they encourage us to know ourselves and to judge others rightly.

They recall to us the possibility of an integral and well-formed world by presenting a straight imitation of English country society, sifted and spruced up, to be sure, but unsullied by imported significance. This copy, the product of a coolly loving contemplation, is made not for penetration but for observation. Its foreground is peopled, while in the background finished humankind carries on its unconscious comedy. And the whole breathes a serene hilarity whose source is the reason and the faith of the authoress.

Perfection, they say, repels love, which is incited rather by flaws. But Jane Austen's six perfect novels say otherwise. For what draws me to reread them cyclically but their peculiar mystery—the captivating enigma of lovable perfection?

Donald Greene

FROM "THE MYTH OF LIMITATION"

I

There is no difficulty in finding material for a study of the charge of "limitation" against Jane Austen. It is the one steady landmark in the swirling waters of Jane Austen criticism, the security blanket to which the critic who is vaguely aware of her greatness but doesn't quite know why, or the critic who can't see what all the shouting is about, desperately clings. There seems little point in attempting a systematic history of the use of this shibboleth—almost everyone who writes on her (there are a very few distinguished exceptions)[1] displays a compulsive need to make use of that blessed word sooner or later, usually sooner.

So for my texts I have merely pulled down at random a few well-known books on the novel. Arnold Kettle writes,

> The silliest of all criticisms of Jane Austen is the one which blames her for not writing about the Battle of Waterloo and the French Revolution. She wrote about what she understood and no artist can do more. But did she understand enough? . . . The limitation and the narrowness of the Hartfield world is the limitation of class society . . . The values and standards of the Hartfield world are based on the assumption that it is right and proper for a minority of the community to live at the expense of the majority . . . Now this charge, that the value of *Emma* is seriously limited by the class basis of Jane Austen's standards, cannot be ignored or written off as a non-literary issue. If the basic interest of the novel is indeed a moral interest, then it can scarcely be considered irrelevant to

face the question that the standards we are called upon to admire may be inseparably linked with a particular form of social organization.[2]

This expression of the popular "class limitation" variety of the charge immediately brings a number of questions to the mind. The implication seems to be that a novel about the Battle of Waterloo or the French Revolution is ipso facto a better novel than one about Hartfield—surely a dubious assumption. And this in turn raises the basic question of just what the function of the novel is, a question to which we shall later return. Anyway, how do we know that Jane Austen did not understand the French Revolution and the Napoleonic War—she lost a relation to the guillotine in the first and had two brothers on active service for many years in the second—as well as Tolstoy, say, who was not born until they were over, or as Arnold Kettle? Indeed, how many even of specialist historians of those events would have the chutzpah to say that they fully "understood" them? And if one of them did so believe, would he not be better occupied in incorporating his understanding in a history than in a novel? In how many ages and regions of the world has there *not* been a "class society"? Are the works of Homer and Sophocles and Shakespeare similarly vitiated by the limitation that they lived in and wrote about one? Did, in fact, the minority of the Hartfield—rather, Highbury—community live at the expense of the majority? Mr. Knightley, like Mr. Darcy and Sir Thomas Bertram in other novels, owned a considerable estate and no doubt spent much of his time managing it—"improving it," as the title of a recent book on Jane Austen puts it[3]—supervising his tenants, farm laborers, and so on, and as a consequence lived in greater material comfort than they. But one understands that even in Soviet Russia commissars have substantially more perquisites and privileges than the workmen they supervise, in recognition of their administrative skills.

Anyway, how does the fact that Jane Austen depicts in her novels the "class society" that she lived in demonstrate the "class basis" of her "standards" or that she calls on us to admire the standards of that society? I would maintain, on the contrary, that her standards, her moral values, have no class basis whatever. She values honesty, decency, clear-sightedness, emotional responsiveness in whatever class they occur: her most contemptible characters—Lady Catherine de Bourgh, Sir Walter Elliot, General Tilney—are often the highest in the scale of wealth and social prestige.

Another variety of the charge of limitation is presented by Lionel Stevenson. "The absence of passion is a graver limitation, since the dominant theme of all her novels is love. She is so suspicious of emotion that when a scene of strong feeling is imperative she tries to avoid narrating it . . . Of the sixteen kisses mentioned in the novels, not one is exchanged by a pair of lovers. Her heroines are so sensible and self-controlled that even in their secret thoughts they do not allow sex to intrude."[4] Stevenson's statistical assiduity is to be admired. One wishes he had gone on to count the number of explicit descriptions of kisses of passion between hero and heroine in the works of those robust, uninhibited male novelists, Scott, Dickens, and Thackeray. Offhand, I can't recollect a single one—perhaps the occasional chaste brushing of the lips against the cheek or forehead of an Agnes or Amelia. And how does Stevenson know what went on in the secret thoughts of Jane Austen's heroines—or for that matter Shakespeare's Rosalind, Portia, or Beatrice? She leaves us in no doubt as to what went on in the secret thoughts of some other women characters, thoughts that were fully acted out by Lydia Bennet, Maria Rushworth, Mrs. Clay, for instance—thoughts in which sex very clearly "intruded."

Stevenson seems to be using the terms *passion* and *emotion* and *feeling* in a highly technical—indeed, "limited"—sense, the sense they began to acquire about the time of Elinor Glyn, who initiated the practice of titillating the prurience of the mass readership of bestsellers by fairly explicit accounts of sexual intercourse; and who will argue that the novel has improved as a result of this development? What an incredible thing to say, after all, that Jane Austen avoids narrating "scenes of strong feeling"! Can Stevenson never have read Chapter 34 of *Pride and Prejudice* or Chapter 46 of *Sense and Sensibility* or Chapter 43 of *Emma*? By any normal use of the term Elizabeth Bennet is a passionate person; so is Darcy; and Jane Austen so deftly presents their personalities that—in case anyone is still worrying about this matter—she leaves me, at any rate, in no doubt that after their marriage they had quite as good a time in bed as Lydia and Wickham; probably better, for, by comparison with Darcy, Wickham is a pretty cold fish.

And Dorothy Van Ghent sums it up in omnibus fashion: "It is the frequent response of readers who are making their first acquaintance with Jane Austen that her subject matter is itself so limited—limited to the manners of a small section of English country gentry, who apparently never have been worried about death or sex, hunger or war, guilt or God—that it can offer no contiguity with modern interests. This is a very real difficulty in an approach to an Austen novel, and we should not obscure it."[5] I began thinking over this list of the six ingredients Professor Van Ghent felt it necessary for a novel to contain in order for it to provide "contiguity"—a nice euphemism for "relevance"—"with modern interests": death, sex, hunger, war, guilt, God. When I cast around in my memory for a modern novel that would eminently qualify, the first that came to my mind was, for some reason, James Jones's *From Here to Eternity,* now so thoroughly forgotten, though it is only a little over twenty years ago that it was the great bestseller of the time and the great movie a little later. It had death; it had sadism; it had hunger—at least it contained large chunks of "social consciousness," which I suppose is what is meant. It had sex—how thrilled we all were at the daring of the famous copulation scene on the Hawaiian beach! It had war—the attack on Pearl Harbor, no less. Indeed it combined the last two ingredients in a short sentence of priceless felicity, to which Jane Austen could never have hoped to aspire: "Pearl Harbor made a queasiness in the testicles." To be sure, the characters in Jones's book are not much more worried about God than were the English country gentry of the late eighteenth century. But then the number of novels, in any time or place, in which God plays a very large part is small. One has, of course, to except those of Tolstoy and Dostoyevsky, though I am not sure that it is for His role in them that most readers find them memorable.

But I still find that Jane Austen's novels offer at least as much "contiguity with modern interests" as Jones's. As usual in such critiques, Professor Van Ghent gives an inaccurate account: she describes the "image" of a Jane Austen novel rather than the reality. The seemingly impending death of a central character forms the climax of one of them: Professor Van Ghent has forgotten the plot of *Sense and Sensibility,* or at least Chapters 42 to 47. The death of Fanny Harville accounts for an important subplot in *Persuasion,* as does the near fatal accident of Louisa Musgrove. Fanny Price in *Mansfield Park* worries about the possible death in action of her brother, and in *Persuasion* the theme of death at sea runs a powerful undertone throughout the novel (" 'Ah!' cried Captain Harville, in a tone of strong feeling, 'if I could but make you comprehend what a man suffers when he takes a last look at his wife and children, and watches the boat he has sent them off in, as long as it is in sight, and then turns away and says 'God knows whether we ever meet again!' "[6]) Illicit sex occurs in all the novels except *Northanger Abbey* and brings about the dénouement of two of them, *Pride and Prejudice* and *Mansfield Park*. Perhaps it is because Jane Austen often takes such matters in her stride that critics overlook them. Not only is Harriet Smith's illegitimacy in *Emma* taken as a matter of course, but Jane Austen can even laugh at "society's" attitude toward it and Emma's romanticizing of it. Harriet turns out in the end to be the child of a tradesman: "Such was the blood of gentility which Emma had formerly been so ready to vouch for! It was likely to be as untainted, perhaps, as the blood of many a gentleman: but what a connection had she been preparing for Mr. Knightley—or for the Churchills—or even for Mr. Elton! The stain of illegitimacy, unbleached by nobility or wealth, would have been a stain indeed."[7] If anyone thinks Jane Austen's tongue is not in her cheek here, he should notice the mention of Mr. Elton and the satiric image "unbleached." (What, by the way, does *untainted* mean? Can she be referring to anything but syphilis?) And there is the notorious account of young Musgrove's death in *Persuasion*: "The Musgroves had had the ill fortune of a very troublesome, hopeless son, and the good fortune to lose him before he reached his twentieth year . . . He had, in fact, though his sisters were now doing all they could for him, by calling him 'poor Richard,' been nothing better than a thick-headed, unfeeling, unprofitable Dick Musgrove, who had never done anything to entitle himself to more than the abbreviation of his name, living or dead." Some readers have held up their hands in horror at the "callousness" of this. Jane Austen can't win, it seems. Either she is characterized as so "limited" that she shudders at the idea of death and sex and cannot bring herself to mention them, or else she is berated for being utterly cynical about them.

As for hunger, one might remember Jane Fairfax on the plight of the young unmarried woman of good birth and education but without financial means:

"When I am quite determined as to the time, I am not at all afraid of being long unemployed. There are places in town, offices, where inquiry would soon produce something—offices for the sale, not quite of human flesh, but of human intellect."

"Oh! my dear, human flesh! You quite shock me; if you mean a fling at the slave-trade, I assure you Mr. Suckling was always rather a friend to the abolition."

"I did not mean—I was not thinking of the slave-trade," replied

Jane; "governess-trade, I assure you, was all that I had in view; widely different certainly as to the guilt of those who carry it on; but as to the greater misery of the victims, I do not know where it lies." [*Emma*]

And on war (and government):

"The Admiralty . . . entertain themselves now and then with sending a few hundred men to sea in a ship not fit to be employed. But they have a great many to provide for; and among the thousands that may just as well go to the bottom as not, it is impossible for them to distinguish the very set who may be least missed." [*Persuasion*]

As James Jones might say, this causes a queasiness in the testicles. Captain Wentworth, the speaker, continues with a lively and detailed account of his naval actions in this tub:

"After taking privateers enough to be very entertaining, I had the good luck in my passage home, the next autumn, to fall in with the very French frigate I wanted. I brought her into Plymouth; and here was another instance of luck. We had not been six hours in the Sound, when a gale came on, which lasted four days and nights, and which would have done for poor old *Asp* in half the time . . . Four-and-twenty hours later, and I should only have been a gallant Captain Wentworth, in a small paragraph at one corner of the newspapers; and being lost in only a sloop, nobody would have thought about me."

Anne's shudderings were to herself alone. [*Persuasion*]

As for guilt, it is the main staple of the novels. The plot of every one of them turns, as much as any Greek tragedy, on the recognition by one or more of the central characters of guilt and the subsequent self-reproach, self-insight, and reparation. No, Jane Austen understood a very great deal about the darker, the more tragic and sordid aspects of life, and did not hesitate to incorporate them in her novels.

II

Of course, Jane Austen was to some extent herself to blame for this label. She dropped one or two remarks about her own performance which later critics, as the easiest solution, seized on and have repeated again and again with the utmost solemnity and literalness. They tend to forget what a consummate ironist she is. There is the famous, or notorious, "two inches of ivory." It is really time that this phrase, useful as it is to Austenian critics, was put back into context. It occurs in a letter, one of her most charming ones, to her young nephew James Edward Austen, who has just left school. It is worth the space to quote the opening of it, by way of recapturing the tone of the letter:

> My dear Edward,
>   One reason for my writing to you now is that I may have the plea-
> sure of directing to you *Esqre*. I give you joy of having left Winchester.
> Now you may own how miserable you were there; now it will gradu-
> ally all come out—your crimes and miseries—how often you went up
> by the mail to London and threw away fifty guineas at a tavern, and how
> often you were on the point of hanging yourself, restrained only, as
> some ill-natured aspersion on poor old Winton has it, by the want of a
> tree within some miles of the city.

A delightful dig at the self-pitying, self-romanticizing, "unhappy school-days" and "unhappy childhood" tradition, which has been responsible for some good and much dreary autobiography and fiction in English and other languages. It was the heyday of Byronism. In the most engaging way, Aunt Jane is warning the boy, who is at the age when the advice is most needed, "Don't act or think like a character out of popular fiction."

Young Edward has been inspired by his aunt's example to try his hand at novel writing. Jane Austen continues with some family news; then,

> Uncle Henry writes very superior sermons. You and I must try to get
> hold of one or two, and put them into our novels; it would be a fine
> help to a volume—

one is sure of what she thinks about novelists who put sermons into their novels to help pad them out (she might have made an exception for Sterne)—

> and we could make our heroine read it aloud of a Sunday evening, just
> as Isabella Wardour in *The Antiquary* is made to read the history of the

Hartz Demon in the ruins of St. Ruth—though I believe, upon recollection, Lovell is the reader.[8]

Nor, clearly, did she approve of long interpolated ghost stories and the like. Jane Austen is somewhat less kind to Scott's novels than he was to hers; which is as it should have been.

Then comes a reference to a mysterious disaster that has occurred to the manuscript of the novel Edward has been working on:

By the bye, my dear Edward, I am quite concerned for the loss your mother mentions in her letters; two chapters and a half to be missing is monstrous! It is well that I have not been at Steventon lately, and therefore cannot be suspected of purloining them—two strong twigs and a half toward a nest of my own would have been something. I do not think however that any theft of that sort would be really very useful to me. What should I do with your strong, manly, spirited sketches, full of variety and glow? How could I possibly join them on to the little bit (two inches wide) of ivory on which I work with so fine a brush as produces little effect? [Letters, 467–469]

It must be kept in mind that this is a forty-year-old woman, who has published four highly successful novels, the last dedicated by request to the Prince Regent and recently given a rave review by Sir Walter Scott in the prestigious Quarterly, writing to an eighteen-year-old schoolboy. I think the modesty of "two inches of ivory" and "produces little effect" needs to be taken with the same number of grains of salt as the praise of the "strong, manly, spirited sketches, full of variety and glow" of the boy, who did, when he was over seventy, publish an excellently written memoir of his aunt, but never managed to get a novel into print. Rather I detect, under the jocosity, a considerable amount of the proper pride of a serious, mature, successful professional artist—and perhaps even a touch of justified "female chauvinism" in the "manly."[9] She who, without having had a chance to go to Winchester or (as Edward was to do) to Oxford, had beaten the great Sir Walter at his own game was not, I think, really apologizing for the inadequacies, the "limitations" of her work to this young male whippersnapper—especially when the passage occurs in a letter already full of snide comments on the kind of book that Jane Austen does not want to write and probably thinks should not be written at all.

Not so often used in evidence against her—indeed it is difficult to do so, so evident is the contempt she holds for the kind of work that has been suggested—is her reply to the Prince Regent's librarian:

> You are very very kind in your hints as to the sort of composition which might recommend me at present, and I am fully sensible that an historical romance, founded on the House of Saxe Cobourg, might be much more to the purpose of profit or popularity than such pictures of domestic life in country villages as I deal in. But I could no more write a romance than an epic poem. I could not sit seriously down to write a serious romance under any other motive than to save my life; and if it were indispensable for me to keep it up and never relax into laughing at myself or other people, I am sure I should be hung before I had finished the first chapter. No, I must keep to my own style and go on in my own way; and though I may never succeed again in that, I am convinced that I should totally fail in any other. [*Letters*, 452–453]

I detect no sense of real limitation in her expression of inability to sit "seriously" down to write a "serious" historical romance about the House of Saxe-Coborg, and I rather think the "laughter" she speaks of is really directed at the idea of such a work and perhaps at "serious historical romances" generally.

Finally, and most damaging, there is the much-cited passage at the beginning of the last chapter of *Mansfield Park:* "Let other pens dwell on guilt and misery. I quit such odious objects as soon as I can." It seems to me astonishing that critics, after exclaiming in pious horror at such voluntary self-limitation, fail to notice that, after Jane Austen has written this, she immediately goes on to dwell, at length, in detail, and one is almost tempted to say, with relish, on the guilt and misery that await Maria Rushworth, Henry Crawford, Mrs. Norris, and others. Jane Austen is one of the great portrayers of guilt, to be ranked along with Sophocles and Dostoyevsky—guilt and its consequences in the way of misery; guilt and its redemption by remorse, self-examination, the acquisition of new insight, expiation. I can think of few English novelists in whose works the word itself occurs more frequently, except her mentor, Richardson. There are no finer self-recognition scenes in literature than those of Marianne Dashwood and Elizabeth Bennet—"How despicably have I acted! I, who have prided myself on my discernment! I, who have valued myself on my abilities! who have often disdained the generous candour of my sister, and gratified my vanity in useless or blameable distrust. How humiliating is this discovery! yet, how just a humiliation! . . . Till this moment I never knew myself" (*Pride and Prejudice*)—and, above all, that of Emma Woodhouse, which continues through several chapters, and stages of increasing intensity:

> Never had she felt so agitated, mortified, grieved, at any circumstance in her life. She was most forcibly struck. The truth of his representation there was no denying. She felt it at her heart. How could she have been so brutal, so cruel to Miss Bates! . . . Time did not compose her. As she reflected more, she seemed but to feel it more. She never had been so depressed . . . Emma felt the tears running down her cheeks almost all the way home, without being at any trouble to check them, extraordinary as they were.

> "O God! that I had never seen her!"
>   The rest of the day, the following night, were hardly enough for her thoughts. She was bewildered amidst the confusion of all that had rushed on her within the last few hours. Every moment had brought a fresh surprise; and every surprise must be matter of humiliation to her. How to understand it all! How to understand the deceptions she had been thus practising on herself, and living under! The blunders, the blindness of her own head and heart! She sat still, she walked about, she tried her own room, she tried the shrubbery—in every place, every posture, she perceived that she had acted most weakly; that she had been imposed on by others in a most mortifying degree; that she had been imposing on herself in a degree yet more mortifying; that she was wretched, and should probably find this day but the beginning of wretchedness.
>   To understand, thoroughly understand her own heart, was the first endeavour.

To reinforce the effect, Jane Austen even introduces one of her rare but always brilliant and significant natural descriptions: "The evening of this day was very long and melancholy at Hartfield. The weather added what it could of gloom. A cold stormy rain set in, and nothing of July appeared but in the trees and shrubs, which the wind was despoiling, and the length of the day, which only made such cruel sights the longer visible." Few other pens have dwelt so long and so convincingly on guilt and misery as Jane Austen's. If the literal-minded critic asks in bewilderment, "Why then does she confuse us by making the statement she does at the end of *Mansfield Park*?" Jane Austen's reply might only be to repeat sardonically her parody of Scott. "I do not write for such dull elves / As have not a great deal of ingenuity themselves" (*Letters*, 298).

Amy Bloom

TERRIBLE JANE

"If I *am* a wild beast, I cannot help it. It is not my own fault."
—from a letter to her sister, Cassandra, 1813

Scenes of avarice and poverty brutal in their cool understatement; cruelty, often enjoyed for its own sake; flirtations begun and abandoned, with no thought to the heart; love sought by people who should, and do, know that there is no such thing; lecherous fathers, neglectful mothers, disappointed and disappointing offspring; a brilliant, ruthless narrator savaging society and its hopeless attempts to hide, dismantle, and deny the truth, whatever it is—*Persuasion* is the most modern of novels. The restrained speech, the author's pronounced admiration for the British navy, the presence of a Dowager Viscountess, and a society that honors such titles are artifacts of a world gone by, but Jane Austen's telling of it is contemporary, in the best sense, and timeless, as great art is: it speaks to us of our own lives, our own hearts, of what one knows and must bear, and who one chooses to be.

Jane Austen was one of eight children brought up in Steventon, Hampshire, England, in a rural, genteelly deprived rectory. Her mother, Cassandra Leigh, the much-petted and precocious child of an aristocratic family, grew up preferring kindness to wealth and comfort to romance, and married George Austen, known in his youth as the "Handsome Proctor." Later in life, she wrote witty, pointed verse for the family's entertainment and to encourage her husband's students to work harder (and to continue to board in the rectory); later still, straitened circumstances and disappointment changed Mrs. Austen from a cheerful wife and mother to a hypochondriac, and then to a broody invalid whose only exercise in imagination lay in concocting maladies and their treatments. George Austen, a hardworking, book-loving country vicar, was generally fond of his children, as Austen's fathers often are, and a particular admirer of his daughter Jane's talents, which he appreciated both for their quality and for their income-producing potential. He was her first agent and not much good at getting her published. Her brother Henry was her second, and he was not much good at getting her money. Aside from occasional and happily extended visits to Kent and to Bath, Jane Austen lived with her parents and her sister, Cassandra, all her life.

There are no great mothers in Austen's work. There are good, even marvelous, fathers—like Mr. Bennet, of *Pride and Prejudice*—and fine father figures, like *Persuasion*'s Admiral Croft, but there are no admirable, if flawed, mothers. There are only fond and foolish mothers (Mrs. Bennet, or Mrs. Musgrove in *Persuasion*) and there are mother surrogates, like Lady Russell. Affectionate toward Anne Elliot, *Persuasion*'s heroine, and striving blindly from beginning to end for what she believes will be Anne's happiness, Lady Russell never knows the young woman she cares for. Anne will suffer from Lady Russell's bad counsel and will have to wait eight years to reunite with Captain Wentworth, whom Lady Russell advised her to snub. And that's the whole of the plot.

For Jane Austen, a devoted aunt herself, and a devoted sister, the maternal instinct is as complete a fiction as interesting children and classless societies. When her brother George was six and his fits and mental impairments were more than his mother could manage, he was sent off to the kindly Cullums, who had cared in a similar way for Jane's neurologically impaired uncle Thomas. Poor George is neither memorialized nor visited nor mentioned in family records or letters again. When it became apparent that the Austens' wealthy cousins, Mr. and Mrs. Knight, could not have children, Jane's brother Edward, handsome and charming, was "given" to them, when Jane was eight. One brother banished and excised for his failings, another, a foundling prince, mistakenly laid at the Austens' grimy doorstep and retrieved at sixteen by the glorious, childless Knights of Godmersham (Edward took the surname Knight in adulthood). The Austens (on both the Austen side and the Leigh side) were two generations of disappointed expectations, legacies suggested, even promised, then gone astray, and always one favorite plucked from rapidly diminishing resources and transplanted with a better life and a proper income—and the lucky ones were not ever Jane's sister or her father or her mother or Jane. "People get so horridly poor and economical in this part of the world that I have no patience with them," she wrote Cassandra in 1798.

There are modern critics who have felt that the great truth about Jane Austen is her clear-eyed and painful exposé of the economic relations and underpinnings of English society—the great houses, the emerging merchants, the rapid rise of entrepreneurs and naval heroes, the near servitude of single women. I don't think Jane Austen thought she was tearing the veil off a terrible secret or analyzing a complex equation whose far-reaching implications only she could see; I think she thought she was telling truths that most people knew, even if she would not say them at a dinner party—truths recognized by everyone but the village idiot and the excessively self-satisfied. Everyone she knew had or was a poor relation; every woman she knew had to weigh the strength of her desire, or even the chance of compatibility, against a lifetime of scrimping and deprivation; hardly anyone could afford to have what they wanted, and those who could did not care overmuch about the concerns of those who couldn't. I think it would have amused her to suppose that anyone sitting in her parlor, including her fourteen-year-old niece, did not know these things.

Jane Austen wrote for the best reasons. She wrote to tell a story that mattered to her, even when she didn't know why, and she wrote to engage her readers, even if they were only a querulous mother, dubious neighbors, and her devoted but deeply restrained sister. As for the critics, they commended her as "a favourite with those who seek for harmless amusement" (*The Monthly Review*) and her books as "amusing if not instructive" (*Gentleman's Magazine*), "amusing, inoffensive and well-principled" (*The British Critic*).

Jane Austen was not modest about her writing, but she did not wish to seem to be overreaching herself. She complained when her work was not published, and she complained when it was not published quickly enough. If she complained that her work was appreciated for all the wrong reasons, and by writers who were not fit to clean her muddy boots, there is no record of it. She wrote cheerful piffle to help with family soirees, she took seriously the literary efforts of her nieces and nephews (who seem to have thought that if dear Aunt Jane could do it, anyone could), and when her back did not hurt too badly and the house was quiet, she sat at her little desk and wrote this short, brilliant book, both romantic and bitter, the year before she died.

Jane Austen had experienced her own Lady Russell, Anne Lefroy, a sensible, class-conscious woman watching over a favorite young person—not Jane, but her Irish suitor, Tom Lefroy. Madame Lefroy counseled her beloved nephew to act with prudence and end a relationship that promised too long a wait (while he pursued his law career) and no financial benefit. Tom Lefroy, like Anne Elliot, took the advice and ended the romance. He married later, and although Jane Austen received two other proposals—one in which she, like Fanny Price of *Mansfield Park,* said yes at night and no the next day—she did not marry. Unlike her own Anne Elliot, Jane was not prudent in her youth, learning the value of romance only after eight years of loss and loneliness. The young Jane Austen was a shameless flirt and a cheerful admirer of gentlemen's assets (one's dark eyes, another's broad shoulders), and delighted in her own ability to catch a man's eye. She did not give up on love, ever, but preferred a profound and loving intimacy with her sister, Cassandra, to the dull sham of an agreeable but empty marriage; she would not be wed, but she would love and be loved, deeply and passionately.

Like Austen's family, many readers have created their own mild and shy Jane Austen. As Virginia Woolf said, in 1923, "Anybody who has the temerity to write about Jane Austen is aware of [two] facts: first, that of all great writers she is the most difficult to catch in the act of greatness; second, that there are twenty-five elderly gentlemen living in the neighborhood of London who resent any slight upon her genius as if it were an insult to the chastity of their aunts." This is no less true today, although one might substitute Janeites and Leavisites and certain feminists for the elderly gentlemen, and something quite different for their aunts' chastity. There seems to be something about the mix of apple blossoms in churchyards, rakish younger sons, country balls, and a single woman of thirty or forty who seems not unlovable that inclines readers toward a Jane who is the witty, reticent maiden aunt, the wistful observer, the companion, like Anne Elliot, who plays so well because she will not dance. Anne Elliot is not meek, but she is quiet, and she speaks only when she feels obliged by social requirements, by probity, by the wild promptings of her heart, or on occasion by a serious discussion of literature. Now forty, clear-eyed about love, and the marriages and losses she has seen and known, Anne Elliot's maker tells every uncomfortable truth with such a mix of astringency and tenderness that the reader laughs, flinches, and then, right on the verge of laughter once more, is deeply moved. Her cool, harsh assessment of Richard Musgrove, lost at sea, and of his grieving mother's "fat sighings over the destiny of a son, whom alive nobody had cared for," is not the observation of a gentle lady, and the further observation that "personal size and mental sorrow certainly have no necessary proportions" is more cold wit, undone by the narrator's own point that despite ridicule, "a large bulky figure has as good a right to be in deep affliction as the most graceful set of limbs in the world." Jane Austen is often unkind, occasionally contemptuous, but almost never wrong.

What is the "persuasion" of this novel? Lady Russell's advice not to undertake a long engagement as a poor suitor tries to become a wealthy man? Anne is not, in fact, persuaded, but she listens and obeys, and we discover that Anne's creator is a modern philosopher and a moral relativist. Her deference to Lady Russell was ". . . one of those cases in which the advice is good or bad only as the event decides," Anne muses as happiness approaches. Captain Wentworth does not persuade, either. He grows up right before it is irretrievably too late, as Austen's heroes do; they become the men they wish to be, better, bigger, and more generous than one might have hoped, exactly the kind of husband one wishes to have, in any century, and most especially in a century in which a divorce would leave you without income or social standing or custody, and an unhappy marriage would leave you in purgatory. He cannot persuade Anne to love him, because she already does. She needs no persuading; she needs only to know that he still loves her. Anne herself is a singularly poor persuader: she changes no one's mind through her sensible remarks, and she bites her tongue discreetly whenever she is tempted to make a strong argument or a sharp retort. She cannot persuade her father, by example or argument, to be kind or prudent; she cannot make her horrid sister Elizabeth love her; she cannot persuade Captain Benwick to be anything other than the sodden, tearful fool that he is (although she does suggest reading more prose as a cure for his hilarious, lachrymose bleating about his dead fiancée); she cannot persuade even herself to forget Wentworth. Mrs. Smith, on whom one of the thinner plot devices turns, does not persuade; she produces the evidence that Anne has longed for, a letter that reveals her cousin and suitor, Mr. William Elliot, to be the superficial, two-faced, scheming bounder Anne has suspected him to be. She is relieved, she is affirmed; she is not persuaded, because, like everyone else, she already knows what she thinks.

Money can make a strong argument, and does, but it is only the constancy of true love that persuades. Sailors may swear that a woman on board is bad luck, but Admiral Croft knows better. One of Austen's eccentric heroes, he is successful on merit, not on birth, generous, dependent on his wife, and unashamed of their mutual need. Admiral and Mrs. Croft, equally beloved by the author, partners in everything from quiet dinners to donkey-cart rides in the rain, are persuaded by love that a life apart is not the life for them, no matter how laughable, eccentric, or quaint that makes them. And although they cannot persuade Captain Wentworth that a man needs his wife, cannot persuade him that the right spouse can make the difference between a terrible voyage and a wonderful one, the Crofts know that it is so, and they hope that Wentworth will have the opportunity to be persuaded, when he is married. True love— rare, unfashionable, unlikely, and inimitable—is the only persuasion Jane Austen recommends and that's why I love her. It's also why I read her. She knows a great deal about what else is persuasive in the world— money, position, and security—and she writes about all of those things with appreciation. She disliked poverty; she loathed being poor, and she was thrilled by the chance to go to a good party, flirt with handsome men, and ride in a comfortable carriage. She had two inadequate agents—her father and her brother—and she despaired of their incompetence and how little money she was able to earn. (She completely eschewed the contemporary and false position of pretending contempt for things, which everyone knows the writer, as well as the reader, could reasonably desire. Jane Austen's moral compass, as an author and as a person, was firmly held and it did not include piety, hypocrisy, or self-deception.) Miss Austen says, thoughtfully, even with a sigh of regret: Those things are really very nice, but they are not better than love and they will not compensate for its absence.

Jane Austen is, for me, the best writer for anyone who believes in love more than in romance, and who cares more for the private than the public. She understands that men and women have to grow up in order to deserve and achieve great love, that some suffering is necessary (that mewling about it in your memoir or on a talk show will not help at all), and that people who mistake the desirable object for the one necessary and essential love will get what they deserve.[1]

Harold Bloom

"Persuasion" is a word derived from the Latin for "advising" or "urging," for recommending that it is good to perform or not perform a particular action. The word goes back to a root meaning "sweet" or "pleasant," so that the good of performance or nonperformance has a tang of taste rather than of moral judgment about it. It is the title of her last completed novel. As a title, it recalls *Sense and Sensibility* or *Pride and Prejudice* rather than *Emma* or *Mansfield Park*. We are given not the name of a person or house and estate, but of an abstraction, a single one in this case. The title's primary reference is to the persuasion of its heroine, Anne Elliot, at the age of nineteen, by her godmother, Lady Russell, not to marry Captain Frederick Wentworth, a young naval officer. This was, as it turns out, very bad advice, and, after eight years, it is mended by Anne and Captain Wentworth. As with all of Austen's ironic comedies, matters end happily for the heroine. And yet each time I finish a rereading of this perfect novel, I feel very sad.

This does not appear to be my personal vagary; when I ask my friends and students about their experience of the book, they frequently mention a sadness which they also associate with *Persuasion,* more even than with *Mansfield Park*. Anne Elliot, a quietly eloquent being, is a self-reliant character, in no way forlorn, and her sense of self never falters. It is not *her* sadness we feel as we conclude the book: it is the novel's somberness that impresses us. The sadness enriches what I would call the novel's canonical persuasiveness, its way of showing us its extraordinary aesthetic distinction.

Persuasion is among novels what Anne Elliot is among novelistic characters—a strong but subdued outrider. The book and the character are not colorful or vivacious; Elizabeth Bennet of *Pride and Prejudice* and Emma Woodhouse of *Emma* have a verve to them that initially seems lacking in Anne Elliot, which may be what Austen meant when she said that Anne was "almost too good for me." Anne is really almost too subtle for us, though not for Wentworth, who has something of an occult wavelength to her. Juliet McMaster notes "the kind of oblique communication that constantly goes on between Anne Elliot and Captain Wentworth, where, though they seldom speak to each other, each constantly understands the full import of the other's speech better than their interlocutors do."

That kind of communication in *Persuasion* depends upon deep "affection," a word that Austen values over "love." "Affection" between woman and man, in Austen, is the more profound and lasting emotion. I think it is not too much to say that Anne Elliot, though subdued, is the creation for whom Austen herself must have felt the most affection, because she lavished her own gifts upon Anne. Henry James insisted that the novelist must be a sensibility upon which absolutely nothing is lost; by that test (clearly a limited one) only Austen, George Eliot, and James himself, among all those writing in English, would join Stendhal, Flaubert, and Tolstoy in a rather restricted pantheon. Anne Elliot may well be the one character in all of prose fiction upon whom nothing is lost, though she is in no danger of turning into a novelist. The most accurate estimate of Anne Elliot that I have seen is by Stuart Tave:

> Nobody hears Anne, nobody sees her, but it is she who is ever at the center. It is through her ears, eyes, and mind that we are made to care for what is happening. If nobody is much aware of her, she is very much aware of everyone else and she perceives what is happening to them when they are ignorant of themselves . . . she reads Wentworth's mind, with the coming troubles he is causing for others and himself, before those consequences bring the information to him.

The aesthetic dangers attendant upon such a paragon are palpable: how does a novelist make such a character persuasive? Poldy, in Joyce's *Ulysses,* is overwhelmingly persuasive because he is so complete a person, which was the largest of Joyce's intentions. Austen's ironic mode does not sanction the representation of completeness: we do not accompany her characters to the bedroom, the kitchen, the privy. What Austen parodies in *Sense and Sensibility* she raises to an apotheosis in *Persuasion:* the sublimity of a particular, inwardly isolated sensibility. Anne Elliot is hardly the only figure in Austen who has an understanding heart. Her difference is in her almost preternatural acuteness of perception of others and of the self, which are surely the qualities that most distinguish Austen as a novelist. Anne Elliot is to Austen's work what Rosalind of *As You Like It* is to Shakespeare's: the character who almost reaches the mastery of perspective that can be available only to the novelist or playwright, lest all dramatic quality be lost from the novel or play. C. L. Barber memorably emphasized this limitation:

> The dramatist tends to show us one thing at a time, and to realize that one thing, in its moment, to the full; his characters go to extremes, comical as well as serious; and no character, not even a Rosalind, is in a position to see all around the play and so be completely poised, for if this were so the play would cease to be dramatic.

I like to turn Barber's point in the other direction: more even than Hamlet or Falstaff, or than Elizabeth Bennet, or than Fanny Price in *Mansfield Park,* Rosalind and Anne Elliot are almost completely poised, nearly able to see all around the play and the novel. Their poise cannot transcend perspectivizing completely, but Rosalind's wit and Anne's sensibility, both balanced and free of either excessive aggressivity or defensiveness, enable them to share more of their creators' poise than we ever come to do.

Austen never loses dramatic intensity; we share Anne's anxiety concerning Wentworth's renewed intentions until the novel's conclusion. But we rely upon Anne as we should rely upon Rosalind; critics would see the rancidity of Touchstone as clearly as they see the vanity of Jacques if they placed more confidence in Rosalind's reactions to everyone else in the play, as well as to herself. Anne Elliot's reactions have the same winning authority; we must try to give the weight to her words that is not extended by the other persons in the novel, except for Wentworth.

Stuart Tave's point, like Barber's, is accurate even when turned in the other direction; Austen's irony is very Shakespearean. Even the reader must fall into the initial error of undervaluing Anne Elliot. The wit of Elizabeth Bennet or of Rosalind is easier to appreciate than Anne Elliot's accurate sensibility. The secret of her character combines Austenian irony with a Wordsworthian sense of deferred hope. Austen has a good measure of Shakespeare's unmatched ability to give us persons, both major and minor, who are each utterly consistent in her or his separate mode of speech, and yet completely different from one another. Anne Elliot is the last of Austen's heroines of what I think we must call the Protestant will, but in her the will is modified, perhaps perfected, by its descendant, the Romantic sympathetic imagination, of which Wordsworth was the prophet. That is perhaps what helps to make Anne so complex and sensitive a character.

Jane Austen's earlier heroines, of whom Elizabeth Bennet is the exemplar, manifested the Protestant will as direct descendants of Samuel Richardson's Clarissa Harlowe, with Dr. Samuel Johnson hovering nearby as moral authority. Marxist criticism inevitably views the Protestant will, even in its literary manifestations, as a mercantile matter, and it has become fashionable to talk about the socioeconomic realities that Jane Austen excludes, such as the West Indian slavery that is part of the ultimate basis for the financial security most of her characters enjoy. But all achieved literary works are founded upon exclusions, and no one has demonstrated that increased consciousness of the relation between culture and imperialism is of the slightest benefit whatsoever in learning to read *Mansfield Park*. *Persuasion* ends with a tribute to the British navy, in which Wentworth has an honored place. Doubtless Wentworth at sea, ordering the latest batch of disciplinary floggings, is not as pleasant as Wentworth on land, gently appreciating the joys of affection with Anne Elliot. But once again, Austen's is a great art founded upon exclusions, and the sordid realities of British sea power are no more relevant to *Persuasion* than West Indian bondage is to *Mansfield Park*. Austen was, however, immensely interested in the pragmatic and secular consequences of the Protestant will, and they seem to me a crucial element in helping us appreciate the heroines of her novels.

Austen's Shakespearean inwardness, culminating in Anne Elliot, revises the moral intensities of Clarissa Harlowe's secularized Protestant martyrdom, her slow dying after being raped by Lovelace. What removes Clarissa's will to live is her stronger will to maintain the integrity of her being. To yield to the repentant Lovelace by marrying him would compromise the essence of her being, the exaltation of her violated will. What is tragedy in *Clarissa* is converted by Austen into ironic comedy, but the will's drive to maintain itself scarcely alters in this conversion. In *Persuasion* the emphasis is on a willed exchange of esteems, where both the woman and the man estimate the value of the other to be high. Obviously outward considerations of wealth, property, and social standing are crucial elements here, but so are the inward considerations of common sense, amiability, culture, wit, and affection. In a way (it pains me to say this, as I am a fierce Emersonian) Ralph Waldo Emerson anticipated the current Marxist critique of Austen when he denounced her as a mere conformist who would not allow her heroines to achieve the soul's true freedom from societal conventions. But that was to mistake Jane Austen, who understood that the function of convention was to liberate the will, even if convention's tendency was to stifle individuality, without which the will was inconsequential.

Austen's major heroines—Elizabeth, Emma, Fanny, and Anne—possess such inward freedom that their individualities cannot be repressed. Austen's art as a novelist is not to worry much about the socioeconomic genesis of that inner freedom, though the anxiety level does rise in *Mansfield Park* and *Persuasion*. In Austen, irony becomes the instrument for invention, which Dr. Johnson defined as the essence of poetry. A conception of inward freedom that centers upon a refusal to accept esteem except from one upon whom one has conferred esteem, is a conception of the highest degree of irony. The supreme comic scene in all of Austen must be Elizabeth's rejection of Darcy's first marriage proposal, where the ironies of the dialectic of will and esteem become very nearly outrageous. That high comedy, which continued in *Emma,* is somewhat chastened in *Mansfield Park,* and then becomes something else, unmistakable but difficult to name, in *Persuasion,* where Austen has become so conscious a master that she seems to have changed the nature of willing, as though it, too, could be persuaded to become a rarer, more disinterested act of the self.

No one has suggested that Jane Austen becomes a High Romantic in *Persuasion;* her poet remained William Cowper, not Wordsworth, and her favorite prose writer was always Dr. Johnson. But her severe distrust of imagination and of "romantic love," so prevalent in the earlier novels, is not a factor in *Persuasion.* Anne and Wentworth maintain their affection for each other throughout eight years of hopeless separation, and each has the power of imagination to conceive of a triumphant reconciliation. This is the material for a romance, not for an ironical novel. The ironies of *Persuasion* are frequently pungent, but they are almost never directed at Anne Elliot and only rarely at Captain Wentworth.

There is a difficult relation between Austen's repression of her characteristic irony about her protagonists and a certain previously unheard plangency that hovers throughout *Persuasion*. Despite Anne's faith in herself she is very vulnerable to the anxiety, which she never allows herself to express, of an unlived life, in which the potential loss transcends yet includes sexual unfulfillment. I can recall only one critic, the Australian Ann Molan, who emphasizes what Austen strongly implies, that "Anne . . . is a passionate woman. And against her will, her heart keeps asserting its demand for fulfillment." Since Anne had refused Wentworth her esteem eight years before, she feels a necessity to withhold her will, and thus becomes the first Austen heroine whose will and imagination are antithetical.

Although Austen's overt affinities remained with the Aristocratic Age, her authenticity as a writer impelled her, in *Persuasion,* a long way toward the burgeoning Democratic Age, or Romanticism, as we used to call it. There is no civil war within Anne Elliot's psyche, or within Austen's; but there is the emergent sadness of a schism in the self, with memory taking the side of imagination in an alliance against the will. The almost Wordsworthian power of memory in both Anne and Wentworth has been noted by Gene Ruoff. Since Austen was anything but an accidental novelist, we might ask why she chose to found *Persuasion* upon a mutual nostalgia. After all, the rejected Wentworth is even less inclined to will a renewed affection than Anne is, and yet the fusion of memory and imagination triumphs over his will also. Was this a relaxation of the will in Jane Austen herself? Since she returns to her earlier mode in *Sanditon,* her unfinished novel begun after *Persuasion* was completed, it may be that the story of Anne Elliot was an excursion or indulgence for the novelist. The parallels between Wordsworth and *Persuasion* are limited but real. High Romantic novels in England, whether of the Byronic kind like *Jane Eyre* and *Wuthering Heights* or of a Wordsworthian sort like *Adam Bede,* are a distinctly later development. The ethos of the Austen heroine does not change in *Persuasion,* but she is certainly a more problematic being, tinged with a new sadness concerning life's limits. It may be that the elegant pathos *Persuasion* sometimes courts has a connection to Jane Austen's own ill health, her intimations of her early death.

Stuart Tave, comparing Wordsworth and Austen, shrewdly noted that both were "poets of marriage" and both also possessed "a sense of duty understood and deeply felt by those who see the integrity and peace of their own lives as essentially bound to the lives of others and see the lives of all in a more than merely social order." Expanding Tave's insight, Susan Morgan pointed to the particular affinity between Austen's *Emma* and Wordsworth's great "Ode: Intimations of Immortality from Recollections of Earliest Childhood." The growth of the individual consciousness, involving both gain and loss for Wordsworth but only gain for Austen, is the shared subject. Emma's consciousness certainly does develop, and she undergoes a quasi-Wordsworthian transformation from the pleasures of near solipsism to the more difficult pleasures of sympathy for others. Anne Elliot, far more mature from the beginning, scarcely needs to grow in consciousness. Her long-lamented rejection of Wentworth insulates her against the destructiveness of hope, which we have seen to be the frightening emphasis of the earlier Wordsworth, particularly in the story of poor Margaret. Instead of hope, there is a complex of emotions, expressed by Austen with her customary skill:

> How eloquent could Anne Elliot have been,—how eloquent, at least, were her wishes on the side of early warm attachment, and a cheerful confidence in futurity, against that over-anxious caution which seems to insult exertion and distrust Providence!—She had been forced into prudence in her youth, she learned romance as she grew older—the natural sequel of an unnatural beginning.

Here learning romance is wholly retrospective; Anne no longer regards it as being available to her. And indeed Wentworth returns, still resentful after eight years, and reflects that Anne's power with him is gone forever. The qualities of decision and confidence that make him a superb naval commander are precisely what he condemns her for lacking. With almost too meticulous a craft, Austen traces his gradual retreat from this position, as the power of memory increases its dominance over him and as he learns that his jilted sense of her as being unable to act is quite mistaken. It is a beautiful irony that he needs to undergo a process of self-persuasion while Anne waits, without even knowing that she is waiting or that there is anything that could rekindle her hope. The comedy of this is gently sad, as the reader waits also, reflecting upon how large a part contingency plays in the matter.

While the pre-Socratics and Freud agree that there are no accidents, Austen thinks differently. Character is fate for her also, but fate, once activated, tends to evade character in so overdetermined a social context as Austen's world. In rereading *Persuasion,* though I remember the happy conclusion, I nevertheless feel anxiety as Wentworth and Anne circle away from each other in spite of themselves. The reader is not totally persuaded of a satisfactory interview until Anne reads Wentworth's quite agonized letter to her:

"I can listen no longer in silence. I must speak to you by such means as are within my reach. You pierce my soul. I am half agony, half hope. Tell me not that I am too late, that such precious feelings are gone for ever. I offer myself to you again with a heart more your own, than when you almost broke it eight years and a half ago. Dare not say that man forgets sooner than woman, that his love has an earlier death. I have loved none but you. Unjust I may have been, weak and resentful I have been, but never inconstant. You alone have brought me to Bath. For you alone I think and plan.—Have you not seen this? Can you fail to have understood my wishes?—I had not waited even these ten days, could I have read your feelings, as I think you must have penetrated mine. I can hardly write. I am every instant hearing something which overpowers me. You sink your voice, but I can distinguish the tones of that voice, when they would be lost on others.—Too good, too excellent creature! You do us justice indeed. You do believe that there is true attachment and constancy among men. Believe it to be most fervent, most undeviating in

F. W.

"I must go, uncertain of my fate; but I shall return hither, or follow your party, as soon as possible. A word, a look will be enough to decide whether I enter your father's house this evening or never."

I cannot imagine such a letter in *Pride and Prejudice,* or even in *Emma* or *Mansfield Park.* The perceptive reader might have realized how passionate Anne was, almost from the start of the novel, but until this there was no indication of equal passion in Wentworth. His letter, as befits a naval commander, is badly written and not exactly Austenian, but it is all the more effective thereby. We come to realize that we have believed in him until now only because Anne's love for him provokes our interest. Austen wisely has declined to make him interesting enough on his own. Yet part of the book's effect is to persuade the reader of the reader's own powers of discernment and self-persuasion; Anne Elliot is almost too good for the reader, as she is for Austen herself, but the attentive reader gains the confidence to perceive Anne as she should be perceived. The subtlest element in this subtlest of novels is the call upon the reader's own power of memory to match the persistence and intensity of the yearning that Anne Elliot is too stoical to express directly.

The yearning hovers throughout the book, coloring Anne's perceptions and our own. Our sense of Anne's existence becomes identified with our own consciousness of lost love, however fictive or idealized that may be. There is an improbability in the successful renewal of a relationship devastated eight years before which ought to work against the texture of this most "realistic" of Austen's novels, but she is very careful to see that it does not. Like the author, the reader becomes persuaded to wish for Anne what she still wishes for herself. Ann Molan has the fine observation that Austen "is most satisfied with Anne when Anne is most dissatisfied with herself." The reader is carried along with Austen, and gradually Anne is also persuaded and catches up with the reader, allowing her yearning a fuller expression.

Dr. Johnson, in *The Rambler* 29, on "The folly of anticipating misfortunes," warned against anxious expectations of any kind, whether fearful or hopeful:

> . . . because the objects both of fear and hope are yet uncertain, so we ought not to trust the representations of one more than the other, because they are both equally fallacious; as hope enlarges happiness, fear aggravates calamity. It is generally allowed, that no man ever found the happiness of possession proportionate to that expectation which incited his desire, and invigorated his pursuit; nor has any man found the evils of life so formidable in reality, as they were described to him by his own imagination.

This is one of a series of Johnsonian pronouncements against the dangerous prevalence of the imagination, some of which his disciple Austen had certainly read. If you excluded such representations, on the great critic's advice, then Wordsworth could not have written at all, and Austen could not have written *Persuasion*. Yet it was a very strange book for her to write, this master of the highest art of exclusion that we have known in the Western novel. Any novel by Jane Austen could be called an achieved ellipsis, with everything omitted that could disturb her ironic though happy conclusions. *Persuasion* remains the least popular of her four canonical novels because it is the strangest, but all her work is increasingly strange as we approach the end of the Democratic Age that her contemporary Wordsworth did so much to inaugurate in literature. Poised as she is at the final border of the Aristocratic Age, she shares with Wordsworth an art dependent upon a split between a waning Protestant will and a newly active sympathetic imagination, with memory assigned the labor of healing the divide. If the argument of my book has any validity, Austen will survive even the bad days ahead of us, because the strangeness of originality and of an individual vision are our lasting needs, which only literature can gratify in the Theocratic Age that slouches toward us.

Diane Johnson

SOME THOUGHTS ON THE CRAFT
OF AUSTEN'S *PERSUASION*

Every novelist has a toolbox of techniques and tricks—traditional elements of the novelist's craft that she must make use of to express its specific themes, subject, and moral universe. The most important are: plot, point of view, dialogue and exposition (proportion of scene to summary), pace, form, language, and a preexisting set of genres and modes to choose from. No one has surpassed Jane Austen in the mastery of these tools, but what is surprising is how often she has flouted modern views of effective novel writing. At the time of her premature death, she had learned enough about the techniques of her art to place her enduringly among its foremost practitioners. Yet no teacher of creative writing today would recommend many of her practices.

There are many ways of reading narrative. Children read for a story—for the suspense, loving the sense of delicious dread, the knowledge they are powerless to alter what will happen. Some readers are also interested in the historical and biographical context—the world of the novelist and the connection of her work to her own life. Apart from these, the most sophisticated readings involve an awareness of how the writer is practicing her tricks, making her artistic decisions, and demonstrating her craft, even though such an awareness of technique can take away some of the naïve pleasures of narrative and remind us too forcibly that the events of fiction are arbitrary—that it's actually Jane Austen who pushes Louisa Musgrove off the slippery rocks. For some this may complicate or even ruin the experience of reading; on the other hand, looking at how and why Austen makes certain choices allows us to appreciate fully one of the greatest practitioners of this complex craft, and to marvel at the way she often produces her magical effects by breaking a number of commonplace writerly rules.

Persuasion, Austen's shortest novel, is perfect in its economy of form.[1] It is a compendium of lessons, and its tone is somewhat different from the high-spirited, eighteenth-century tone of her earlier works. *Persuasion* is the story of Anne Elliot, an unmarried daughter of Sir Walter Elliot, a vain, extravagant English baronet. In her teens Anne had been *persuaded* by a family friend, Lady Russell, against her heart to refuse a marriage offer from a dashing sea captain, Frederick Wentworth. Now the captain is back in England, living nearby, and much richer than he was eight years before. But the course of true love cannot be expected to run smoothly.

Austen was a novelist of manners. Each genre contains coded signals about what the reader must expect from works within it, and though writers are free to flout the pattern or obey it, they can't escape the fact that readers bring a set of expectations and criteria with which to experience the work. If the writer violates these too drastically, the work fails in some way. When we say "novel of manners" we think of a depiction, comic and often lightly satirical, of the ways of a given society, with characters who best represent it, usually its middle- or upper-class members—the same people who will read it. Choosing to write a novel of manners is probably a matter of temperament as well as fashion, and it suited Jane Austen's particular genius so well she might have invented the genre—though she didn't.

A novel of manners has certain rules, the same that govern comedy, and the first rule of comedy is that things will turn out all right in the end, at least for the obligatory young lovers. Knowing it's a comedy of manners, we have no undue anxiety about the outcome of *Persuasion*— Captain Wentworth and Anne Elliot must end up together, and the interest of the story will arise from each impediment or reverse they experience along the way. The interest lies not in matters of metaphysical anguish but in details of social behavior, focusing on subjects like embarrassment and chagrin, matrimonial fate, social climbing, vulgarity, and so on. People who defy the tenets of the society are usually punished, either like Lydia Bennet in *Pride and Prejudice* by falling a few notches in the social register, or by ridicule or financial failure; but sometimes, like Thackeray's Becky Sharp, they are allowed to prosper at least for a while as a way of making the author's comment on the values and practices of her day. If death and misery come into it, these usually befall the characters who "deserve" their misfortune, and their fates don't pain the reader at all—the Musgroves' ne'er-do-well sailor son, for example, even if his only crime was to have not been bright.

Austen is exquisitely mindful of the tradition she's working in, and one interesting thing for the modern reader is to see how she works within this tradition, subtly modifying it, beginning with making the hero and heroine past their first "bloom," as Margaret Drabble points out in her brilliant introduction to *Persuasion*.[2] Anne and Wentworth are older than the average hero and heroine of books at the time, and each has experienced first love and disappointment (albeit with each other). Some of the disappointment readers have felt about Austen's *Mansfield Park* has to do with genre confusion; it doesn't quite fit into the comic paradigm, rather like the "problem plays" of Shakespeare.

Like any novel, a comedy of manners has, of course, a serious didactic nexus or underlying theme, often overlooked in the genial glow of the work. A recent instance in my own experience involves my novel *Lulu in Marrakech*, which has as a more or less overt subject the role of women in modern Islamic societies. Austen's great serious subject was the precariousness of the lives of women in early-nineteenth-century England, and, lacking other options, the urgent need for them to establish themselves by marriage. Austen scholarship has certainly noted this, but Ruth Perry (*Novel Relations: The Transformation of Kinship in English Literature and Culture 1748–1818*) has recently argued that by the time *Persuasion* was written, the social arrangements of earlier periods, "kinship orientation based on blood relations,"[3] were in the throes of change. The family you married into was becoming more important than the one you were born into. Women who found themselves on the cusp of this broad social shift in real life, like the heroines of fiction, depended on marriage for the happiness and the financial security that might have formerly come from their birth family. Perry finds evidence that in Austen's day, moreover, manners and morals were becoming more strict, and women's place more restricted and precarious, than at previous periods in English life; these deformations of earlier customs are explored in all of Austen's books. Austen herself was affected by a period that had started with sprightly eighteenth-century values and was slowly becoming Victorian.

Inheritance issues drive most of Jane Austen's plots and subplots; and because she was on the cusp of changes in attitude that would increasingly commodify women and virginity for the marriage market, trends masked by conventions of romantic love, she came to seem to some later readers somewhat hard-hearted in the practicality of her views. For instance (in Perry's example), her implicit mockery in *Sense and Sensibility* of Marianne Dashwood's "ardent belief in a first and only love" would have made no sense in an earlier period, when a third of all marriages were second marriages anyhow, but was fashionably new in Marianne's day. Today's heroine has a broader choice of dénouement—like my own heroine Lulu, she can go off to join the Peace Corps or the CIA.

Incidentally, seeing the plots of eighteenth- and early-nineteenth-century novels in the light of these broad social changes goes a long way to explaining why many do not move us today; the reunion of long-lost fathers and daughters, for instance, or the intense relation of brother and sister, no longer seem compelling. Will *Mansfield Park* make more sense to us now if we look at which scenes Austen chose to dramatize compared to what happens offstage? She doesn't show us the scene where the docile Fanny refuses the dashing Henry Crawford, the suitor her benefactors think is perfect for her; the important scene for Austen is the one in which Fanny defies Sir Thomas, her adopted father. In the emotional hierarchy of the period the kinship issue is the more dramatic, but the less so for us.[4]

The changes in and the absence of social norms in today's Western societies are limitations on the modern novelist of manners, since comedy depends for effect on a stable community whose rules are known and agreed on, against which transgression shows off in comic or cautionary relief. In the case of *Lulu in Marrakech,* I tried to approximate such a community by limiting the novel to the world of expatriates in Morocco, and by inventing a job for the heroine that would explain her presence there and authorize her to snoop around.

Besides its genre, an early clue to what any novel is about is of course its title. If *Persuasion* had been called *The Elliots,* as apparently Jane Austen intended, we might not have noticed the persuasion theme at first and read the novel as being simply about the Elliot family fortunes, with asides on the subjects of money and the navy; and of course it's about these things too. The title *Persuasion* was added after her death, taken from the text, which is mined with the word "persuasion" used as both noun and verb. Such verbal clues are a great guide to the rudderless reader, but we should also remember that titles are often under the control of publishers, who think they know more than authors—and often do—about what will make people read the book; in this case the title was chosen by her relatives after her death, shortly after the book was finished. *Pride and Prejudice,* on the other hand, was renamed by Austen herself from her original title, *First Impressions,* possibly because there were other recent novels with that name.

Besides genre and title, the writer must adjust the proportion of scene and summary in the text. Though conventional wisdom instructs writers to begin with an exciting action moment (*in medias res*), here Austen doesn't bother, unlike her practice in *Pride and Prejudice.* Instead, she launches into an analysis of the characters we'll be concerned with, especially their defects and frailties—Sir Walter's vanity, Elizabeth's complacence and self-satisfaction, Anne's quiet nature and more modest expectations, cousin William Elliot's negligent lack of family feeling, Mary Musgrove's hypochondria, and so on. These things are "told" us by an omniscient narrator, as opposed to shown us—another direct flouting of modern writing manuals. She also defies them by not telling us much about the physical appearance of the characters beyond the information that Elizabeth, pushing thirty, is as good-looking as ever, and that poor Anne has somewhat faded at twenty-seven.

Austen also manages to "get in," in the Jamesian sense, the main plot lines—that is, conflicts, for plot is conflict. She outlines these almost in the manner of a soap opera digest: by the end of the first chapter we know that Sir Walter is in financial difficulties that only Anne and a family friend, Lady Russell, are facing up to, and we know the complicated situation of inheritance that will leave Anne and Elizabeth impoverished and dependent when Sir Walter dies. We also know that both Anne and Elizabeth are unmarried and over the hill, a dire plight for women at this time. These matters are laid out with no frills, entirely in summary—that is, with no dialogue, and in no one's voice but that of the omniscient narrator, which may or may not be the same as that of Jane Austen, but which we take to be that of Austen herself. The tone is occasionally facetious. For instance, when Elizabeth and Sir Walter hit on the idea of economizing by cutting out charitable donations and Anne's yearly allowance, the narrator comments that "these measures, *however good in themselves* [italics mine], were insufficient for the real extent of the evil."

Another truism of the creative writing class is flouted by Austen's practice at the beginning of the novel: the belief that the reader must have someone to identify with. Initially, the heroine is problematic here. Anne is faded, disappointed, and not very forceful—an anti-heroine if ever there was one. Nor are the interfering Lady Russell and the vain, pretty sister suitable candidates. Almost the first dialogue of the novel is an immensely long speech by Lady Russell demonstrating her bossiness:

> "If we can persuade your father to all this . . . much may be done. If he will adopt these regulations, in seven years he will be clear, and I hope we may be able to convince him and Elizabeth, that Kellynch Hall has a respectability in itself which cannot be affected by these reductions; and that the true dignity of Sir Walter Elliot will be very far from lessened, in the eyes of sensible people, by his acting like a man of principle. What will he be doing, in fact, but what very many of our first families have done, or ought to do?—there will be nothing singular in his case; and it is singularity which often makes the worst part of our suffering, as it always does of our conduct. I have great hope of our prevailing. We must be serious and decided—for, after all, the person who has contracted debts must pay them, and though a great deal is due to the feelings of the gentleman, and head of the house, like your father, there is still more due to the character of an honest man."

Though Austen has prepared us to like Lady Russell, this speech makes her sound, at least to our modern ears, both pompous and self-righteous, if undoubtedly wise, and we immediately question her interference in Anne's life. Austen challenges the truism, not supported by the novel in its opening pages, that we must identify with somebody. We see we will have to be alert to Austen's attitudes; and for that matter, to Anne.

In general, this peculiar need of fiction—finding someone for a reader to identify with—seems to be an absolute, and lies at the heart, too complicated to go into, of why we read. Of course we can, in some circumstances, identify with villains, and Cousin William Elliot is in a tradition of charming Austenian rogues. (William Elliot is more subtly drawn than, say, Mr. Collins in the early *Pride and Prejudice;* we must listen carefully to detect the cynical intentions beneath his polished charm.) In *Persuasion,* we come to identify with Anne, but only after a while, which is, of course, Austen's plan.

Early on in the novel, we notice that Austen uses very little dialogue, another deviance from "showing." Reading further confirms our impression that even when she does give us speeches, she seldom uses them to advance the plot. Instead, she uses them to give her characters the power of self-characterization and self-parody to mock them implicitly, as with Lady Russell's long speech. It's as if the novelist steps back, throws up her hands—and claims she can't stop her characters from say-ing the silly, pompous, earnest, ebullient, or sincere things they say that reveal their personal flaws. It may surprise us to see how consistent this practice is, and it probably accounts in part for the distinctive Austenian tone, which is beloved but seldom successfully imitated. Only occasion-ally does dialogue in Austen serve the end of both plot and characteriza-tion; a famous example where it does both is the opening of *Pride and Prejudice,* where Mrs. Bennet enters saying "Netherfield Park is let at last."

Great novels vary a lot in how much they show or tell; some novels are much talkier than others. Obviously, if a whole novel were to be dramatized—people speaking, with no exposition—we would have a play, or at least a novel by Ivy Compton-Burnett, and it could be ex-tremely cumbersome. Over eighty pages into this novel, we've heard Anne Elliot say very little, and nothing endearing. There's very little dia-logue except in Chapter 7, where we have two long speeches by Anne lecturing her sister Mary on her maternal duties and offering to babysit her little nephew, who has broken his collarbone. Mary wants to go to a party with her husband. We are apt to find what Anne has to say a little prissy:

> "Mary, I cannot wonder at your husband [planning to go]. Nursing does not belong to a man, it is not his province. A sick child is always the mother's property, her own feelings generally make it so."

Mary retorts,

> "I hope I am as fond of my child as any mother—but I do not know that I am of any more use in the sickroom than Charles, for I cannot always be scolding and teasing a poor child when it is ill, and you saw, this morning, that if I told him to keep quiet, he was sure to begin kicking about. I have not nerves for the sort of thing."
> "But could you be comfortable yourself, to be spending a whole evening away from the poor boy?"
> "Yes, you see his papa can, and why should not I?"

At this point in the book, Anne's sententiousness doesn't endear her to the reader.

As part of their plan to economize, the Elliots rent their house to an

Admiral Croft and move to the neighboring city of Bath. One might draw attention to, without wishing to exaggerate, the strong biographical elements in *Persuasion*. In 1801, the Austen family, like the Elliots, was obliged to move to Bath. The story is told that Jane, upon hearing the news, apparently traumatized and upset, fainted away. As far as is known, she didn't write for some three years after the move. Modern critics have scruples of various kinds, depending on academic fashion, about assuming that things that happen in the writer's life influence the subjects of her books, or about guessing at biographical details from events in her books; but both writers and readers know how directly the things that happen to you or someone you know get into your books, directly or tangentially; to read without this knowledge is a somewhat naïve form of reading. Knowing that Austen discussed her writing with her family explains some things about *Persuasion* that were surely intended to amuse them as much as or more than her other readers—the naval talk, for example. Two of her brothers were in the British navy (both eventually rose to the rank of admiral), and Mrs. Croft's comments about life at sea must have made the family laugh a lot.

Much is to be learned from the formal shape of a work. *Persuasion* is short (some might say too short), comprised of two books of almost exactly the same length, of twelve chapters each, elegantly balanced. Book One is concerned with introducing the characters, establishing their interaction, and developing the plot. It ends with a cliff-hanger: flighty Louisa Musgrove has fallen from a stile and has a severe head injury. Will she die? And does Captain Wentworth's immense concern reflect his love for her or his feelings of guilt? These are the issues that end Book One on a note of suspense. You can't help but notice that the ladylike Austen ends her chapters with shameless narrative hooks.

Book Two, told mostly from the point of view of Anne Elliot, by means of amusing ups and downs, resolves these questions. Since Jane Austen was careful never to write a scene with no women present, there are no scenes without women—in this case Anne—there to observe them. This restriction has the effect of limiting Austen's ability to reveal certain things; and because we are fully in Anne's point of view toward the end of the novel, we too are in suspense.

The point-of-view management of any novel is the most crucial technical decision the writer will have to make. Austen's management of the point of view here would be disapproved by most creative writing teachers, but it is very adroit. In *Persuasion,* Book One, up to Chapter 5, all is very much managed by the intrusive omniscient narrator, a device very much out of fashion now. This is the Jane Austen–like person who tells us what Lady Russell, Anne, and even Charles Musgrove think, makes her own comments, even adds expressions of personal surprise in her characteristic ironic tone:

> Oh! Could the originals of the portraits against the wainscot, could the gentlemen in brown velvet and the ladies in blue satin have seen what was going on, have been conscious of such an overthrow of all order and neatness!

Book One is still very much managed by this intrusive omniscient narrator, but we notice that by Book Two she has more or less disappeared. We are almost entirely in Anne's consciousness, and liable, with Anne, to misjudge things. In a sort of narrative bait and switch, Anne's unreliable consciousness—what Henry James called "limited omniscience"—has taken the place of the Jane Austen figure's reliable asperities. Why has this happened? Looking back, beginning with Chapter 6, we find the slide into Anne's point of view almost imperceptibly gradual, rendered at first in a form of peculiarly Austenian indirect speech: "she must now submit to feel that another lesson, that of knowing our own nothingness beyond our own circle, was becoming necessary for her." This could be either Anne's or Jane's thought. Notice too, from this concise writer, the extra verb—she must not just feel, but "submit to feel," emphasizing the helplessness, as Anne feels it, of her position as the unmarried sister.

Anne is more intelligent and sensitive than the other characters—she already understands that she was misled by Lady Russell, and is aware of the motives and limitations of her father and sisters—but because of her youth and inexperience, she is apt to make mistakes. Once we are in Anne's consciousness, we have to keep in mind that her perception of events is not altogether reliable. For example, she mistakenly believes that Captain Wentworth is in love with Louisa Musgrove:

> There could not be a doubt, to her mind there was none, of what would follow [Louisa's] recovery. A few months hence, and the room so deserted, occupied but by her silent, pensive self, ought to be filled again with all that was happy and gay, all that was glowing and bright in prosperous love, all that was most unlike Anne Elliot!

This is Anne's self-pitying perception that her life is hopeless, Captain Wentworth is sure to marry Louisa, and everyone in the world is happy but herself. She misinterprets Captain Wentworth's attentions to Louisa, but because we're in her head we have only her analysis. We too fall in with her misinterpretation, and all the better is the surprise when we, a little sooner than Anne, come to understand that he merely felt guilty about having let Louisa jump.

Anne's understanding is limited because of her age, inexperience, gender, and so on, and she makes other mistakes: she is taken in by her charming cousin William Elliot. She is also a woman of her time, the early nineteenth century, who sees the world in romantic terms:

> An hour's complete leisure for such reflections as these, on a dark November day, a small thick rain almost blotting out the very few objects ever to be discerned from the windows . . .

This reminds us that Austen is writing at the height of the Romantic period, with its pathetic fallacies, where trees weep in tandem with the heroine's emotions, and skies lower at times of danger, a mode Austen is only partly satirical in imitating.

Austen had a stern set of rules governing point of view—for instance, she chose never to go into the minds of servants or of men. If she had stepped outside the experience of women, the novels would be entirely different, but certainly not better, and probably no longer comedies of manners. It's always revealing to think about the alternatives to the point-of-view choice the author has made, for the interest of seeing what was to be lost and gained by an alternative. A bolder novelist than I might have chosen to go into the minds of my Islamic characters and report their feelings of fear, panic, and resentment, but then the tone would have been different; it would have been another novel, perhaps overtly tragic, and perhaps better suited to the serious subject. Here and there Austen does break her own rules, as when in Book Two we go momentarily into Lady Russell's mind, even though the point of view of the story has shifted to Anne's. When Lady Russell hears that Captain Wentworth and Louisa are a number, aloud she wishes them well,

> but internally her heart revelled in angry pleasure, in pleased contempt that the man who at twenty-three had seemed to understand somewhat

of the value of an Anne Elliot, should, eight years afterwards, be charmed by a Louisa Musgrove.

Here, Austen cannot resist this exploration of *schadenfreude,* or whatever we would call the undoubted satisfaction of having one's darkest opinions confirmed.

Our reading of other novels has shown us that great works often take a turn, about half or three quarters of the way through, when they reveal themselves to concern something other than what they appeared to be about at the beginning. I've always supposed this reflects the novelist's increased understanding, as she goes along, of her true subject, which usually turns out to be a bit or very different from her plan at the outset. This shift is good, maybe essential, if a work is going to rise above the formulary confinement of the author's original plan. One such shift in *Persuasion* is noticeable. It isn't till the second half of the book, when we have become firmly fixed in Anne's consciousness, that we begin to understand its true nature as a psychological drama of developing self-confidence. The novel charts a young woman's passage from docility and dependence to moral independence, a crucial subject for Austen and for the society in which she was raised.

The shift finds its formal expression; just when we were thinking that this is a novel without much dialogue, we suddenly have pages of it, observed, overheard, or reported by Anne herself. The other characters have long discussions about the day's program, the music, and naval matters. Sometimes their talk takes the form of wounding gossip. The high point of this is when someone tells Anne that Captain Wentworth has said she was "so altered he should not have known her," which she of course takes to mean she is altered for the worse. Our—and Anne's—anxiety is increased when the chapter ends with her hearing that he means to marry: "anybody between 15 and 30 may have me for asking. A little beauty and a few smiles, and a few compliments to the navy and I am a lost man." He wants "a strong mind with sweetness of nature," and adds, "Something a little inferior I of course will put up with, but it must not be much. If I am a fool, I shall be a fool indeed, for I have thought on the subject more than most men." Anne, of course, thinks he is describing Louisa Musgrove, and from here on the novel must find its way to the resolution of this mistake.

The formal elements we want to examine when reading any beloved book are all perfectly traditional elements of the craft of the novel, considerations that exist apart from the specific subject, theme, or moral of the work: the title, the genre, the way characterization is done, how the principal conflict is introduced, the proportion of scene—the dramatized bits—to exposition, whether there is someone to identify with, how dialogue is used, biographical connections to the author's life, the general form and management of point of view, and finally, an aspect of form, a shift or acceleration that enlarges our understanding of the meaning of the work. To these I might have added Austen's language—the special tool of her art. The witty precision of Austen's style has entertained readers for nearly two hundred years without losing its freshness and power to delight, a testimony to her unparalleled genius and to the enduring powers of the English language.

Margot Livesey

NOTHING BUT HIMSELF

When last spring I finally made a pilgrimage to Winchester Cathedral, one of the guides apologized to me for the lack of flowers on Jane Austen's grave; the Cathedral does not allow them during Lent. "But during the rest of the year," she assured me, "you can find her grave by the flowers. People are always bringing Jane bouquets." Austen is buried in the north aisle of the nave and her grave has not one but two markers. The older one, the stone slab in the floor, contains no mention of her work but remarks on "The benevolence of her heart, the sweetness of her temper, and the extraordinary endowments of her mind." Nearby, a bronze plaque on the wall praises her novels. Reading these touching inscriptions, I thought how typical the guide's remark was of the affection that Austen, and her work, inspire. People who love her novels also seem to feel admitted to her uneventful life: Dear Jane. She is buried not far from a casket said to contain the bones of King Canute, the great eleventh-century Viking king who helped to convert England to Christianity.

There are no kings in Austen's work. Her six novels, as she herself was among the first to comment, revolve around a limited set of concerns, are set in small communities, and are comedic rather than tragic. Her plots are mostly predictable, though she is capable of surprises, like Louisa's famous fall from the Cobb in Lyme, or Emma's rudeness to Miss Bates. As for characters, she has certain types to which she steadfastly returns: the foolish parent, the snob, the misguided daughter, the social climber, the easily overlooked estimable young woman, the reserved man of integrity. These characters show up in book after book, and for the most part, although they contribute to the events of the narrative, remain unchanged by them. Only her major characters—the heroine and hero—are transformed by the last page.

I first encountered Austen's work at the age of fourteen, when I had to read *Pride and Prejudice* for school. At that time, I lived in a community that Austen herself, in some parallel universe, might have relished as subject matter: a boys' school in Scotland, ten miles from the nearest town. Everyone who lived in the valley of Glenalmond, except for two farmers, was in some way connected with the institution. We knew what it was like to deal with the same small number of people week after week, year after year; to have a keen sense of hierarchy: the headmaster came before his deputy who came before the bursar . . . And then, of course, we also knew what it was like to have occasional visitors who called that hierarchy into question.

But seeing the world around me mirrored, however obliquely, was not part of the appeal of *Pride and Prejudice.* I read to escape my environment, and made no connection between the two. Nor could I have said exactly why Austen's characters gave me such pleasure. Compared with those in, say, *Wuthering Heights,* they were painfully sedate. No one promised to love anyone from beyond the grave. No suitor threatened to break every bone in another's body. But there was this feeling of something moving beneath the surface of Austen's calm prose that made me, even as I finished the book, want to turn back to the opening page.

Decades later, I still find myself struggling to understand what makes Austen's novels so alluring, and what, as a writer, I can learn from her. A few years ago I gained new insight when I decided to follow, humbly, in her footsteps and write a romance: a novel titled *Banishing Verona.* While trying to figure out how I could make such familiar subject matter new again, I identified a few major "rules" (by which I do not mean to suggest for a moment that Austen consciously devised, or followed, such guidelines). The lovers must meet early and then be separated—either physically or emotionally—for most of the narrative. There must be significant obstacles, internal, or external, or both. A subplot, or two, is required to keep the lovers apart, to allow time to pass, and, ideally, to act as a foil to the main plot. Crucially, and most mysteriously of all, the reader must come to feel that this romance is not merely a matter of personal preference between two people, but that a whole world order is in question until these two find each other.

I use the verb "find" deliberately. Although Jane Austen's characters go on the most modest of journeys—never more than an hour or two on foot or a few hours by carriage—somehow we end up feeling that they have covered a long distance. They travel from a place where the self is poorly known and where various major landmarks have been misidentified—a windmill is mistaken for a library; attraction is mistaken for antipathy—to a place where the self is recognized and understood. The couple do not so much decide upon as discover each other, and in the course of their discovery something profound is revealed. It seems likely that Austen, given her family's pleasure in theatre, would have known *A Midsummer Night's Dream,* in which three couples (I include Titania and Bottom) enter a dark forest where they part and come together in a complicated dance.

But Austen does not go in for forests any more than for kings. Another of the rules that govern the world of her novels is her commitment to realism, and nowhere, I would argue, is that commitment more obvious than in her last novel, *Persuasion.* In the typical world of romance, flaws vanish and virtues are exaggerated, but in *Persuasion* Austen achieves a compelling romance that comes out of a hard-won realism. Again I think of the Brontës, where love conquers all and good looks and/or virtue make up for lack of social standing or income. *Persuasion* offers no such rosy view of the world; we see two flawed characters grappling with a flawed society. When Captain Wentworth first proposes to Anne Elliot, he has nothing to recommend him but himself, and that is not enough, at least not in the eyes of Anne's advisor, the somewhat irritating Lady Russell. Nor, I would argue, for Austen. When Wentworth proposes again at the end of the novel, he has not only himself to recommend him but also a good fortune, good connections, and a good career. Love needs the things of the world.

In balancing the demands of realism with those of romance, Austen must do battle with the reader. Critics have long noted the role of the reader in creating the text, and no subject matter makes readers more ardently creative than romantic love. From the reader's point of view, it is a truth universally acknowledged that, if a single man and a single woman are in the same story, they are going to end up together. This devotion to matchmaking has, as Austen seems to have known all along, and I painfully discovered, several repercussions for the writer. In their eagerness to unite characters, readers tend to be oblivious to such quotidian concerns as class, money, and family. I was partly commenting on this myopia when, in *Banishing Verona,* I made my twenty-nine-year-old hero look like a Raphael angel and my thirty-seven-year-old heroine resemble the famous bust of Beethoven. (Austen perhaps had some similar thought when she made Sir Walter Elliot, Anne's father, a remarkably handsome man.) I knew that, almost irrespective of the difficulties with which I burdened my characters, readers would be expecting this unlikely couple to end up together. A large question for the novel was how to manage those expectations and delay realizing them, without either boring or frustrating the reader.

Here Austen sets a wonderful example in making admirable use of both prose and plot. At fourteen, I was too young to recognize that, while I thought I was reading *Pride and Prejudice* to see who married whom, I was really reading for the unswerving music of Austen's sentences, which, from first to last, carry the reader effortlessly along. This book, single-handedly, contradicts the famous descriptions of the novel as a baggy monster, or a piece of prose with something wrong with it. Selfishly, when I began to write my own novels, I was glad to learn that *Pride and Prejudice* had not sprung full-blown onto the page, but was the product of hard work, deep thought, and revision.

Paragraph by paragraph, I do not think that *Persuasion* offers quite the lustrous pleasure of this earlier work. It is more complicated in tone, less steady in voice, and (I feel like a heretic saying this) sometimes a bit plodding. To reread the novel, for me, is always a perplexing experience. Although Austen writes with exhilarating freedom about her heroine's feelings, I do not love every sentence. There are passages that seem pedestrian or where I can see the wheels turning—and yet, when I reach the last page, I discover that the novel, from first to last, is once again complete and shimmering in my imagination. *Persuasion* is one of those rare works that become much more than the sum of their sentences. If the reader helps to create the text, then the author also helps to create the reader, and in her last novel Austen creates readers who feel more intelligent, more compassionate, and more empathetic than most of us are in real life.

Like Trollope and Dickens, Austen is acutely aware of how social distinctions and money—usually the lack thereof—shape the lives of her characters. The plot of *Persuasion* revolves around the tension between Sir Walter's poverty and his vanity. Both aspects of his character are introduced in the opening pages and become a major force, along with health, in propelling the novel. Anne is simply a helpless bystander as her father decides to rent out his house and take lodgings in Bath. As she tells Captain Harville (and Wentworth), this is the fate of women. "We live at home, quiet, confined, and our feelings prey upon us." Passive characters in fiction are often judged unsympathetic, but Anne is active in all the ways she properly can be, taking care of her family, thinking and feeling even when she can't act, and, when Louisa falls from the Cobb, rising, superbly, to the occasion.

The opening pages also introduce an important theme. The only book, we are told, that Sir Walter enjoys reading, under any and all circumstances, is the Baronetage. He has already edited his own entry to make it more accurate, and he wishes that he could make still further changes involving his oldest daughter, the almost equally vain and foolish Elizabeth. *Persuasion* is often said to be about second chances, but to my mind it is more about revision—for what use are second chances if we don't see things differently, and act differently? Our star-crossed lovers, Anne and Captain Wentworth, find themselves in each other's company less than a quarter of the way through the novel, but initially Wentworth sees Anne in much the same way as her father and sisters do: "only Anne," a counterpart to his "nothing but himself." The two lovers don't really see each other until the penultimate chapter.

This crucial chapter provides an excellent example of not just her characters revising, but of Austen herself doing so. We still have the first version she wrote, a year before her death, in which she brings Anne and Captain Wentworth together and allows them, almost immediately, to dispel the cloud of misunderstandings that has kept them apart. In the revision—the ending as we know it—Austen writes a much more complicated scene in which, rather than leave the two lovers alone, she has them address each other through an intermediary. Anne and Captain Harville argue about which gender is the more steadfast when it comes to romantic love. Meanwhile, Captain Wentworth sits nearby, listening, and, rather than speaking his feelings, writes them in a letter.

Being less skillful than Austen, I adopted a different strategy in my novel *Banishing Verona:* after bringing my lovers together in the first chapter, I separated them not merely by misunderstandings but also by an energetic plot that forced them to travel thousands of miles. When, however, after many vicissitudes, I finally allowed them to meet again in the last chapter, I did pay homage to Austen by using a book to bring them together.

My plot was also, I hoped, a way of overcoming a confusing contradiction: while readers themselves may engage in ardent matchmaking, heterosexual love is often deemed slight, or unworthy, subject matter for fiction. Many factors fuel this contradiction, but one that seems relevant to *Persuasion* is the apparently random nature of romance, both in its early stages and its later outcome. Austen, I think, embraces that randomness on behalf of her minor characters—Louisa falls off the Cobb, out of one relationship and into another—but her hero and heroine are held to more stringent standards. Readers have been hoping that Anne and Captain Wentworth will be reunited for most of the novel, but what makes this ending so satisfying is not merely our partisan feelings, but our sense that each of these characters has, over the course of the novel, slain various dragons, withstood the sirens, and remained true to themselves while honoring the strict mores of the period. Captain Wentworth, who has earlier seemed ready to settle for any obliging young woman, now recognizes that only Anne's superior nature can answer his needs. Bravely—and this takes as much courage as embarking on a stormy voyage—he risks being rejected again. As for Anne, she has become a woman who can recognize both the truth of her own affections and the inescapable foolishness of the father and sister she must leave behind in order to claim her place in the world. There is nothing random about their union.

In his conversation with Anne, Harville argues that he has never "opened a book in my life which had not something to say upon woman's inconstancy . . . But perhaps you will say, these were all written by men." "Perhaps I shall," says Anne. ". . . I will not allow books to prove anything." This is a subject, she continues, on which we may have opinions but no proof. I can offer no absolute proof as to how Austen convinces us in this wonderful scene that Anne's and Wentworth's lives hang in the balance, but I hazard the opinion that she practices a kind of synecdoche; the part, romance, stands in for the whole, their social and spiritual beings. Her characters have gone on a pilgrimage and are now able to offer each other nothing but themselves in the best sense of that phrase, which is to say the selves which comprise both their accomplishments and the part of them that will endure even if these accomplishments are stripped away. Together Anne and Wentworth are ready to follow the excellent example of Admiral and Mrs. Croft and face whatever dangers the world holds, on land and at sea.

And as readers, we, too, practice a kind of synecdoche. We put aside the part of ourselves that pretends to want literature to uphold values different from those we have in life, that censures novels for, mostly, not bringing news of war, famine, and revolution. And we accept, even embrace, the delicate, tremulous part of ourselves that yearns for the great good fortune of intimate connection and understanding. I read Austen first as a teenager, then in the company of a long romance, later still as a single woman, and now as a married woman. And in each of these incarnations I have understood that Austen is speaking to me, and about me, and about that deep need to have the world we live in—be it Bath, or Lyme Regis, or the Lower East Side—make sense.

Virginia Woolf

JANE AUSTEN AT SIXTY

It is probable that if Miss Cassandra Austen had had her way, we should have had nothing of Jane Austen's except her novels. To her elder sister alone did she write freely; to her alone she confided her hopes and, if rumor is true, the one great disappointment of her life; but when Miss Cassandra Austen grew old, and the growth of her sister's fame made her suspect that a time might come when strangers would pry and scholars speculate, she burnt, at great cost to herself, every letter that could gratify their curiosity, and spared only what she judged too trivial to be of interest.

Hence our knowledge of Jane Austen is derived from a little gossip, a few letters, and her books. As for the gossip, gossip which has survived its day is never despicable; with a little rearrangement it suits our purpose admirably. For example, Jane "is not at all pretty and very prim, unlike a girl of twelve . . . Jane is whimsical and affected," says little Philadelphia Austen of her cousin. Then we have Mrs. Mitford, who knew the Austens as girls and thought Jane "the prettiest, silliest, most affected, husband-hunting butterfly she ever remembers." Next, there is Miss Mitford's anonymous friend "who visits her now [and] says that she has stiffened into the most perpendicular, precise, taciturn piece of 'single blessedness' that ever existed, and that, until *Pride and Prejudice* showed what a precious gem was hidden in that unbending case, she was no more regarded in society than a poker or firescreen . . . The case is very different now," the good lady goes on; "she is still a poker—but a poker of whom everybody is afraid . . . A wit, a delineator of character, who does not talk is terrific indeed!" On the other side, of course, there are the Austens, a race little given to panegyric of themselves, but nevertheless, they say, her brothers "were very fond and very proud of her. They were attached to her by her talents, her virtues, and her engaging manners, and each loved afterwards to fancy a resemblance in some niece or daughter of his own to the dear sister Jane, whose perfect equal they yet never expected to see." Charming but perpendicular, loved at home but feared by strangers, biting of tongue but tender of heart—these contrasts are by no means incompatible, and when we turn to the novels we shall find ourselves stumbling there too over the same complexities in the writer.

To begin with, that prim little girl whom Philadelphia found so unlike a child of twelve, whimsical and affected, was soon to be the authoress of an astonishing and unchildish story, *Love and Freindship,* which, incredible though it appears, was written at the age of fifteen. It was written, apparently, to amuse the schoolroom; one of the stories in the same book is dedicated with mock solemnity to her brother; another is neatly illustrated with watercolor heads by her sister. There are jokes which, one feels, were family property; thrusts of satire, which went home because all little Austens made mock in common of fine ladies who "sighed and fainted on the sofa."

Brothers and sisters must have laughed when Jane read out loud her last hit at the vices which they all abhorred. "I die a martyr to my grief for the loss of Augustius. One fatal swoon has cost me my life. Beware of Swoons, Dear Laura . . . Run mad as often as you chuse, but do not faint . . ." And on she rushed, as fast as she could write and quicker than she could spell, to tell the incredible adventures of Laura and Sophia, of Philander and Gustavus, of the gentleman who drove a coach between Edinburgh and Stirling every other day, of the theft of the fortune that was kept in the table drawer, of the starving mothers and the sons who acted Macbeth. Undoubtedly, the story must have roused the schoolroom to uproarious laughter. And yet, nothing is more obvious than that this girl of fifteen, sitting in her private corner of the common parlor, was writing not to draw a laugh from brothers and sisters, and not for home consumption. She was writing for everybody, for nobody, for our age, for her own; in other words, even at that early age Jane Austen was writing. One hears it in the rhythm and shapeliness and severity of the sentences. "She was nothing more than a mere good tempered, civil, and obliging young woman; as such we could scarcely dislike her—she was only an object of contempt." Such a sentence is meant to outlast the Christmas holidays. Spirited, easy, full of fun, verging with freedom upon sheer nonsense—*Love and Freindship* is all that, but what is this note which never merges in the rest, which sounds distinctly and penetratingly all through the volume? It is the sound of laughter. The girl of fifteen is laughing, in her corner, at the world.

Girls of fifteen are always laughing. They laugh when Mr. Binney helps himself to salt instead of sugar. They almost die of laughing when old Mrs. Tomkins sits down upon the cat. But they are crying the moment after. They have no fixed abode from which they see that there is something eternally laughable in human nature, some quality in men and women that forever excites our satire. They do not know that Lady Greville who snubs, and poor Maria who is snubbed, are permanent features of every ballroom. But Jane Austen knew it from her birth upward. One of those fairies who perch upon cradles must have taken her a flight through the world directly she was born. When she was laid in the cradle again she knew not only what the world looked like, but had already chosen her kingdom. She had agreed that if she might rule over that territory, she would covet no other. Thus at fifteen she had few illusions about other people and none about herself. Whatever she writes is finished and turned and set in its relation, not to the parsonage, but to the universe. She is impersonal; she is inscrutable. When the writer, Jane Austen, wrote down in the most remarkable sketch in the book a little of Lady Greville's conversation, there is no trace of anger at the snub which the clergyman's daughter, Jane Austen, once received. Her gaze passes straight to the mark, and we know precisely where, upon the map of human nature, that mark is. We know because Jane Austen kept to her compact; she never trespassed beyond her boundaries. Never, even at the emotional age of fifteen, did she round upon herself in shame, obliterate a sarcasm in a spasm of compassion, or blur an outline in a mist of rhapsody. Spasms and rhapsodies, she seems to have said, pointing with her stick, end *there;* and the boundary line is perfectly distinct. But she does not deny that moons and mountains and castles exist—on the other side. She has even one romance of her own. It is for the Queen of Scots. She really admired her very much. "One of the first characters in the world," she called her, "a bewitching Princess whose only friend was then the Duke of Norfolk, and whose only ones now Mr. Whitaker, Mrs. Lefroy, Mrs. Knight and myself." With these words her passion is neatly circumscribed, and rounded with a laugh. It is amusing to remember in what terms the young Brontës wrote, not very much later, in their northern parsonage, about the Duke of Wellington.

The prim little girl grew up. She became "the prettiest, silliest, most affected husband-hunting butterfly" Mrs. Mitford ever remembered, and, incidentally, the authoress of a novel called *Pride and Prejudice,* which, written stealthily under cover of a creaking door, lay for many years unpublished. A little later, it is thought, she began another story, *The Watsons,* and being for some reason dissatisfied with it, left it unfinished. Unfinished and unsuccessful, it may throw more light upon its writer's genius than the polished masterpiece blazing in universal fame. Her difficulties are more apparent in it, and the method she took to overcome them less artfully concealed. To begin with, the stiffness and the bareness of the first chapters prove that she was one of those writers who lay their facts out rather baldly in the first version and then go back and back and back and cover them with flesh and atmosphere. How it would have been done we cannot say—by what suppressions and insertions and artful devices. But the miracle would have been accomplished; the dull history of fourteen years of family life would have been converted into another of those exquisite and apparently effortless introductions; and we should never have guessed what pages of preliminary drudgery Jane Austen forced her pen to go through. Here we perceive that she was no conjurer after all. Like other writers, she had to create the atmosphere in which her own peculiar genius could bear fruit. Here she fumbles; here she keeps us waiting. Suddenly, she has done it; now things can happen as she likes things to happen. The Edwardses are going to the ball. The Tomlinsons' carriage is passing; she can tell us that Charles is "being provided with his gloves and told to keep them on"; Tom Musgrove retreats to a remote corner with a barrel of oysters and is famously snug. Her genius is freed and active. At once our senses quicken; we are possessed with the peculiar intensity which she alone can impart. But of what is it all composed? Of a ball in a country town; a few couples meeting and taking hands in an assembly room; a little eating and drinking; and for catastrophe, a boy being snubbed by one young lady and kindly treated by another. There is no tragedy and no heroism. Yet for some reason the little scene is moving out of all proportion to its surface solemnity. We have been made to see that if Emma acted so in the ballroom, how considerate, how tender, inspired by what sincerity of feeling she would have shown herself in those graver crises of life which, as we watch her, come inevitably before our eyes. Jane Austen is thus a mistress of much deeper emotion than appears upon the surface. She stimulates us to supply what is not there. What she offers is, apparently, a trifle, yet is composed of something that expands in the reader's mind and endows with the most enduring form of life scenes which are outwardly trivial. Always the stress is laid upon character. How, we are made to wonder, will Emma behave when Lord Osborne and Tom Musgrove make their call at five minutes before three, just as Mary is bringing in the tray and the knife case? It is an extremely awkward situation. The young men are accustomed to much greater refinement. Emma may prove herself ill bred, vulgar, a nonentity. The turns and twists of the dialogue keep us on the tenterhooks of suspense. Our attention is half upon the present moment, half upon the future. And when, in the end, Emma behaves in such a way as to vindicate our highest hopes of her, we are moved as if we had been made witnesses of a matter of the highest importance. Here, indeed, in this unfinished and in the main inferior story are all the elements of Jane Austen's greatness. It has the permanent quality of literature. Think away the surface animation, the likeness to life, and there remains to provide a deeper pleasure, an exquisite discrimination of human values. Dismiss this too from the mind and one can dwell with extreme satisfaction upon the more abstract art which, in the ballroom scene, so varies the emotions and proportions the parts that it is possible to enjoy it, as one enjoys poetry, for itself, and not as a link which carries the story this way and that.

But the gossip says of Jane Austen that she was perpendicular, precise, and taciturn—"a poker of whom everybody is afraid." Of this too there are traces; she could be merciless enough; she is one of the most consistent satirists in the whole of literature. Those first angular chapters of *The Watsons* prove that hers was not a prolific genius; she had not, like Emily Brontë, merely to open the door to make herself felt. Humbly and gaily she collected the twigs and straws out of which the nest was to be made and placed them neatly together. The twigs and straws were a little dry and a little dusty in themselves. There was the big house and the little house; a tea party, a dinner party, and an occasional picnic; life was hedged in by valuable connections and adequate incomes; by muddy roads, wet feet, and a tendency on the part of the ladies to get tired; a little money supported it, a little consequence, and the education commonly enjoyed by upper-middle-class families living in the country. Vice, adventure, passion were left outside. But of all this prosiness, of all this littleness, she evades nothing, and nothing is slurred over. Patiently and precisely she tells us how they "made no stop anywhere till they reached Newbury, where a comfortable meal, uniting dinner and supper, wound up the enjoyments and fatigues of the day." Nor does she pay to conventions merely the tribute of lip homage; she believes in them besides accepting them. When she is describing a clergyman, like Edmund Bertram, or a sailor, in particular, she appears debarred by the sanctity of his office from the free use of her chief tool, the comic genius, and is apt therefore to lapse into decorous panegyric or matter-of-fact description. But these are exceptions; for the most part her attitude recalls the anonymous lady's ejaculation—"A wit, a delineator of character, who does not talk is terrific indeed!" She wishes neither to reform nor to annihilate; she is silent; and that is terrific indeed. One after another she creates her fools, her prigs, her worldlings, her Mr. Collinses, her Sir Walter Elliots, her Mrs. Bennets. She encircles them with the lash of a whip-like phrase which, as it runs round them, cuts out their silhouettes for ever. But there they remain; no excuse is found for them and no mercy shown them. Nothing remains of Julia and Maria Bertram when she has done with them; Lady Bertram is left "sitting and calling to Pug and trying to keep him from the flower beds" eternally. A divine justice is meted out; Dr. Grant, who begins by liking his goose tender, ends by bringing on "apoplexy and death, by three great institutionary dinners in one week." Sometimes it seems as if her creatures were born merely to give Jane Austen the supreme delight of slicing their heads off. She is satisfied; she is content; she would not alter a hair on anybody's head, or move one brick or one blade of grass in a world which provides her with such exquisite delight.

Nor, indeed, would we. For even if the pangs of outraged vanity, or the heat of moral wrath, urged us to improve away a world so full of spite, pettiness, and folly, the task is beyond our powers. People are like that—the girl of fifteen knew it; the mature woman proves it. At this very moment some Lady Bertram finds it almost too trying to keep Pug from the flower beds; she sends Chapman to help Miss Fanny, a little late. The discrimination is so perfect, the satire so just that, consistent though it is, it almost escapes our notice. No touch of pettiness, no hint of spite, rouses us from our contemplation. Delight strangely mingles with our amusement. Beauty illumines these fools.

That elusive quality is indeed often made up of very different parts, which it needs a peculiar genius to bring together. The wit of Jane Austen has for partner the perfection of her taste. Her fool is a fool, her snob is a snob, because he departs from the model of sanity and sense which she has in mind, and conveys to us unmistakably even while she makes us laugh. Never did any novelist make more use of an impeccable sense of human values. It is against the disc of an unerring heart, an unfailing good taste, an almost stern morality, that she shows up those deviations from kindness, truth, and sincerity which are among the most delightful things in English literature. She depicts a Mary Crawford in her mixture of good and bad entirely by this means. She lets her rattle on against the clergy, or in favor of a baronetage and ten thousand a year with all the ease and spirit possible; but now and again she strikes one note of her own, very quietly, but in perfect tune, and at once all Mary Crawford's chatter, though it continues to amuse, rings flat. Hence the depth, the beauty, the complexity of her scenes. From such contrasts there comes a beauty, a solemnity even which are not only as remarkable as her wit, but an inseparable part of it. In *The Watsons* she gives us a foretaste of this power; she makes us wonder why an ordinary act of kindness, as she describes it, becomes so full of meaning. In her masterpieces, the same gift is brought to perfection. Here is nothing out of the way; it is midday in Northamptonshire; a dull young man is talking to rather a weakly young woman on the stairs as they go up to dress for dinner, with housemaids passing. But, from triviality, from commonplace, their words become suddenly full of meaning, and the moment for both one of the most memorable in their lives. It fills itself; it shines; it glows; it hangs before us, deep, trembling, serene for a second; next, the housemaid passes, and this drop in which all the happiness of life has collected gently subsides again to become part of the ebb and flow of ordinary existence.

What more natural then, with this insight into their profundity, than that Jane Austen should have chosen to write of the trivialities of day-to-day existence, of parties, picnics, and country dances? No "suggestions to alter her style of writing" from the Prince Regent or Mr. Clarke could tempt her; no romance, no adventure, no politics or intrigue could hold a candle to life on a country-house staircase as she saw it. Indeed, the Prince Regent and his librarian had run their heads against a very formidable obstacle; they were trying to tamper with an incorruptible conscience, to disturb an infallible discretion. The child who formed her sentences so finely when she was fifteen never ceased to form them, and never wrote for the Prince Regent or his librarian, but for the world at large. She knew exactly what her powers were, and what material they were fitted to deal with as material should be dealt with by a writer, whose standard of finality was high. There were impressions that lay outside her province; emotions that by no stretch or artifice could be properly coated and covered by her own resources. For example, she could not make a girl talk enthusiastically of banners and chapels. She could not throw herself wholeheartedly into a romantic moment. She had all sorts of devices for evading scenes of passion. Nature and its beauties she approached in a sidelong way of her own. She describes a beautiful night without once mentioning the moon. Nevertheless, as we read the few formal phrases about "the brilliancy of an unclouded night and the contrast of the deep shade of the woods" the night is at once as "solemn, and soothing, and lovely" as she tells us, quite simply, that it was.

The balance of her gifts was singularly perfect. Among her finished novels there are no failures, and among her many chapters few that sink markedly below the level of the others. But, after all, she died at the age of forty-one. She died at the height of her powers. She was still subject to those changes which often make the final period of a writer's career the most interesting of all. Vivacious, irrepressible, gifted with an invention of great vitality, there can be no doubt that she would have written more, had she lived, and it is tempting to consider whether she would not have written differently. The boundaries were marked; moons, mountains, and castles lay on the other side. But was she not sometimes tempted to trespass for a minute? Was she not beginning, in her own gay and brilliant manner, to contemplate a little voyage of discovery?

Let us take *Persuasion,* the last completed novel, and look by its light at the books she might have written had she lived. There is a peculiar beauty and a peculiar dullness in *Persuasion.* The dullness is that which so often marks the transition stage between two different periods. The writer is a little bored. She has grown too familiar with the ways of her world; she no longer notes them freshly. There is an asperity in her comedy which suggests that she has almost ceased to be amused by the vanities of a Sir Walter or the snobbery of a Miss Elliot. The satire is harsh, and the comedy crude. She is no longer so freshly aware of the amusements of daily life. Her mind is not altogether on her object. But, while we feel that Jane Austen has done this before, and done it better, we also feel that she is trying to do something which she has never yet attempted. There is a new element in *Persuasion,* the quality, perhaps, that made Dr. Whewell fire up and insist that it was "the most beautiful of her works." She is beginning to discover that the world is larger, more mysterious, and more romantic than she had supposed. We feel it to be true of her-self when she says of Anne: "She had been forced into prudence in her youth, she learned romance as she grew older—the natural sequel of an unnatural beginning." She dwells frequently upon the beauty and the melancholy of nature, upon the autumn where she had been wont to dwell upon the spring. She talks of the "influence so sweet and so sad of autumnal months in the country." She marks "the tawny leaves and withered hedges." "One does not love a place the less because one has suffered in it," she observes. But it is not only in a new sensibility to na-ture that we detect the change. Her attitude to life itself is altered. She is seeing it, for the greater part of the book, through the eyes of a woman who, unhappy herself, has a special sympathy for the happiness and un-happiness of others, which, until the very end, she is forced to comment upon in silence. Therefore the observation is less of facts and more of feelings than is usual. There is an expressed emotion in the scene at the concert and in the famous talk about woman's constancy which proves not merely the biographical fact that Jane Austen had loved, but the aes-thetic fact that she was no longer afraid to say so. Experience, when it was of a serious kind, had to sink very deep, and to be thoroughly disinfected by the passage of time, before she allowed herself to deal with it in fic-tion. But now, in 1817, she was ready. Outwardly, too, in her circum-stances, a change was imminent. Her fame had grown very slowly. "I doubt," wrote Mr. Austen-Leigh, "whether it would be possible to men-tion any other author of note whose personal obscurity was so com-plete." Had she lived a few more years only, all that would have been altered. She would have stayed in London, dined out, lunched out, met famous people, made new friends, read, traveled, and carried back to the quiet country cottage a hoard of observations to feast upon at leisure.

And what effect would all this have had upon the six novels that Jane Austen did not write? She would not have written of crime, of passion, or of adventure. She would not have been rushed by the importunity of publishers or the flattery of friends into slovenliness or insincerity. But she would have known more. Her sense of security would have been shaken. Her comedy would have suffered. She would have trusted less (this is already perceptible in *Persuasion*) to dialogue and more to reflec-tion to give us a knowledge of her characters. Those marvelous little speeches which sum up, in a few minutes' chatter, all that we need in order to know an Admiral Croft or a Mrs. Musgrove forever, that short-hand, hit-or-miss method which contains chapters of analysis and psychology, would have become too crude to hold all that she now perceived of the complexity of human nature. She would have devised a method, clear and composed as ever, but deeper and more suggestive, for conveying not only what people say, but what they leave unsaid; not only what they are, but what life is. She would have stood farther away from her characters, and seen them more as a group, less as individuals. Her satire, while it played less incessantly, would have been more stringent and severe. She would have been the forerunner of Henry James and of Proust—but enough. Vain are these speculations: the most perfect artist among women, the writer whose books are immortal, died "just as she was beginning to feel confidence in her own success."

Jay McInerney

BEAUTIFUL MINDS

We love Jane Austen through her heroines. Knowing so little about her, we worship her surrogates. And generally speaking, unless we are cranky scholars or celibate critics, we love and rank the novels according to our regard for the female principals. I can't help finding my own response to the novels colored by the degree to which I find the heroines attractive, although over the course of some thirty years of reading and rereading I find my admiration shifting among the young ladies; unlike Frederick Wentworth, longtime lover of *Persuasion*'s leading lady Anne Elliot, I could be accused of inconstancy, but I like to think my tastes show an underlying consistency.

Like most Austen readers I first loved Elizabeth Bennet, the protagonist of *Pride and Prejudice,* and I loved her more for reminding me of the great love of my freshman year in college, or perhaps it would be just as accurate to say that I loved Christine better for reminding me of Elizabeth. Later, I came under the spell of Emma Woodhouse, the eponymous heroine of Austen's penultimate novel, believing this to be a more mature love. By the time I read *Emma* I was a graduate student and I may have been susceptible to the general academic opinion that *Emma* was the more serious achievement. There is no question though, that I imagined her to share many desirable qualities, as well as a few not quite so desirable qualities, with my fiancée. My affections have oscillated between these two most spirited of the Austen protagonists over the course of the years, although just lately, much to my surprise, I have developed a bit of a sneaker for Fanny Price. If my actual romantic life has sometimes been influenced by superficial considerations, as an Austen reader the basis of my affections has been almost entirely cerebral. I have fallen under the spell of beautiful minds—though it couldn't be otherwise, since we seldom get a very precise physical description of our heroines, and they are never the prettiest girls in the neighborhood.

In *Heroines of Fiction,* an infatuated W. D. Howells was among the earlier Janeites to judge the novels on the basis of the temperament of their heroines, as have thousands of readers before and since. "People will prefer Anne Elliot to Elizabeth Bennet according as they enjoy gentle sufferance in women more than a lively rebellion; and it would not be profitable to try converting the worshippers of the one to the cult of the other." Anne certainly has her fans: a celebrated English novelist of my acquaintance prefers her to all the others. But her cult is undoubtedly much smaller than that of the second Miss Bennet, Austen's most lovable and vivacious heroine.

Catherine Morland, the heroine of *Northanger Abbey,* is the crude prototype of the Austen heroine, a teenage provincial whose worldview, such as it is, has been shaped by her extensive reading of gothic novels. Just seventeen years old when she embarks on her first trip beyond the family manor to the great resort of Bath, Catherine is good-natured but gullible. She befriends the duplicitous and supercilious Isabella Thorpe and gradually falls for the wellborn, well-read cleric Henry Tilney. Though she is not always quick nor erudite enough to understand Tilney, her attraction to him suggests, despite much evidence to the contrary, that she is capable of good judgment. The narrator, who keeps popping up to wink at us, seems determined to exploit Catherine's lack of experience and infatuation with Romantic fiction for comic effect. When she is invited to the Tilney family seat by Henry's sister Eleanor, she insists on infusing the environs of Northanger Abbey with gothic menace, and while she seems to be cured of this tendency after a few weeks at the Abbey, the best we can say of young Catherine is that she may someday grow up to be the kind of heroine who populates the later novels.

Elinor and Marianne Dashwood, the two sisters at the center of *Sense and Sensibility,* seem in many ways to add up to a single Austen protagonist. Elinor is too sensible by half and Marianne too impulsive and romantic. You'd much rather take Marianne to the dance, or to bed, for that matter, if such a thing can be contemplated in the world of Jane Austen. In her second novel Austen would unite a playful, blithe spirit with sagacity and judgment in a single protagonist. If *Pride and Prejudice* is Jane

Austen's most popular novel, much of the credit belongs to Elizabeth. Smart, funny, by turns passionate and sensible, irreverent and feisty, the second of Mr. Bennet's five daughters embodies virtues that appeal to both sexes. How many female readers have imagined themselves to be *just* like Mr. Darcy's beloved, and how many male readers have become infatuated with her spirit and her wit? Unlike Mr. Bennet, Elizabeth's father, who fell for the future Mrs. Bennet solely on the basis of her beauty, male readers have little opportunity to become enamored with Elizabeth for superficial reasons, since we have only a very sketchy notion of her appearance. Unlike some of her Victorian counterparts, with their belief in phrenology and their elaborately detailed descriptions of their characters, Austen is not much of a portraitist.

We know that Jane Bennet, the eldest, is the great beauty of the family; Mr. Bingley, whose arrival in the neighborhood sets the events of the book in motion, on first meeting declares her "the most beautiful creature I ever beheld," whereas the first assessment of Elizabeth's appearance, from Bingley's great friend Mr. Darcy, is unpromising: "She is tolerable, but not handsome enough to tempt *me*." Later, on the basis of brief acquaintance, Darcy revises his opinion. "No sooner had he made it clear to himself and his friends that she had hardly a good feature in her face than he began to find it was rendered uncommonly intelligent by the beautiful expression of her dark eyes. To this discovery succeeded some others equally mortifying. Though he had detected with a critical eye more than one failure of perfect symmetry in her form, he was forced to acknowledge her figure to be light and pleasing . . ." This is hardly the stuff of sonnets, nor is it very pictorial, but it allows those of us who are already falling under Elizabeth's spell the freedom to imagine her as pretty. But she is no prettier than she was a few pages earlier at the dance. Darcy's improved opinion of her beauty is a function of his growing appreciation for her character. In spite of himself, and his pride, Darcy seems to appreciate Elizabeth Bennet's independence, her irreverent wit, her refusal to be daunted by him. After his second proposal has been tacitly accepted, he tells her that he fell in love with "the liveliness of your mind." And most of us can concur. She's smart, and we feel smarter for being privy to her thoughts and observations through the novel. *Pride and Prejudice* has all the lightness and brightness of Elizabeth's lively sensibility. (Austen herself worried that it lacked gravitas. "The work is rather too light, and bright and sparkling," she wrote in an 1813 letter, as she was composing *Mansfield Park*. "It wants shade; it wants to be stretched out here and there with a long chapter of sense." To which we can only reply, nonsense.)

For all of her good sense and penetration, Elizabeth is fallible. She badly misjudges Mr. Wickham, the handsome officer attached to the regiment billeted in the town of Meryton not far from her home. Taken in by a pretty face and easy manners, she uncritically accepts Wickham's slander of Darcy. If she were not quite so charmed by his attentions, she might have questioned the impropriety of his confiding in her so quickly and thoroughly. It seems quite possible that Elizabeth might have been misguided enough to fall in love with Wickham if his attentions had not been diverted by a young lady with ten thousand pounds.

Fanny Price, the diffident and timorous heroine of *Mansfield Park,* turns out to be infallible; she is the only character in the novel who judges everything and everyone correctly. Virtuous, yes. Is she lovable, or even likable? That's the central question that has complicated the response to this beautifully constructed, somewhat stately novel. Is she even plausible to readers two hundred years later? Fanny is a child of ten when she arrives at the home of her rich uncle, Sir Thomas Bertram of Mansfield Park, and for many pages it's not entirely clear that she is the protagonist. Neither Sir Thomas, nor his supremely lazy and self-absorbed wife, Lady Bertram, pays much attention to her, while Lady Bertram's sister Mrs. Norris seems determined to keep her in her place and constantly remind her of how unworthy she is of the honor of residing at Mansfield Park. A sturdier plant than Fanny might thrive in this soil, but she is barely able to make her voice heard in this household, which includes four older children, two daughters and two sons. Only Edmund, the second son, takes an active interest in her welfare. Edmund treats her with kindness and takes a hand in her education. "He knew her to be clever," we are told, "to have a quick apprehension as well as good sense, and a fondness for reading which, properly directed, must be an education in itself."

Fanny's quickness and good sense are gradually demonstrated, but she is a passive figure through most of the novel who silently observes the folly of her adoptive family: her vain and frivolous cousins, Julia and Maria, their clueless elder brother Tom, and the officious Mrs. Norris. Hers is a kind of negative virtue—she shines in contrast to the others, and by virtue of her superior perception and judgment—but in its first volume, at least, *Mansfield Park* is effectively a novel without a heroine, a fact that makes it much less inviting than its predecessor.

Fanny's gratitude to her cousin Edmund slowly ripens into romantic love. Edmund is the only other sensible character in the book, although he proves himself less acute than Fanny by overestimating the virtues of Henry and Mary Crawford, the brother and sister who give the book and the neighborhood a much-needed infusion of energy when they arrive for an indeterminate stay with their half sister, who occupies the vicarage adjacent to Mansfield Park. The Crawfords represent a newer, more cosmopolitan, less-rooted England than the gentry of Mansfield Park.

The rich, dashing Henry Crawford makes a hobby of toying with the affections of the women he comes into contact with, and he snares the hearts of both Bertram girls, much to Fanny's chagrin. When Crawford turns his attentions to Fanny, it is at first only for sport, but he ends up falling in love with her. Even though the reader is clued in to Crawford's blossoming affection long before Fanny, he may be no less surprised than she is. To the astonishment of all her little circle, Fanny violently and persistently rejects the proposal, and though it seems that she may have been mistaken in her harsh assessment of Crawford's character, or that his love for her may have improved it, her judgment is eventually vindicated when Crawford runs off with Fanny's married cousin, Maria. Of course, it is not only her low opinion of Crawford, but her love for her cousin Edmund that influences her decision, even though she has every reason to believe that Edmund is about to propose to Mary Crawford.

We can't help liking Fanny, if only because she is practically the only candidate for our sympathy, surrounded by boors and boobs, but she's harder to love than Elizabeth Bennet. The fact is that she's far too good and too noble for those of us who are not clergymen, or saints. One can't help suspecting a kind of penitential impulse in the novel, and in the righteousness of its heroine, as if Austen were trying to atone for the lightness and the "lack of shade" with which she taxed herself in her previous novel. Reaction, or overreaction, to the previous work is a fairly common impulse in authors, and this seems evident in Austen's oeuvre. It's hard to imagine that the home performance of a play would have been a scandal in *Pride and Prejudice,* as it is in *Mansfield Park,* or that Elizabeth Bennet would have been horrified by the idea. Fanny is a sweet soul, but you wouldn't want to take her to a party.

Emma Woodhouse could hardly be more different than her predecessor: "handsome, clever, and rich, with a comfortable home and a happy disposition." You can't help feeling that Austen was a little sick of Fanny's virtue and modesty, that she is once again reacting against her previous creation. When we meet Emma in her twentieth year she has just married off Miss Taylor, her governess and companion of many years (her mother having died when she was very young). "The real evils indeed of Emma's situation were the power of having rather too much her own way, and a disposition to think a little too well of herself." Austen announces Emma's flaws right at the start, and then provides ample evidence of them. If Elizabeth is mistaken mainly in her judgment of Wickham, Emma is constantly misreading character and intention. She self-importantly adopts a foolish young protégé named Harriet Smith, sabotages the girl's budding romance with a local farmer (beware when your mentor says "Do not imagine that I want to influence you"), and attempts to set her up with the local vicar, whose interest in her she misreads as interest in her friend. She imagines herself to be the romantic object of Frank Churchill, the handsome and eligible young stepson of her governess Miss Taylor, failing to realize that he's secretly engaged to her neighbor Jane Fairfax. And she undervalues Jane, out of jealousy of her beauty and accomplishments. All in all, she's on the verge of qualifying as a rich bitch. Emma is the only one of Austen's protagonists who is at certain points viewed from such an objective distance as to nearly become a comic character, as when the narrative describes Emma as "highly esteeming Miss Taylor's judgement, but directed chiefly by her own." Austen fluidly moves between an omniscient point of view and the limited third-person perspective of Emma's consciousness, employing the former partly to compensate for the defects in Emma's judgment and partly to give us a clearer view of Emma herself.

Emma's flaws are almost flaunted. In the end the list includes heedless cruelty, after she insults the blithering, good-hearted spinster Miss Bates during the expedition to Box Hill. But she deeply regrets and repents this particular sin, and gradually learns to acknowledge and regret all of her mistakes in judgment and comportment. It's a very coldhearted reader who isn't standing by ready to forgive her, or to share Mr. Knightley's feelings when he declares his love. In the end, for all her flaws she seems far more human than Fanny, and the novel to which she gives her name seems far richer in emotion and more full of life, despite its much more limited compass. *Emma* is the most constricted of all the novels in terms of event and geographic range, if not in amplitude of feeling.

The protagonist of *Persuasion,* Austen's final novel, is much more in the mold of Fanny Price. Anne Elliot is a passive and dependent figure whose good nature and acuity are largely unrecognized and unappreciated by the fools and narcissists who form most of her society. Her father, Sir Walter Elliot, is a monstrous snob who favors her older sister, Elizabeth, a selfish, self-important bitch. Sir Walter's vanity, and his obsession with physical appearance, produce a few comic moments, but Austen's great gift for satirizing vice and vanity is not nearly so evident here as it was in *Pride and Prejudice*. If *Pride and Prejudice* had "a lack of shadow" as Austen claimed, there are plenty of dark corners and overcast afternoons in *Persuasion*. Sir Walter and Miss Elliot are unpleasant and oppressive, and treat Anne as if she were a foundling. Among the faults her father charges to Anne, when he thinks of her, is a loss of beauty. "A few years before, Anne Elliot had been a very pretty girl, but her bloom had vanished early; and as even in its height, her father had found little to admire in her, (so totally different were her delicate features and mild dark eyes from his own); there could be nothing in them now that she was faded and thin to excite his esteem."

Anne's only real ally is her late mother's friend, Lady Russell, although Lady Russell had a hand in blighting Anne's future when she advised her against accepting the proposal of Frederick Wentworth, with whom Anne was in love some eight years before the novel opens. Wentworth's lack of fortune and standing were among her chief objections to the match. Gradually we learn that Anne has regretted her decision ever since, and when Captain Wentworth of the Royal Navy comes back into the neighborhood with a new fortune and honors, this old wound is reopened. Thrown into Wentworth's company, Anne can detect no trace of his former passion—in fact she believes she sees only resentment and bitterness—and her own behavior is so ridiculously circumspect that Wentworth has no clue that her heart has remained constant over the intervening years, despite her formal rejection.

Contemporary readers may find too much reticence on both sides, though Wentworth has the excuse of hurt pride. Whether Anne was exercising prudent caution when she rejected him, or weakness of character in allowing herself to be persuaded against his suit, is a question that remains open to debate. The author seems to give her heroine the benefit of the doubt. When Wentworth finally declares himself a second time, in Bath, Austen seems to suggest that they are all the better for having waited. "There they returned again into the past, more exquisitely happy, perhaps, in their reunion, than when it had been first projected; more tender, more tried, more fixed in a knowledge of each other's character, truth and attachment; more equal to act, more justified in acting." The reader has only a sketchy retrospective glimpse of their early courtship, but the author is suggesting that it was less informed, and less rational, than this second installment. Austen believes in passion, but only when it's allied with reason—Elinor Dashwood's sense and Marianne Dashwood's spirit combined.

Near the end of Mansfield Park we hear that the caddish and inconstant Henry Crawford "lost the woman whom he had rationally, as well as passionately, loved." *Rationally as well as passionately* could stand as her prescription for true love. "Critics have remarked that there is no real delineation of true love in Jane Austen and that is true enough," David Daiches claims in an influential and otherwise sensible essay entitled "Jane Austen, Karl Marx and the Aristocratic Dance." "Austen knew only too well that in that kind of society genteel young ladies cannot afford true love. The only object must be marriage, and marriage with someone eligible. In Jane Austen, only the poor can afford passion." It's hard to believe a reader of sense could be so preposterously obtuse and misguided, although Charlotte Brontë made a similar argument a hundred years earlier. ("The passions are perfectly unknown to her.") For all of their differences, a belief in true love, with passion as its signal component, is precisely what distinguishes Austen heroines from most of their contemporaries. Elizabeth Bennet, when she rejects Mr. Darcy's first proposal, rejects the great estate of Pemberley and ten thousand pounds a year—a far greater prize than her friend Charlotte Lucas sacrificed herself to in accepting the proposal of the odious Mr. Collins—for the simple reason that all of her passion is against him. She can't bring herself to marry Darcy for purely prudent and mercenary reasons. Fanny turns down Henry Crawford, and Anne Elliot turns down Charles Musgrove in large part because passion is missing. But Austen clearly believes that passion without reason is dangerous.

There have been some recent attempts to enlist Jane Austen into the Romantic movement, despite the famous disapprobation of Charlotte Brontë. But Austen would have been appalled by William Blake's avowal that "those who control their passions do so because their passions are weak enough to be controlled." Lydia Bennet and Maria Bertram are the pathetic examples of those who let their passion overrule their reason. Given the choice between rationality and emotion, Austen chooses both.

And yet, the most important quality that all the Austen protagonists share is a capacity for passion, and a commitment to the concept of romantic love. Personally I'm inclined to be most passionate about those, like Elizabeth and Emma, who are not always perfectly rational and measured, whose passion sometimes gets the better of their reason.

Notes

"Introduction," by Susannah Carson

1. David Nokes, *Jane Austen: A Life* (New York: Farrar, Straus, Giroux, 1997).

"A Life Among the Manuscripts: Following in the Steps of Dr. Chapman," by Brian Southam

1. Henry Austen, "Biographical Notice of the Author," dated December 13, 1817, preface to the first edition of *Northanger Abbey and Persuasion* (1817), in the Oxford edition, p. 7.
2. All these features are detailed in my Oxford edition of *Volume the Second,* 1963.
3. See her letter to Charles Austen, written from Chawton, May 9, 1843, in which she names him as "residuary Legatee," describes her effects and to whom within the family they should be distributed on her death. The final sentence reads: "And as I have leisure I propose ticketing some of the other articles I have named" (Jo Modert, *Jane Austen's Manuscript Letters in Facsimile,* 1990, p. xxi).
4. James Edward Austen-Leigh, *Memoir of Jane Austen* (1870), p. 61.
5. Published in London on June 12, 1922, it was reprinted in the same month and again in July, with a fourth printing in January 1923 and a further two printings in 1929. The American edition, published by the Frederick A. Stokes Company, New York, in 1922, met with equal success, with four printings. Nor was it any surprise to find the book widely reviewed in academic journals, including the *Yale Review,* and in the literary and cultural weeklies. These included, in London, *The Times Literary Supplement.*
6. In Edmund Clerihew Bentley, *Biography for Beginners* (1905), unpaginated. The Austen clerihew is sometimes attributed to Bentley.
7. Jane Austen, *Love and Freindship and Other Early Works* (1922), Preface, pp. xi, xiv.

8. *The New York Times Book Review,* September 17, 1922, p. 1.

9. Virginia Woolf, review of *Love and Freindship, New Statesman,* July 15, 1922, vol. xix, pp. 419–20.

10. Virginia Woolf, "Jane Austen at Sixty," *Nation and Athenaeum,* December 15, 1923, p. 433.

11. R. W. Chapman, *The Times Literary Supplement,* June 15, 1922, p. 393.

12. There were, of course, six novels, but volume five was a double volume containing the two shorter novels, *Northanger Abbey* and *Persuasion.*

13. Frederick Page, senior Oxford University Press editor at the London office, to R. W. Chapman, March 11, 1924.

14. RWC to Watt, September 19, 1931. Regarding his work on Austen's letters, Chapman's hand may have been forced by the announcement of a first "collected edition" of forty-four letters (already available elsewhere), also published in London in 1925, under the editorship of Richard Brimley Johnson.

15. Ibid.

16. Watt to RWC, October 23, 1931.

17. RWC to Watt, October 26, 1931.

18. Watt to RWC, November 3, 1931.

19. RWC to Watt, November 4, 1931.

20. RWC to R. A. Austen-Leigh, November 4, 1931. One can understand Chapman's annoyance. Richard Brimley Johnson was an established presence in the Austen world long before him. Johnson's Dent edition of 1892 (reused in other Dent editions in 1898 and 1899) was the first to be prepared with any regard to textual issues, returning, as he put it, to "the text of the last editions revised by the author" (vol. 1, p. lx). In 1902, Johnson published his own Hampshire edition, issued in New York in 1903 by Putnam's. Textually, however, the Hampshire edition took a step backward, for Johnson announced that "There has been no attempt to retain the author's antique and often careless spelling . . ." Phenomenally industrious, Johnson followed the Hampshire edition with the lavish Old Manor House edition published in New York by Holby in 1906, and republished, also in 1906, both as the Chawton edition and as the Manydown edition, in 1907 as the Illustrated Cabinet edition, in 1912 as the Winchester edition, and again in 1915, all these variations and recyclings published in America. In 1906, Johnson was also the editor of the enduring Everyman editions of the novels, all of them published in London by Dent and in New York by Dutton. Moreover, Johnson's name was also attached to a considerable number of other books and editions (over three hundred literary items are listed under his name in the British Library catalogue), and it is hardly surprising to find Agnes Repplier, the prominent American essayist and critic, opening her review of Johnson's *Jane Austen,* 1930, with a tribute that must have riled Chapman: "No man living knows more, or as much, about Jane Austen as does Mr Johnson" (*Commonweal,* May 13, 1931).

21. This confusion may have arisen because one branch of the Austen-Leigh family had settled in North America: in 1910 Lionel Arthur Austen-Leigh (who

was later to inherit *Volume the Third*) went to live in Victoria, British Columbia, where his family settled.

22. R. W. Chapman, *Minor Works* (1954), p. 2.

23. In fact, as late as mid-1950, Chapman had been anticipating earlier publication. *The Times* report of the July 1950 annual general meeting of the Jane Austen Society noted Chapman's announcement that the volume was due for publication "early in 1952, or even perhaps before that time." As he also said that he would be "glad to know about any scrap of prose or verse written by Jane Austen at about 17," he may have hung on, hoping for such late discoveries to come in. (*The Times,* July 10, 1950).

24. RWC to Brian Southam, August 26, 1959.

25. Twelve years earlier, *Volume the Third,* "The Property of the late Lionel A. Austen-Leigh," had been sold at Sotheby's and purchased by "Maxwell" for £30,000 (Lot 172, December 14, 1976).

26. *The New York Times,* September 28, 1988.

27. Material from Oxford University Press archives is reprinted by permission of the secretary to the delegates of Oxford University Press, and for archival advice and assistance I am particularly grateful to Dr. Martin Maw, the press archivist. In the preparation of this essay I have been advised by several members of the Austen family: Mrs. Caroline Bell; Patrick Stokes, chairman of the Jane Austen Society; Ronald Dunning; and Di Gardener. I am also grateful for advice received from Professors Barbara Britton Wenner, Peter Sabor, and Joseph Wiesenfarth; Margaret Wilson; Christine Nelson and Clara Drummond, Pierpont Morgan Library; Tara Craig, Butler Library, Columbia University; Michael Riordan, archivist, St. John's and The Queen's College, Oxford; Jean Rose, library manager, Random House Group Archive and Library; Johnnie Kerne, practice manager, Mowll and Mowll; Nancy Fulford, Special Collections Service, University of Reading; Emily Kitchin; A. P. Watt; Tessa Milne, director, Department of Books and Manuscripts, Sotheby's; Rachel Foss, curator of modern literary manuscripts, British Library. Finally, I would also like to thank Susannah Carson, the editor of this volume, for her support and guidance.

"Reading *Northanger Abbey*," by Susannah Carson

1. *Northanger Abbey,* initially titled *Susan,* was first drafted in 1798–99, revised and sold in 1803, and then revised again as *Northanger Abbey* in 1817.

2. Harold Bloom, *How to Read and Why* (New York: Simon & Schuster, 2000), p. 159.

"From 'Why We Read Jane Austen,' " by Lionel Trilling

1. Clifford Geertz, "From the Native's Point of View: On the Nature of Anthropological Understanding," *Bulletin of the American Academy of Arts and Sciences,* vol. xxviii, no. I.

"Jane Austen and *Pride and Prejudice*," by W. Somerset Maugham

1. Jane Austen was the seventh of eight children; a younger brother, Charles John Austen, was born in 1779.

"A Note on Jane Austen," by C. S. Lewis

1. H. W. Garrod, "Jane Austen: A Depreciation," *Essays by Divers Hands: Transactions of the Royal Society of Literature,* VIII (1928), pp. 21–40.
2. *Jane Austen,* Cambridge, 1936, p. 33.
3. Chastisement.
4. "Cinna wants to seem poor and he is" (i.e., not worth much). Martial, *Epigrams* viii, no. 19.
5. Rudyard Kipling, "The Janeites," *Debits and Credits,* 1926.

"Fanny Was Right: Jane Austen as Moral Guide," by James Collins

1. Tony Tanner, "Knowledge and Opinion: *Pride and Prejudice*" in *Jane Austen,* edited by Harold Bloom (Philadelphia: Chelsea House, 2004), p. 155.
2. Quoted in *Early Auden* by Edward Mendelson (Cambridge: Harvard University Press, 1983), p. 177.
3. Virginia Woolf, "Jane Austen" in *Jane Austen,* edited by Ian Watt (Englewood Cliffs, N.J.: Prentice-Hall), 1963, p. 20.
4. Lionel Trilling, "Mansfield Park" in *The Opposing Self* (New York: Viking Press, 1955).
5. Kingsley Amis, "What Became of Jane Austen?" in *Jane Austen,* edited by Ian Watt, pp. 20, 142.

"Why I Like Jane Austen," by Janet Todd

1. www.citizenofthemonth.com/2005/10/27/jane-austen-and-the-pussycats
2. janeaustenaddict.com/thebook/press

"Why Do We *Read* Jane Austen?" by John Wiltshire

1. Brian Southam, ed., *Jane Austen: The Critical Heritage* (London: Routledge, 1995), p. 159.
2. Andrew Higson, *English Heritage, English Cinema: Costume Drama Since 1980* (Oxford: Oxford University Press, 2003).
3. Oscar Wilde, *The Importance of Being Earnest,* Act 3.
4. Janet Todd, *Gender, Art, and Death* (New York: Continuum, 1993).
5. John Keats, *Letters* (Oxford: Oxford University Press, 1970), pp. 36–37.
6. Peter Sabor, ed., *Juvenilia, The Cambridge Edition of the Works of Jane Austen* (2006), frontispiece.

7. I discuss this in more detail in my chapter "By Candelight; Jane Austen, Technology and the Heritage Film" in *The Cinematic Jane Austen: Essays on the Filmic Sensibility of the Novels* (McFarland: Jefferson and London, 2009), pp. 38–56.
8. Emma Thompson, *The* Sense and Sensibility *Screenplay and Diaries: Bringing Jane Austen's Novel to Film* (New York: Newmarket Pictorial Moviebooks, 1995), p. 71.

"Reading and Rereading *Emma*," by David Lodge

1. Reginald Farrer, "Jane Austen, *ob.* July 18, 1817," *Quarterly Review,* ccxxviii (1917), pp. 24–28.
2. W. J. Harvey, "The Plot of Emma," *Essays in Criticism,* xvii (1967), pp. 48–63.
3. James Edward Austen-Leigh, *A Memoir of Jane Austen* (1870); ed. R. W. Chapman (1926), p. 203.
4. Marvin Mudrick, *Jane Austen: Irony as Defense and Discovery* (1952), pp. 181–206.
5. D. W. Harding, "Regulated Hatred: An Aspect of the Work of Jane Austen," *Scrutiny,* viii (1940), pp. 346–62.
6. Ian Watt, *The Rise of the Novel,* Penguin edition (1963), pp. 300–301.
7. R. W. Chapman, *Jane Austen: Facts and Problems* (1948), pp. 201–2.

"From '*Emma* and the Legend of Jane Austen,'" by Lionel Trilling

1. *The Question of Our Speech; The Lesson of Balzac: Two Lectures* (1905).
2. D. W. Harding, "Regulated Hatred: An Aspect of the Work of Jane Austen," *Scrutiny,* viii (1940).
3. Marvin Mudrick, *Jane Austen: Irony as Defense and Discovery* (1952).
4. Reginald Farrer, "Jane Austen," *Quarterly Review* 228, July 1917.
5. Alexis de Tocqueville, *The Old Regime and the French Revolution,* Anchor edition, pp. 82–83. Tocqueville should not be understood as saying that there was no class system in England but only that there was no caste system, caste differing from class in its far greater rigidity. In his sense of the great advantage that England enjoyed, as compared with France, in having no caste system, Tocqueville inclines to represent the class feelings of the English as being considerably more lenient than in fact they were. Still, the difference between caste and class and the social and political importance of the "gentleman" are as great as Tocqueville says.
6. Harold Rosenberg, "Revolution and the Idea of Beauty," *Encounter,* December 1953.
7. See Abram Kardiner, *The Psychological Frontiers of Society* (1945), p. 410. In commenting on the relatively simple society which is described in James West's *Plainville, U.S.A.,* Dr. Kardiner touches on a matter which is dear, and all too dear, to Emma's heart—speaking of social mobility in a democratic, but not classless, society, he says that the most important criterion of class is "manners," that "knowing how to behave" is the surest means of rising in the class

hierarchy. Nothing is more indicative of Jane Austen's accurate awareness of the mobility of her society than her concern not so much with manners themselves as with her characters' concern with manners.

"From 'The Myth of Limitation,'" by Donald Greene

1. Such as G. K. Chesterton: "She was naturally exuberant. Her power came as all power comes, from the direction and control of exuberance. But there is the presence and pressure of that vitality behind her thousand trivialities; she could have been extravagant if she liked. She was the very reverse of a starched or a starved spinster; she could have been a buffoon like the Wife of Bath if she chose" (*Love and Friendship* [New York: Frederick A. Stokes, 1922], p. xv).
2. Arnold Kettle, *An Introduction to the English Novel* (New York: Harper, 1960), 1: pp. 98–99.
3. Alistair M. Duckworth, *The Improvement of the Estate: A Study of Jane Austen's Novels* (Baltimore: Johns Hopkins Press, 1971).
4. Lionel Stevenson, *The English Novel: A Panorama* (Boston: Houghton Mifflin, 1960), pp. 189–90.
5. Dorothy Van Ghent, *The English Novel: Form and Function* (New York: Harper, 1953), p. 99.
6. In quotations from Jane Austen and Samuel Johnson, I have modernized spelling and punctuation.
7. One wonders whether it was Jane Austen's publishers or her family who were responsible for the deletion from the second edition of *Sense and Sensibility* ("in the interests of propriety": R. W. Chapman) of the last sentence in the following passage:

"And who is Miss Williams?" asked Marianne.

". . . She is a relation of the Colonel's, my dear; a very near relation. We will not say how near, for fear of shocking the young ladies." Then, lowering her voice a little, she said to Elinor [aged nineteen], "She is his natural daughter."

. . . Lady Middleton's delicacy was shocked; and in order to banish so improper a subject as the mention of a natural daughter, she actually took the trouble of saying something about the weather.

8. Her memory is good: Isabella wrote out the story, and Lovell read it aloud. The congratulations to Isabella at the end make it sound as though she were the reader.
9. One wonders whether the caption on the title page of Jane Austen's first published work, "By a Lady," is not rather a challenge than an expression of modesty. It seems to have confused whoever wrote the advertisements for it: "A new novel by Lady ———" and "Interesting Novel by Lady A———."

"Terrible Jane" by Amy Bloom

1. I am indebted to David Nokes's *Jane Austen: A Life* (New York: Farrar, Straus, Giroux, 1997) for biographical information.

"Some Thoughts on the Craft of Austen's *Persuasion*," by Diane Johnson

1. This essay is mostly based on my afterword to an edition of *Persuasion,* her last novel (Signet Classics, 2008), with some additional discussion of her other novels and some illustrative examples from my own experience, where a contemporary novelist has hoped to profit from her discoveries, or failed to.
2. Austen, *Persuasion* (New York: Signet Classic, 1996).
3. Ruth Perry, *Novel Relations: The Transformation of Kinship in English Literature and Culture 1748–1818* (Cambridge: Cambridge University Press, 2004), p. 466.
4. A further exploration of such issues can be found in Richard Jenkyns's interesting *A Fine Brush on Ivory: An Appreciation of Jane Austen* (Oxford: Oxford University Press, 2004).

Contributor Biographies

Kingsley Amis (1922–95) was an English novelist, poet, and critic. He wrote experimental novels such as *The Anti-Death League* (1966), but is best known for the wry irreverence of such novels as *Lucky Jim* (1954), *Take a Girl Like You* (1960), and the Booker Prize–winning *The Old Devils* (1986).

Martin Amis (b. 1949) is known for the innovative narrative techniques and themes of novels such as *Money* (1984), *London Fields* (1989), *Time's Arrow* (1992), and *Yellow Dog* (2003). *The War Against Cliché* (2001) is a collection of critical essays and articles. He is professor of creative writing at the University of Manchester.

Louis Auchincloss (b. 1917) is a novelist, short-story writer, essayist, historian, and lawyer. He has written over thirty novels, many of which are novels of manners depicting the moral dilemmas of upper-class New England society, such as *The House of Five Talents* (1960), *Portrait in Brownstone* (1962), *East Side Story* (2004), and *Last of the Old Guard* (2008).

Amy Bloom (b. 1953) has written the novels *Love Invents Us* (1997) and *Away* (2007). Her short stories have appeared in anthologies such as *The Best American Short Stories* and *The O. Henry Prize Stories,* and have been collected in *Come to Me* (1993) and *A Blind Man Can See How Much I Love You* (2000). Her articles have been published in *The New Yorker, The New York Times Magazine, The Atlantic Monthly,* and *Vogue.* Bloom was the creator of the television series *State of Mind* (2007). She teaches at Yale. Her next book is a collection of short stories, *Where the God of Love Hangs Out* (2010).

Harold Bloom (b. 1930) is a literary critic whose work ranges from the poetics of influence to studies of the Judeo-Christian tradition. His books include *The Anxiety of Influence* (1973), *The Western Canon* (1994), *Shakespeare: The Invention of the Human* (1998), *How to Read and Why* (2000), and *Where Shall Wisdom Be Found* (2004). Bloom was awarded the American Academy of Arts and Letters Gold Medal for Criticism in 1999. He is Sterling Professor of the Humanities at Yale University. He is currently working on a book entitled *The Living Labyrinth*.

Eva Brann (b. 1929) was born in Berlin and emigrated to the United States in 1941. She is the author of *Homeric Moments: Clues to Delight in Reading the Odyssey and the Illiad* (2002), *The Music of the Republic: Essays on Socrates' Conversations and Plato's Writings* (2004), and *Feeling Our Feelings: What Philosophers Think and People Should Know* (2008). Brann was awarded a National Humanities Medal in 2005. Since 1957, she has taught at St. John's College, Annapolis, Maryland.

A. S. Byatt (b. 1936) is a British novelist, short-story writer, and poet who combines realism and fantasy in short stories such as those collected in *The Matisse Stories* (1993) and in novels such as *Still Life* (1985), which won the PEN/Macmillan Silver Pen Award, and *Possession* (1990), which won the Booker Prize.

Susannah Carson (b. 1975) is a doctoral candidate in French at Yale University. Previous degrees include an M.Phil. from the Sorbonne-Paris III, as well as MAs from the Université des Lumières-Lyon II and San Francisco State University. Her work has appeared in the journal *Seventeeth-Century French Studies,* as well as in the collection *Religion, Ethics, and History in the French Long Seventeenth Century* (2007).

Susanna Clarke (b. 1959) is known for a style that combines fairy-tale magic with Dickensian realism. Her first novel, *Jonathan Strange & Mr. Norrell* (2004), won the Hugo Award and the World Fantasy Award. She has also written a number of shorter pieces, many of which have been collected in *The Ladies of Grace Adieu and Other Stories* (2006). She was raised in northern England and Scotland, and currently resides in Cambridge and Derbyshire.

James Collins (b. 1958) is a writer and editor whose first novel, *Beginner's Greek* (2008), is a study in romantic irony and optimism. He has been a frequent contributor to *The New Yorker,* and he has written and served as editor for *Time* and *Spy* magazines. He is a New Yorker who currently resides in rural Virginia.

Alain de Botton (b. 1969) has written novels such as *Essays in Love* (1993) and essayistic books such as *How Proust Can Change Your Life* (1997), *The Consolations of Philosophy* (2000), *The Art of Travel* (2002), *Status Anxiety* (2004), *The Architecture of Happiness* (2006), and *The Pleasures and Sorrows of Work* (2009). He was born in

Zurich, Switzerland, and currently lives in London where he helps to run The School of Life.

E. M. Forster (1879–1970) wrote short stories and novels characterized by their ironic tone and humanistic intent. Differences of class, culture, and sexuality are themes that run through his major works, *Where Angels Fear to Tread* (1905), *A Room with a View* (1908), *Howards End* (1910), *A Passage to India* (1924), and *Maurice* (1971). In his *Aspects of the Novel* (1927), he examines the craft of novel writing. Forster was a member of the London literary society the Bloomsbury Group.

Donald Greene (1914–97) was a Canadian academic who specialized in Samuel Johnson. His works include *The Politics of Samuel Johnson* (1960), *The Age of Exuberance: Backgrounds to Eighteenth-Century English Literature* (1970), and *Samuel Johnson* (1984). He also wrote on Jane Austen, Evelyn Waugh, and Graham Greene. Greene taught in several universities in both Canada and the United States before finishing his career at the University of Southern California (1968–84).

Amy Heckerling (b. 1954) is a director, writer, and producer. Her films include *Fast Times at Ridgemont High* (1982), *National Lampoon's European Vacation* (1985), *Look Who's Talking* (1989), and *Clueless* (1995). She was born in the Bronx, and currently divides her time between New York and Los Angeles.

Diane Johnson (b. 1934) is the author of the satirical, cross-cultural novels *Le Divorce* (1997), for which she won the California Book Awards gold medal, as well as *Le Mariage* (2000), *L'Affaire* (2004), and *Lulu in Marrakech* (2008). She is a long-term, frequent contributor to *The New York Review of Books*. Johnson was born in Moline, Illinois, and currently divides her time between San Francisco and Paris.

C. S. Lewis (1898–1963) was a Northern Irish novelist, broadcaster, and academic who taught medieval literature at Oxford and Cambridge. In addition to *The Screwtape Letters* (1942) and *The Chronicles of Narnia* (1950–56), he wrote works of criticism such as *The Allegory of Love* (1936) and *The Discarded Image* (1964).

Margot Livesey (b. 1953) is a Scottish-born novelist, essayist, and short-story writer. Her novels include *The Missing World* (2000), *Eva Moves the Furniture* (2001), *Banishing Verona* (2005), and *The House on Fortune Street* (2008), which won the L. L. Winship Award. Her work has also appeared in *The New Yorker* and *The Atlantic Monthly*. Livesey lives in the Boston area, and is writer-in-residence at Emerson College.

David Lodge (b. 1935) is Emeritus Professor of English Literature at the University of Birmingham, where he taught from 1960 to 1987. The academic world is fictionalized in many of his novels, which include *Changing Places* (1975), *Small World* (1984), *Nice Work* (1988), and, most recently, *Deaf Sentence* (2008). Lodge's critical works include *The Modes of Modern Writing* (1977), *The Art of Fiction* (1992), *Consciousness and the Novel* (2003), and *The Year of Henry James* (2006).

W. Somerset Maugham (1874–1965) was a British playwright, novelist, short-story writer, travel writer, and spy. His many novels include *Of Human Bondage* (1915), *The Painted Veil* (1925), *Christmas Holiday* (1939), *Up at the Villa* (1941), and *The Razor's Edge* (1944). *The Gentleman in the Parlour* (1930) is a collection of travel essays, and *A Writer's Notebook* (1949) is a selection of his journal entries.

Jay McInerney (b. 1955) is the author of seven novels which serve as iconoclastic depictions of upper-middle-class urban life. His trendsetting *Bright Lights, Big City* (1984) was followed by *Story of My Life* (1988), *Brightness Falls* (1992), *The Last of the Savages* (1997), *Model Behavior* (1998), and *The Good Life* (2006). McInerney has also written essays on wine, which have been collected in *Bacchus & Me* (2000) and *A Hedonist in the Cellar* (2006). *How It Ended* (2009) is his latest collection of short stories.

Rebecca Mead (b. 1966) has been a staff writer at *The New Yorker* magazine since 1997, where she has profiled institutions and individuals ranging from the Metropolitan Opera to Spring Break and from Santiago Calatrava to Shaquille O'Neal. She was born in London, and was educated at Oxford University and NYU. Her first book, *One Perfect Day: The Selling of the American Wedding,* was published in 2007. She lives in New York.

Benjamin Nugent (b. 1977) is the author of *American Nerd: The Story of My People*. His fiction has appeared in *Tin House* and his nonfiction in *GQ, The New York Times Magazine, Time,* and *n+1*. He grew up in Amherst, Massachusetts. An Iowa Arts Fellow at the Iowa Writers' Workshop, he lives in Iowa City. He is currently working on a memoir entitled *The Shapeshifters*.

J. B. Priestley (1894–1984) was a British writer whose many works include the novel *The Good Companions* (1929), the play *An Inspector Calls* (1946), the critical survey *Literature and Western Man* (1960), and the episodes of his BBC broadcast *The Postscript* (1940–41).

Anna Quindlen (b. 1952) has written bestselling novels including *One True Thing* (1994), *Black and Blue* (1998), *Blessings* (2002), and *Rise and Shine* (2006). Her non-fiction includes *How Reading Changed My Life* (1998), *A Short Guide to a Happy Life* (2000), and her latest book, *Good Dog. Stay* (2009). Her *New York Times* column "Public and Private" was awarded the Pulitzer Prize for Commentary (1992).

Ignês Sodré is a Brazilian psychologist who has lived and practiced in London since 1969. In addition to writings on clinical psychoanalysis, she has published criticism on classical authors such as George Eliot and Shakespeare.

Brian Southam (b. 1931) is esteemed for the exhaustive and essential historical research he has conducted into Jane Austen's life, family, and manuscripts. He served as chairman of the Jane Austen Society of North America from 1990 to 2005. His books include *Jane Austen and the Navy* (2000, 2005) and *Jane Austen's Literary Manuscripts: A Study of the Novelist's Development* (1964, 2000). He has edited several volumes of past and contemporary critical essays, and has produced editions of *Sanditon* (1975), *Jane Austen's "Sir Charles Grandison"* (1980), and the first fully collated edition of *Volume the Second* (1969). He is working on two further books: *Jane Austen and the Professions* and *Jane Austen Beside the Seaside: A Romantic Tale, from Sidmouth to "Sanditon."*

Janet Todd (b. 1942) is a Welsh-born academic who specializes in British women's literature from the seventeenth through the early nineteenth centuries. She is the author of *The Secret Life of Aphra Behn* (1996), *The Revolutionary Life of Mary Wollstonecraft* (2000), and *The Cambridge Introduction to Jane Austen* (2006); she is editor of *The Cambridge Edition of the Works of Jane Austen* (2005–9). Todd is president of Lucy Cavendish College, Cambridge.

Lionel Trilling (1905–75) was an American literary critic who studied and taught at Columbia University (from 1921) and was a member of the New York Intellectuals. His essays chronicle the moral history of literature; they are collected in *The Liberal Imagination* (1950), *The Opposing Self* (1955), *Beyond Culture* (1965), *Sincerity and Authenticity* (1972), and *The Moral Obligation to Be Intelligent* (2001).

Ian Watt (1917–99) was a British literary critic who taught at the University of California, Berkeley (1952–62) and Stanford University (1964–99). His *Rise of the Novel: Studies in Defoe, Richardson, and Fielding* (1957) was a founding work of sociohistorical literary criticism.

Fay Weldon (b. 1931) is a feminist novelist, essayist, and playwright. Her novels include *The Life and Loves of a She-Devil* (1985), *The Bulgari Connection* (2001), and *The Stepmother's Diary* (2009). Her *Letters to Alice on First Reading Jane Austen* (1984) is a series of epistolary essays. She wrote the screenplay for the BBC adaptation of *Pride and Prejudice* (1980). She currently holds the post of professor of creative writing at Brunel University, West London.

Eudora Welty (1909–2001) was a Mississippi-based writer and photographer whose work captures the essence of Southern society throughout the course of the twentieth century. She won the Pulitzer Prize for her novel *The Optimist's Daughter* (1972) and the Rea Award (1992) for short stories ranging from the early "Death of a Traveling Salesman" (1936) to the later "Moon Lake" (1980).

John Wiltshire (b. 1941) is a British-born academic living in Australia who specializes in the work of Jane Austen, Samuel Johnson, and Fanny Burney. His work on Austen includes the Cambridge edition of *Mansfield Park* (2005), and the books *Jane Austen and the Body: "The Picture of Health"* (1992), *Recreating Jane Austen* (2001), *Jane Austen: Introductions and Interventions* (2003), and *The Cinematic Jane Austen* (with David Monaghan and Ariane Hudelet) (2009). He is emeritus professor of English at La Trobe University, Australia.

Virginia Woolf (1882–1941) was a novelist, essayist, and short-story writer. Her modernist novels include *Mrs. Dalloway* (1925), *To the Lighthouse* (1927), *Orlando* (1928), and *The Waves* (1931), and her nonfiction includes the feminist essayistic book *A Room of One's Own* (1929). She was a member of the London literary society the Bloomsbury Group.

Permissions Acknowledgments

Grateful acknowledgment is made to the following for permission to include new and previously published material:

A P Watt Ltd: "Jane Austen and *Pride and Prejudice*" by W. Somerset Maugham. Reprinted by permission of A P Watt Ltd on behalf of The Royal Literary Fund.

Eva Brann: "The Perfections of Jane Austen" by Eva Brann, originally a lecture given at Annapolis on January 31, 1975. Reprinted by permission.

James Collins: "Fanny Was Right: Jane Austen as Moral Guide," copyright © 2009 by James Collins.

The C. S. Lewis Company: "A Note on Jane Austen" by C. S. Lewis from *Essays on Criticism,* copyright © 1954 by C. S. Lewis Pte. Ltd. Reprinted by permission.

Farrar, Straus and Giroux, LLC, and the Wylie Agency LLC: Excerpt from "Why We Read Jane Austen" from *The Moral Obligation to Be Intelligent: Selected Essays* by Lionel Trilling, copyright © 2000 by The Estate of Lionel Trilling. Rights in the United Kingdom are controlled by the Wylie Agency LLC. Reprinted by permission of Farrar, Straus and Giroux, LLC, and the Wylie Agency LLC.

The Gersh Agency: Introduction by Amy Bloom to *Persuasion* by Jane Austen published by the Modern Library in 1992, copyright © 1992 by Amy Bloom. Reprinted by permission of The Gersh Agency.

Amy Heckerling: "The Girls Who Don't Say, 'Whoo!' " copyright © 2009 by Amy Heckerling.

SUSANNAH CARSON is a doctoral candidate in French at Yale University. Her previous degrees include an M.Phil from the Sorbonne Paris III, as well as MAs from the Université Lyon II and San Francisco State University. She has lectured on various topics of English and French literature at Oxford, the University of Glasgow, Yale, Harvard, Concordia, and Boston University.

www.whyjaneausten.com